The Way and the Light

The Way and the Light

An Illustrated Guide to the Saints and Holy Places of Britain

Mick Sharp

AURUM PRESS

Dedication

To St Veronica, patron of photographers: the 'true image' (L. *vera*, G. *ikon*) whose very existence is open to question.

10030?546X

First published in Great Britain
2000 by Aurum Press Ltd
25 Bedford Avenue, London WC1B 3AT

Text and photographs copyright © 2000 by Mick Sharp

Design by Sandra Oakins

A catalogue record for this book is available from the British Library.

ISBN 1 85410 722 4 paperback

ISBN 1 85410 751 8 hardback

10 9 8 7 6 5 4 3 2 1
2004 2003 2002 2001 2000
Printed and bound in Singapore by Imago

Contents

Acknowledgements

In the course of ten years' research, travel, photography and writing, I accumulated too many debts to acknowledge here individually, but I am grateful to all who contributed to this book, and to the few who were obstructive, as that too spurred me on.

Lesley and Roy Adkins and Richard Bryant and Carolyn Heighway were particularly helpful and supportive during the protracted gestation.

The following people provided valuable information on saints and places, or influenced the book's form in some way: Lindsay Badenoch, Stuart Booth, Nancy Edwards, Michael Hare, Dave and Marianne Longley, Maggy Mason, Dave Morgan, David Murphy, Huw Price, Susan Seright, Dave Thompson and Diane Williams.

Of all the sources listed in the Bibliography, David Hugh Farmer's *Oxford Dictionary of Saints* was most often the starting point for my research.

Kate Geary of the Gwynedd Archaeological Trust's Sites and Monuments Record supplied details on some of the locations in north-west Wales.

My thanks to all who facilitated, or kindly granted permission for photography, including the Bardsey Island Trust, Hexham Abbey Parochial Church Council, the Deans and Chapters, administrators and vergers of the featured cathedrals, especially Chester, St Albans, Peterborough and Worcester, and the vicars, wardens and key-keepers of the churches, particularly Evelyn Davies at Pennant Melangell.

Other much appreciated help was provided by Phil Abramson, Claire Adamson, Brian and Lynn Ayers, Julie and Phill Barker, Mrs Bartlett, Hubert and Monica Beales, Simant Bostock, Steve Boyle, Georgina Brown, Anne-Marie Ehrlich, Susan Gathercole, Andrew Jones, Jim Killgore, Pat Lynch, Ann MacSween, Frank and Louise Moran, Charlotte Roberts, Roger and Tania Simpson, Janet Smithies, Tricia Snell, Philip Steele, Charles Thomas, Alex Turner, Brian Williamson and Kathleen Williamson.

Thanks also to Sheila Murphy and Aurum Press for making a book of my words and pictures.

Jean Williamson produced the location map, and I was most fortunate to enjoy her assistance, company and understanding throughout this project.

Finally to those who gave me friendly warnings on the lines of 'you must be mad' or 'hagiography can be a nightmare', thank you: you were right.

St, Michael's Mount, Marazion,
Penzance, Cornwall

1.
A Land of Saints and Pilgrims
Introduction

Stories about saints, their miracles and relics exhibit a fabulous mixture of pagan and Christian elements, down-to-earth practicality and paranormal encounters, extremes of austerity and avarice, chastity and sexual desire, simple faith and gross manipulation, purity and wanton cruelty, courage and self-doubt, sin and repentance. Their *Lives* contain extraordinary storytelling flourishes mixed in with touchingly believable personal details and everyday events. Historical accuracy is variable, plots are borrowed from biblical stories and – despite some heavy-handed moral and social instruction – most manage to be entertainingly didactic, compelling as any modern soap opera. Many details are credible even without the benefit of faith, others are frankly fantastic, but anyone wondering about medieval credulity could reflect on our own appetite for unsubstantiated media opinions. Almost every part of Britain has some connection with a saint or pilgrims: most places had a local saint and many became associated with the cult of a national or international one. Church dedications and place names throughout the country – from St Levan in Cornwall to North Rona off north-west Scotland, Hibaldstow in Lincolnshire to Llandderfel in Gwynedd – bear witness to a multitude of obscure local holy men and women. Following the Norman takeover of 1066, many unfamiliar Celtic and English dedications were replaced by high-profile martyrs and biblical saints, original dedications surviving best in the Celtic and marginal areas where Norman influence was weakest. Most popular in England is the Virgin Mary with over 2000 dedications, followed by St Peter (Heaven's doorkeeper, patron of the Church and papacy) with around 1,100 and St Michael with more than 650.

Archangel Michael (Hebrew: who is like the Lord?) is regarded as the 'great prince' charged with weighing souls, guiding them through the perils of death and protecting humankind from Satan (evil, the dragon) and his fallen angels. Frequently appearing in visions, he is associated with the former haunts of pagan deities, especially high places. Medieval pilgrims to St Michael's Mount would invoke his protection by sitting in the saint's 'chair' – a rock-projection above a deadly drop to the sea – where he was reputed to have been seen. An equally perilous perch atop the chapel tower is named after St Keyne, a young woman of exceptional beauty who sought the joys of solitude rather than marriage. The first of a pair of newlyweds to sit in the stone beacon-container was believed to gain the upper hand in their relationship. A similar legend concerning the water of St Keyne's Well (Cornwall) was recorded by Carew in 1602 and made the subject of a ballad by Southey: a husband ran from church to be first at the spring, leaving his wife calmly drinking from a bottle of well-water she had taken to the service.

Christianity was brought to Britain during the Roman occupation. Its early fortunes were intimately connected with the political struggles, expedient changes of belief and policy of the Roman emperors which affected the whole empire from Jesus's Palestine (Galilee and Judaea) on the eastern margin to its western-most province of Britain. Christian Jews and Greek-speaking traders first spread the faith; eastern Mediterranean merchants and converts in the army brought it to the cosmopolitan urban communities of Roman Britain. Initially proscribed and generally covert, Christianity underwent a dramatic change in status after 312 when Emperor Constantine I ('the Great') won a remarkable victory against a rival emperor. Instructed in a dream to fight under the sign of the Cross, Constantine's outnumbered army of pagan soldiers triumphantly bore the Christian monogram XP (intersecting the first two letters of the Greek word *Christos*) on their shields. From 313, the Christian Church was officially tolerated, but Constantine himself combined Christian worship with that of the *Sol Invictus* (the Unconquered Sun whose feast was chosen as Christ's official birthday) until he gained control of both halves of the empire split by Diocletian. Constantine installed monotheistic Christianity as the official religion and chose Byzantium – rebuilt as Constantinople (Istanbul, Turkey) – for his capital in the east, leaving the office of Bishop of Rome (the future papacy) as the most prominent in the west.

Romano-British Christianity was in competition with residual native paganism and that introduced by the incoming Saxons and other Germanic peoples, but Christian 'heresies' were of equal concern. Pelagius, a British-born law student turned theologian, taught that 'man' was not 'fallen' or capable only of evil, but free to choose good and take the first steps towards salvation without God's supernatural assistance (grace). Denial of the doctrine of Adam's transmission of original sin to his descendants also became an attractive element of Pelagianism, influencing a substantial number of Christians in

Britain, especially among the wealthy Romano-British aristocracy. The Gaulish Church sent St Germanus (Bishop of Auxerre) in 429 to confront the British heretics at a public meeting at Verulamium (St Albans, Hertfordshire). Bede describes a huge crowd of magnificently robed and ornamented Pelagians attended by flattering followers. Germanus won the argument for the official doctrine, performed a healing miracle and placed relics in the tomb of St Alban. He then trained and led British troops in a spectacularly successful ambush of a combined Pictish and Saxon army. Endless questions of Christian doctrine, custom and date (Jesus was born in the period 8BC–4BC rather than the year inaccurately fixed in our calendar by a Roman monk in 525, so the Christian millennium occurred somewhere in 1992–6) were being argued out; many aspects of the religion in the first millennium – such as the appearance of Christ – would be unrecognizable to modern followers: early depictions based on the sun-god Apollo show a clean-shaven blond with curly hair rather than the familiar medieval image of a dark, bearded, long-haired Jesus.

The first Christian saints to be the subjects of a cult were martyrs (witnesses) from the Roman persecutions whose memories were venerated much in the manner of earlier Jewish patriarchs: monuments were erected over their collected bones ('more precious than jewels of great price'), their 'heavenly birthdays' were celebrated each year with communal meals at the tomb. Those who had died for Christ were undoubtedly in Heaven and capable of interceding on behalf of those who prayed to them. Saints were first declared by popular acclaim based on persecution, martyrdom, miracle-working, virginity, holiness and incorruption of the body after death; local bishops became involved in the procedure and Rome eventually reserved the right to create official saints. From around 1200, papal commissions including a 'Devil's Advocate' were appointed to investigate the life, virtues and miracles of candidates for canonization. The Vatican's Congregation for Causes of the Saints is still hard at work and, although '99 out of 100' alleged miracles fail the currently stringent scientific tests, Pope John Paul II has created nearly 500 of the c. 11,000 officially recorded saints.

Every church in Britain contained images, and relics were considered to give protection, healing and status to the building which housed them. Each parish church was dedicated to a saint whose feast day was observed as a parish holiday (holy day): a cross between festival and fair, with stalls set out in nave and churchyard, processions, singing and dancing. Christian celebrations incorporated ancient universal elements too strong to remove, their performance deemed acceptable if done in Christ's name: as Catherine Rachel John (John 1986) has commented about Cornwall's Helston Furry Dance: 'Christianity is the fulfilment of humanity, not its denial'. In fifteenth-century London, on the commemoration day of St Paul's Cathedral the head of a buck killed at the high altar and fixed on a pole was carried in procession.

Being human men and women, saints provided an accessible link between worshippers and the rather daunting Christian Trinity of Father, Son and Holy Spirit; their acts providing inspiration, comfort and guidance. Children were named after them and placed under their special protection. Towns, trades and guilds adopted appropriate saints as patrons: for instance, medieval wool-combers chose the fourth-century martyr St Blaise, who was ripped open by iron combs prior to beheading. St Clement (Bishop of Rome after St Peter), thrown into the sea tied to an anchor, was the perfect choice for the beacon-ships and lighthouses of Trinity House. Crispin and Crispinian were noble Romans martyrs who made a living as shoemakers and became patrons of their craft. An English legend had them setting up shop in Faversham (Kent), and Shakespeare's Henry V invokes them at Agincourt before the battle fought on their feast. The apostle Jude, martyred with St Simon in Persia, is considered patron of difficult situations and hopeless cases.

Henry VIII (1509–47) obsessively dismantled the shrines in Britain to end Rome's influence and greatly enrich his Treasury. In the times of Edward VI (1547–53) and the Commonwealth (1649–53) the 'cleansing' continued with the breaking of images, the burning of rood screens, the destruction of stained glass and wall paintings. Before the Reformation, saints featured actively and significantly in the everyday lives of the whole population and they have an influence on modern life beyond the Orthodox and Catholic Churches. Motorists often carry a medallion of Christopher, patron saint of travellers, the legendary giant who bore the weight of Christ. It was believed that seeing Christopher's image would protect the viewer from sudden death that day, which is why scenes of him carrying the Infant Jesus across a river were painted inside medieval churches opposite the southern door.

Santa Claus, that inveterate giver of Christmas presents, has his origins in Nicholas, a fourth-century bishop of south-west Turkey who is patron saint of children. The late twelfth-century black Tournai marble font in Winchester Cathedral depicts episodes from St Nicholas's legendary life, including him reviving three murdered boys pickled in a brine tub and giving bags of gold as marriage dowries to three young women to save them from prostitution. The pagan Romans gave presents between Saturnalia on 21 December and the Sun's birthday on 25th December. St Valentine was reputedly martyred in the third century on 14 February, traditionally the day on which birds were believed to pair. Exchanging love tokens in Valentine's name is another dilution of pagan custom: on the eve of Lupercalia, young women and men drew lots for sexual partners ready for the following day's festivities in honour of Februa, late-winter moon goddess of love and fertility.

The church at St Merryn (Cornwall) is associated with the legendary seventh-century St Marina who, disguised as a boy, was taken by her father into a monastery where she became a saintly 'monk'. After many years Marina/Merryn was forced to leave when accused by a local woman of fathering her child. St Wilgefortis was a beautiful, virtuous Portuguese princess who miraculously grew a beard and moustache to repel the King of Sicily. Greatly annoyed, her pagan father had her crucified; during her suffering she prayed to be able to remove the troubles and encumbrances of those who invoked her. Women in medieval England would offer oats to a statue of 'St Uncumber' to rid them of their husbands. Her legend may have been prompted by the existence of crucifixes showing a bearded Christ wearing shoes, his body covered by a robe.

Many people are strongly drawn by the continuing power of Britain's ancient holy places, the distinctive atmosphere, capricious weather and subtle beauty of the land. In these 'millennium times' there is a yearning for things sacred and spiritual, a strong curiosity in the history of ideas and places, in knowledge and 'human interest' stories from earlier cultures which are relevant to those of today. My interest is in the saints as remarkable individuals, in religious beliefs generally, and in the widely varying consequences of faith, ambition, power and certainty. In common with other religions, the history of Christianity and the stories of its saints – real or otherwise – have much to teach us about the darkness and light of what it is to be human.

St Gwyndaf's Church, Llanwnda,
Pembrokeshire

2.
Old Gods and Wandering Souls
Celtic Saints

During the fifth to eighth centuries AD, *many charismatic Celtic saints carried their burning love of Christ throughout Britain. It was a murky period covering the gradual breakdown of Roman Britain, the making of 'England' and the continuation of distinctly different societies in the south-west, west and north. By Celtic, I mean native-born Britons and the Romano-British, the missionaries from Celtic-speaking countries such as Brittany and Ireland and other miscellaneous individuals of non-Germanic stock who spread Christianity throughout Britain in 'Celtic' styles and locations. As Christianity was gaining ground in the Roman world, the empire was losing its cohesion: it had effectively collapsed by 406, and came to an end in the West in 476. Roman control in Britain was weakened during the fourth century by successive military reorganizations, raids and revolts, removal of troops by central government and usurpers, and the subsequent expulsion of Roman officials. In 410, the year when Alaric the Visigoth sacked the city of Rome, Emperor Honorius received a request for instructions and aid from the British leaders. His reply, that they must see to their own defence, formally marked the end of Rome's interest in its far-flung province, but another plea was sent to Rome around 446: 'to Aetius, thrice consul, come the groans of the Britons ... the barbarians drive us into the sea, the sea drives us back to the barbarians...'. It went unanswered, leaving relatively small numbers of rebellious federate Saxon troops and other pagan Germanic migrants from across the North Sea to settle on the eastern fringes of what eventually came to be England. Much of the native population stayed put, but there was some displacement westwards, and a significant number of Britons moved to Brittany and the Loire during the period 460–70.*

Aspects of Roman life did survive the initial intrusions – there was a British bishop named Manseutus at the Council of Tours in 462 – but by the mid-sixth century pagan Anglo-Saxon expansion and the decay of former state structures had created a 'Celtic-speaking fringe' which was neither Romano-British nor English. The few remaining bishops and clergy came under the power of local tribal chieftain-kings and the retreat into monasticism accelerated. Christian monasticism, initially inspired by the ascetic values of the desert communities of fourth-century Egypt, was fuelled by increasing perceptions of the secular world as evil and irrelevant. Advancing barbarians were seen as signs of God's displeasure, and devastating climatic events recorded in Asia and Europe from around 536 were also viewed as 'biblical' punishments. Comets filled the skies while dust veils covered the sun; earthquakes, floods, chill winds and summer snow caused crop failures and famine; and in 540 the first recorded outbreak of bubonic plague occurred in Egypt then spread across Europe, creating panic and disorder. Into this world strode the Celtic missionaries like Old Testament prophets, full of certainty and zeal, preaching against an undeniably corrupt and disintegrating secular system: this was the 'Age of Saints'.

The Christianity kept alive or reintroduced to Celtic areas of Britain was essentially that of the wider Catholic Church. Pilgrimages and official visits were made to Rome, there was free movement between monasteries, training in dogma and theology was international and Latin, through study of the scriptures, served as the common language. However, significant differences in organization and approach existed. The Celtic Church, relying more on individuals than rigid structures, was influenced by family loyalties, obligations and the powers of tribal leaders. Its administration was monastic rather than diocesan: an abbot had ecclesiastical jurisdiction over the surrounding area, a Celtic bishop was part of the monastic community and subject to his abbot. Positions often became hereditary with extended, extravagant pedigrees being just as important to Celtic clerics and saints as they were to their pagan contemporaries and forbears.

The Roman clerical tonsure resembled Christ's crown of thorns with a circle of hair around a shaved centre and sides. Celtic clergy also shaved the front of their heads from ear to ear, leaving an arc of long hair around the back: a striking and 'primitive' style attributed by Roman opponents to the sorcerer Simon Magus who bewitched the citizens of Samaria (Acts 8:9–24).

The Celtic Church came into conflict with Roman missionaries and their converts chiefly over the calculation of Easter. Commemoration of Christ's resurrection was originally linked to the Passover full moon, observed on the fourteenth day of the Jewish month of Nisan (March/April) and, as in Britain, originally a pastoral spring equinox celebration requiring a 'bright, triumphant moon'. From the second century, Easter in Rome was celebrated on a Sunday, which had become the Christian weekly day of worship and was held to be the original day of resurrection. Roman practice was imposed on the Celtic Church in 664 at the Synod of Whitby, but it was not until 768 that the Church in North Wales was persuaded to adopt the change by Bishop Elfod (Elfoddwy) of Bangor. Formalization of the Celtic Church, started by Romano-Gaulish missionaries and their Anglo-Saxon converts, was completed in the twelfth century under the Anglo-Normans, whose social and religious influence caused dioceses to be established at some of the old monastic centres. A system of clearly defined parishes was also created, dedications to a local saint often being replaced by an officially approved universal one.

Celtic saints often took over ancient sacred sites and displayed the powerful attributes of former pagan gods and heroes, including the ability to reunite severed heads and bodies. They also assumed some of the functions of druids and bards, and were not afraid to use the legally recognized techniques of fasting and cursing to gain redress. In a battle at Chester around 615, the Northumbrian King Athelfrith slaughtered over 1000 monks of Bangor-is-Coed (Flintshire) who supported the Britons of Powys. The monks, who had fasted for three days and were grouped apart from the armies, were attacked first by Athelfrith in order to end their prayers against him.

Austerities, physical magic and spiritual powers were used to impress Celtic royalty and to overwhelm their pagan priests and advisers, much as Moses and Aaron did with the Pharaoh in Egypt. An affinity with the natural world runs through the Celtic stories, in particular an influence over animals and the weather: St Carantoc tamed a troublesome dragon for King Arthur; St Kew impressed her brother St Docco by making a wild boar obey her; St Ciaran of Saighir was helped by a fox, wolf and a badger; an otter regularly brought salmon to St Kevin who allowed a blackbird to lay and hatch an egg in his outstretched hand, and several saints milked does and used stags to draw their ploughs. Many Celtic saints had an 'edge' about them, being anything but meek or compassionate: several deliberately killed people by magic or more traditional means; the saints of Ireland (except Columba) were so jealous of St Ciaran of Clonmacnoise that they prayed and fasted for his early death; there were violent quarrels concerning ownership of magic bells and decorated gospels; and SS Aedan and Gwynda came to blows over the dedication of a Pembrokeshire well. In The Journey Through Wales (1188), Gerald of Wales wrote: 'both the Irish and the Welsh are more prone to anger and revenge in this life than other nations, and similarly their Saints in the next world seem much more vindictive'. In contrast to this, St Teilo's answer to St Cadoc's question 'what is the greatest wisdom in a man?' was 'to refrain from injuring another when he has power to do so'.

Celtic saints were tough, determined individualists who often sought out remote hostile places to cleanse their souls by battling with privation and the elements. St Ronan, troubled in the seventh century by the evil-tongued women of the Butt of Lewis

(Outer Hebrides), escaped with the help of a whale to Rona island forty miles to the north-east, where he built a drystone tent-shaped oratory and fought off attacks by demons. St Finan traditionally founded the early monastery of Skellig Michael (Co. Kerry), where drystone beehive huts and oratories cling to the island's steep shoulders. Monks carried over mainland soil in wicker boats to create a terraced garden on the barren Atlantic rock. The Breton St Winwaloe, commemorated at Gunwalloe (Cornwall), wore a hair shirt underneath his goat skins, drank only water flavoured with wild herbs, ate coarse barley bread mixed with ashes, prayed for long periods with his arms painfully outstretched and slept on a bed of sand (which can be very comfortable) with a stone for a pillow.

Today, Celtic Christianity is undergoing yet another revival as its emphasis on a direct individual relationship with God, celebration of the natural world, asceticism and mysticism appeal to the many currently seeking a simpler, more personal expression of spirituality. Although most Celtic saints are 'unofficial' or uncanonized — the epithet 'saint' being very freely applied to church-founders — a special quality of holiness shines out from their human weakness and eccentricity, giving valuable inspiration and guidance to anyone with intimations of something beyond the material.

At first glance St Celynin's Church, high above Rowen in the Conwy valley, appears to lie in an empty waste, but the site is an ancient one, carefully chosen. The area is rich in prehistoric remains and the church stands where healing springs bubble to the surface and footpaths and walled trackways meet. There used to be an inn here, and a stable attached to the churchyard wall. A renovated holy well at its southern corner (lower right in photograph on p.10) was popular for cures in the nineteenth century: sickly children were dipped there in the early morning, then carried in blankets to sleep at a nearby farmhouse. If a child's clothes floated when placed on the water the patient would recover but there was no hope if they sank. There is a fort on the summit of Cerrig y Ddinas north-east of the church, a hut circle to the south. The well was undoubtedly significant before St Celynin's sixth-century 'arrival': he may have taken over the hut of the spring's guardian or he may simply be a Christian personification of the pagan spirit of place. His name derives from the holly (*celynnen*), a Celtic sacred tree believed to give refuge to the sun in winter, planted by the Romans to protect their houses from lightning and evil spirits.

St Tecla's Well, Llandegla, beside the River Alun, south-west of her church, may be named after the fourth-century hermit-princess of Gwynedd, murdered on a tidal islet where the Wye joins the Severn estuary. It had a reputation for curing epilepsy – known locally as St Tecla's disease (*Clwyf Tecla*) – and was considered effective against king's evil or scrofula, a form of tuberculosis of the lymphatic glands. A collection of Celtic stone heads from the area suggests that the well was a powerful pagan place before being

St Celynin's Church, Llangelynin, Conwy

assigned to a Christian saint. The complicated healing ritual for epilepsy involved washing hands and feet in the water after sunset on a Friday, walking three times round the well carrying a live cock in a basket while reciting the Lord's Prayer, then throwing into the water a pin used to draw blood from the cock. The church was circled in the same manner before the patient spent the night under the Communion Table with the Bible as a pillow. Next morning the disease was transferred to the cock by blowing into its beak and leaving it to die in the church. Payment was made to the church and to the

Ffynnon Degla, St Tecla's Well, Llandegla, Denbighshire

parish clerk who assisted at the well. Excavations have uncovered coins in the well going back to the eighteenth century, as well as pins, fragments of pottery, and, at the lowest levels, dozens of pieces of quartz and calcite.

The ritual use of pleasingly attractive, rounded white stones goes right back to the time of the megalithic tombs. Quartz, rock crystal and white pebbles were associated with healing, burial and folk-magic throughout the Celtic world, and often included in monastic burials as on Iona and at St Docco's in Llandough (Vale of Glamorgan). Revelation 2:17 mentions the reward of a white stone containing a secret spiritual name. Many small, remote wells in Wales were regularly honoured with such offerings or a charm stone was dipped into water to make a potent drink for sick people or animals. Prominent Highland families possessed charm stones believed to deliver cures, prophecies and victory in battle. Rounded stones placed in rock hollows were 'turned' to make curses, grant wishes, and – as at Kilchoman (Islay) – aid the conception of a son. Pilgrims to holy wells, especially in Ireland, still make offerings of white stones and add them to cairns at sacred sites. Wells such as the one destroyed at Llanelian (Conwy) were considered so powerful that they were reputed to cause injury or death.

St Piran's (Perran) name is attached to a local ale and several landscape features around Penhale Sands south-west of Newquay. It also occurs along the route linking the Atlantic coast and the Fal estuary which was taken by missionaries and pilgrims, travelling between Ireland or South Wales and Brittany, who wished to avoid the dangerous sea journey around Land's End. As Cornwall's best-loved saint, a rich legacy of devotion, cult practice and legend is attached to his name but he has no authentic *Life* of his own. His thirteenth-century story, written for Exeter Cathedral who owned the manor and church of Perranzabuloe (Piran in the Sand) and claimed to possess an arm relic of the saint, seems to be an adaptation of the fabulous life of St Ciaran (Kieran) of Saighir with the addition of Piran/Ciaran leaving Ireland for Cornwall near the end of his days, having lived for 200 years without losing a tooth, thanks to his mother swallowing an intensely bright star after his conception.

St Piran's Cross, Perranporth, Cornwall

Irish tradition has Ciaran dying at his monastery in Co. Offaly and 'Piran' is now considered a separate individual whose genuine biographical details were already lost by the Middle Ages.

St Piran is also commemorated in Brittany, especially at Trézélidé, near St Pol de Léon, where there are statues of him in the church and a wayside shrine. His earliest mention in Cornwall is the place-name *Carnperan* in an Anglo-Saxon charter of 960 which calls the Celtic cross 'Christ's Mace'. He is said to have died on 5 March sometime around 480. A nave-and-chancel chapel, resembling an early Irish oratory with its sculptured corbels, zigzag ornament and clay-mortared rough stones, lies buried in the dunes. This monastic centre, constantly threatened by encroaching sand, was abandoned by Norman times and a new parish church built on higher ground to the east on the boundary of the Church lands marked by Christ's Mace. According to an inventory of 1281 the church contained the head of St Piran in a wooden box bound and locked with iron, his pastoral staff covered with gold, silver and precious stones, his copper bell, his platter, the bier on which his body was carried and a silver cross containing further small relics. Piran's shrine was maintained into the reign of Mary I (1553–8), his relics being carried in procession at festivals (especially Rogation Days in April and May) to other associated parishes for veneration and fund-raising. The north-west wind continued to drive sand before it; the whole parish was almost 'drowned' in 1704, the church finally being overwhelmed a century later. The present (third) parish church of Perranzabuloe, completed in 1805, is two miles inland to the south. Shifting sands in the early nineteenth century revealed St Piran's lost oratory. Three headless skeletons were found buried beneath the chancel floor, their feet underlying the altar, their skulls nearby. One attribution of the remains is that they are those of St Piran, his mother and a companion such as St Ia (Ives). Other burials

Portable altar,
St David's Cathedral,
Pembrokeshire

laid out east-west were found just west of the oratory. An ugly concrete shelter was built in 1910 to give protection from the elements and rapacious tourists, but by the 1970s the chapel was being destroyed by the ever-present sand, rising water and persistent vandals. In 1980 the oratory inside its bunker was buried beneath a mound topped with a commemorative stone. Piran is the patron saint of miners (especially Tinners) who continued up to the nineteenth century to take a paid holiday around 5 March in his honour. Their reputation for enjoying themselves was such that anyone exhibiting signs of overindulgence was called a Perraner. The Cornish flag carries St Piran's Cross: a white cross on a black ground, said to represent gospel truth glowing amongst falsehood, as tin released from ore.

St Piran is claimed as the first surfer, credited with crossing the sea on a millstone. SS Carantoc and Petroc floated over on altar-stones, St Kea in a stone trough, St Ia on a leaf enlarged to the size of a boat and St Bride (Bridget) on a square of turf. Celtic priests carried small stone altars to celebrate the Eucharist, circular Irish examples possibly giving rise to tales of millstones. Flimsy-looking but highly buoyant and manoeuvrable wicker-framed coracles and keeled, sea-going currachs may have inspired ideas of leaves and sods.

St Sithney's Church, Sithney, Cornwall: a modern carving of the saint

Sithney, near Helston (Cornwall), is first mentioned as the saint's sanctuary in 1230, and in 1478 William Worcester stated that St Sithney was buried in the church 'neath the blood red stone'. His shrine was probably under the red-tinged arch of the Norman north transept which survives in the present church, built around 1450. Worcester also said that bad weather on Sithney's feast (19 September) caused the cross and banners to process without human aid. He is venerated in Brittany under the name of Sezni: at Guissény (on the coast north-east of Brest) his wooden statue above the church door looks north-west to meet the gaze of a stone companion on the south-east pinnacle of Sithney church tower. An eighteenth-century accounts entry for white silk ribbons and flowers for the 'Garland' refers to the ancient practice of 'crowning' the pinnacle statue with flowers and greenery on Sithney's feast. John Lelant (official historian to Henry VIII) found a *Life* of St Breaca surviving in Breage Church in the 1530s, which suggested that Sithney travelled with her group of missionaries from Ireland to Cornwall in the sixth century, but the detail 'Sinninus the Abbot who was with St Patrick in Rome' is borrowed from St Ciaran's story, as are most other details in the Guissény *Life*. It is not clear whether Sithney's cult originated in Britain, was carried from Ireland to Brittany possibly via Cornwall, or if Bretons fleeing Norman persecution in the tenth century brought or reintroduced the saint's relics to Cornwall. The carved statue brought to Sithney in 1986 by seven Breton priests is a modern copy by René Ragout of the one at Guissény. A popular Breton story tells how God revealed to Sezni that he was to become the patron saint of girls; greatly alarmed, the holy man complained he would have no peace from their requests for husbands and fine clothes. Offered mad dogs instead, Sithney expressed his strong preference for the stricken animals which are still taken to his well for cures. Wooden statues of other healing saints in Brittany with canine connections include Hubert, considered good for sores and dog-bites, and Tugen whose key when touched invests other keys with the power to drive off mad dogs.

St Pabo's Church, Llanbabo, Anglesey

During the fifth century determined individuals roamed the Celtic West preaching the Gospel of Christ, establishing hermitages, churches and monasteries. The majority of these buildings were simple structures of timber and thatch, often set within an enclosure delimited by an earthen bank or wattled fence (*bangor* in Welsh). The *Lives* of many early Celtic saints (e.g., lltud, Cadoc) describe them marking out a burial enclosure in which to site their church and cell. As these sacred spaces were usually curvilinear, a circular or oval graveyard surviving around a later church often indicates an early foundation. At Llanbabo an enclosure associated with a legendary fifth-century saint encircles a twelfth-century church. The east wall was rebuilt in the late fourteenth century when the present window was inserted; other windows have been added to the original walls and the whole building restored. Reset chevron carvings are above the modernized southern doorway, along with three stone faces of unknown date. Romantically referred to as St Pabo, his son and his daughter, they stare down at their churchyard burial places assigned by ancient parish tradition.

Inside the church is a memorial to St Pabo, who is depicted as a bearded king, crowned and holding a sceptre. Dating from around 1380, it is one of three, low relief carvings made by the same sculptor for Gruffudd ap Gwilym who had inherited land in Anglesey and married a Llanbabo heiress. The Eva Stone in Bangor Cathedral and St Iestyn in his church at Llaniestyn (SE Anglesey) make up the trio. Pabo (d. *c.* 510) is a shadowy figure: known as Pabo Post Prydain (the 'Prop' or 'Pillar of Britain'), he belongs to a semi-legendary dynasty of warriors and saints descended from Coel Godebog, a chieftain of the Scottish border area, who was part of a reputed movement of northern Britons into north-west Wales in late Roman times. Stories of Cunedda and his eight sons of the Votadini tribe moving south from the Firth of Forth to drive out Irish settlers and establish a new ruling family can be seen as an example of the Roman practice of using client tribes against hostile natives and raiders, or as

A fourteenth-century carving of St Pabo dressed as a king inside his church at Llanbabo, Anglesey

deliberate myth-making by the ninth-century rulers of Gwynedd wishing to justify their own intrusions. St Pabo is presented as a brave warrior who, having lost his northern territory to invaders, settled among his transplanted kinsmen where he took up the religious life by establishing a 'monastery' on Anglesey. He is claimed as the grandfather of St Asaph, and of St Deiniol who established the monastic enclosure which gave its name to Bangor Cathedral (Gwynedd). Whatever the truth of Pabo's existence or origins, it seems certain that the beautiful churchyard beside a small stream at Llanbabo is an authentic early Christian foundation.

St Woolos Cathedral, Newport

King Brychan, who gave his name to the Brecon area of mid Wales in the sixth century, may be illustrated with his progeny in the sixteenth-century stained glass of St Neot church (Cornwall), although an alternative interpretation is God the Father with souls in His lap. Brychan reputedly produced a brood of twenty-four saintly children (twelve daughters, twelve sons), but varying sources credit him with anything from 12 to 48 or beyond. Early Welsh texts document a Christian royal family, possibly with a *llys* (court) on the artificial island in Llangorse Lake east of Brecon, whose activities were mainly confined to Wales. The *Life of St Nectan*, written in the twelfth century for the monks of Hartland (Devon) who tended his shrine, deals with the missionary activities of St Brychan's vast family in Cornwall and north Devon, including many saints who do not appear in the older lists such as Clether, Endellion, Morwenna and Nectan himself. Research and excavation led Charles Thomas (Thomas 1994) to suggest that Brychan gave up his kingdom of Brycheiniog for a hermitage on Lundy Island (Bristol Channel) where he died, resting in a specially marked grave-monument until his relics were translated to Hartland for veneration under his adopted spiritual name of *Nechtan* ('washed').

Dubious lists of saints and their descendants were often drawn up by medieval monasteries and churches to authenticate their desire for extended territory and status: high-profile saints were claimed as original patrons while more obscure examples were attached to the church or principal founder to extend influence, gain authority and increase pilgrim revenues via the holding of a wide selection of relics. Stories were recycled or invented to explain inconsistencies and fill the terrible voids of unknowing. Variant forms of names within one language, attempts to spell unfamiliar spoken words, inconsistent translations and basic copying errors added to the confusion. Differing uses of such words as 'father' caused the later compilers considerable trouble: saints could be 'brothers (or sisters) in Christ', a spiritual instructor or mentor was often called 'father' or 'uncle'. Add the Celtic customs of fostering and hostage-exchange and it becomes clear just how unreliable the genealogies of saints can be.

Welsh texts concerning Brecknockshire tell of an arranged marriage between St Brychan's daughter Gwladys and Gwynllyw, prince of the territory to the south-east whose encampment overlooked the mouth of the Usk at Newport. The site is now called Stow Hill and Gwynllyw has been anglicized to Woolos. In spite of a Christian upbringing, Gwladys and her husband are reputed to have led a life of armed violence until persuaded by their son, St Cadoc, to adopt ways more devout. Their newly-austere regime included

daily dips in the Usk, walking naked to and from the river. Cadoc's opposition caused his mother to leave and, as an act of penitence, his father built a wattle church whose site is marked by a Galilee chapel, or narthex, sandwiched between the fifteenth-century tower and Norman nave. The subdued light of the pre-Conquest chapel dedicated to St Mary provides an atmospheric approach to the nave which is framed by a Norman archway incorporating Corinthian columns salvaged from Roman Caerleon. Stained glass windows in the south aisle include early twentieth-century representations of Cadoc and his parents. After leaving Newport, Gwladys lived near the Ebbw river before moving north-west to the high moorland above Gelligaer (Caerphilly). A Celtic-style memorial within the restored footings of a medieval chapel marks the site of her sixth-century foundation. Gelligaer parish church contains a ninth-century cross-slab found during excavations at Gwladys' chapel. The church is dedicated

St Cadog's Church, Llancarfan, Vale of Glamorgan

to her son St Cattwg (Cadoc) and a cup-marked boulder called Maen Cattwg lies nearby.

Cadoc was a leading saint in south-east Wales where his churches cluster around Roman sites. Llancarfan was his most celebrated monastery which he ran and protected as a proud tribal chief. Cadoc's community included scholars and scribes, soldiers and workmen, cooks, bakers and officials responsible for the food supply, a steward, sexton and doctor; retainers, guests, family members and dependants, since the hereditary structure of Celtic monasteries allowed for married clergy. It possessed herds, crops, barns, threshing floors, and used the island of Flat Holm (Echni) as a retreat and sheepwalk. His monks would fast for three days to influence events and Cadoc would punish with a curse any slight to his community or honour. Men attacking his barn were blinded, thieves of meat and drink were swallowed up by the earth after having their heads shaved and the lips and ears cut from their horses. Cadog caused the deaths of two careless disciples, an inefficient steward, an insubordinate servant and a peasant who refused him live coals. Wolves were turned to stone and Cadoc fasted against St David for attending a synod in his absence. Danes destroyed the monastery in 988, but it recovered in time to be taken over by the incoming Normans around 1094, given to St Peter's Monastery (Gloucester) and reduced to the status of a parish church.

In addition to the flow of missionaries from Ireland and Wales to Cornwall, Devon and Brittany, Welsh texts claim a reciprocal movement, notably featuring the Breton St Cadfan. His many followers included Tydecho who made cells at Llanymawddwy and Mallwyd, and yoked stags to the plough after his oxen were confiscated by Maelgwn, the tyrant of Gwynedd. Also listed is Trillo who established his shore-side oratory over a spring used for baptisms and had a healing well dedicated to him at Llandrillo, near Corwen (Denbighshire), over thirty miles inland to the south-east. As Bowen (Bowen 1956) has pointed out, the unreliable lists of Cadfan's 'disciples'

St Trillo's Chapel, Rhos-on-Sea, Conwy

Bardsey Island (Ynys Enlii), Llŷn, Gwynedd

are based on other dedications close to his churches. Their distribution strongly suggests church-founders arriving by boat, establishing bases near the coast before moving further inland via river valleys and surviving Roman roads. That the sea was the highway of these Celtic *peregrini* is certain, but their relationships and countries of origin are hard to define.

Cadfan (fifth–sixth century), grandson of Emyr of Brittany, founded his first monastery in Wales at Tywyn (Gwynedd) where a church and healing well preserve his name, but he is best known for developing a monastic community on Enlli off the tip of the Llŷn peninsula. The island may originally have been the sanctuary of a pagan Celtic deity, then home to Christian solitaries including Einion, a prince of Llŷn. Enlli may also have served as a Lenten retreat for a mainland community at Capel Anelog (north of Aberdaron) where tombstones of the Celtic priests Senacus and Veracius of *c.* 500 have been found. The Latin inscriptions show Greek and Gaulish influences, and the description of Senacus lying with 'a multitude of the brethren' may have given rise to the tradition of 20,000 saints buried on Enlli. St Deiniol retired from his monastery at Bangor to die on Bardsey around 584, and St Dyfrig (Dubricius) from Herefordshire and South Wales did likewise. When the grave of

Dyfrig was recognized in 1120 his body was translated to Llandaff (Cardiff) along with those of Elgar, an English hermit who had lived a 'lean' life on Enlli for more than fourteen years. Elgar dug a grave in his oratory and lay down to die beside it: while still just warm he was found and buried by passing sailors. Gerald of Wales described a community of Culdees (Celtic 'servants of God' not attached to a Roman monastic order) in 1188 but by 1212 there were Augustinian canons on the island, the abbey remaining under that order until abolition in 1536–7.

St Dwynwen is the patron saint of Welsh lovers, her feast celebrated on 25 January. One of King Brychan's many reputed offspring, she lived here in a hermitage commemorated by a Latin cross; the modern Celtic cross is a memorial to shipwreck victims. Her legend has her betrothed to Maelon but in love with another. Aware of her distress, God turned the would-be 'ravisher' to icy stone causing Dwynwen to make three pleas: that Maelon should be restored, that she might never wish to marry and that all true-hearted lovers could win their chosen one or be freed from desire. The fourteenth-century poet Dafydd ap Gwilym wrote a prayer to Dwynwen, imploring her to be a persuasive messenger of love to elusive Morfudd, his longed-for sweetheart. Dafydd describes Dwynwen's church as a place of 'great

Llanddwyn Island, Newborough, Anglesey

resort' with vigils and blazing candles in the chancel. A late fifteenth-century description mentions the saint's statue, miracles wrought at her holy well, and crowds of young people bearing candles and offerings. By 1710 Dwynwen was said to have been martyred at her well which was believed to tell fortunes and indicate likely success in love. An attendant read omens by watching the movements of small eels or fish when lovers' handkerchiefs were spread on the water. A rag or feather was also used. If the object was taken under it denoted unfaithfulness in the lover. Bubbling or 'boiling' of the water while the ceremonies were in progress was a favourable sign. The lovelorn hoped to be cured by drinking the water or, if this failed, by total immersion. A poem of 1852 describes Ceiriog

OPPOSITE: Bardsey Island, St Mary's Abbey, Gwynedd.
The main remnant of the church, chapels, oratory, domestic accommodation, barns, orchards and gardens of St Mary's Abbey is the thirteenth-century tower standing in a later graveyard surrounded by 'model' farmhouses of the 1870s. A seventh-century cross-inscribed stone, a tenth-century grave slab bearing a figure in a pleated 'skirt' and lumps of masonry and dressed sandstone also survive. Many burials were disturbed during the digging of new foundations west (right) of the tower and some of the long bones were used in fences. Skeletons arranged with feet to the east were discovered in long cists under the present roadway.

OPPOSITE: St Nonna's Well, Pelynt, Cornwall.

Offerings of pins for the 'little people' used to be made at Ninnie's or Piskies' well where ferns, mosses and a decorated basin glow green in the dark interior.

BELOW: St Non's, St David's, Pembrokeshire.

A modern Celtic-style chapel at St Non's is dedicated to Our Lady and St Non. A retreat house, shrine to Our Lady, St Non's Well and a ruined chapel are nearby.

St Non's Chapel, St David's, Pembrokeshire

jumping into the well but emerging 'twice as much in love as ever before'. Pilgrimages continued late into the sixteenth century, when the chancel – the main survival of the cruciform church – was rebuilt. The well, reduced to an uninspiring trickle of water emerging from the cliff, is beneath a cleft rock visible through the chancel's north window: the rock split in response to Dwynwen's dying request for a view of her final sunset.

Pelynt parish may be named after Non, the mother of St David or an obscure local saint. Non died in Brittany and her connection with Cornwall is uncertain, but a 'Nonnita' is named on the sixth-century Cuby Stone at Tregony Church and in the Middle Ages her relics were kept at Altarnun (the altar of Non) where she is patron of the church and holy well. The adjoining parish of Davidstow mirrors similar Non–David pairings in

Pembrokeshire and Brittany, but some believe the dedications are to a male companion of David, the stories of his birth to a 'nun' pure invention.

Non's story is told in the *Life of St David* written by Rhigyfarch, son of the Bishop of St David's, in the 1090s. She was made pregnant by a chieftain (and/or monk) named Sant (Saint) from the Cardigan area. An angel told both St Patrick and St Gildas that their missionary work in Pembrokeshire would be taken over by 'David', and a local ruler was warned by his seers of the birth of a boy with great spiritual power. David's traditional birthplace – which shone with light during the delivery in a violent storm – is commemorated by a chapel and well. St Non moved to Brittany (via Cornwall?) where Dirinon (Finistère) combines the Breton word for oaks with the name of the saint, who set up a hermitage among pagan trees. Dirinon has a cenotaph chapel and finger relic of St Non. Her *pardon* or feast is held there on the third Sunday after Easter when a procession with cross and banners is made between St Non's Well and St Divy's Chapel. (St David's story is told in Chapter 7.)

St Samson (Sampson) was a Welsh missionary who died around 565 as Bishop of Dol in Brittany. His *Life*, written by a monk of Dol about sixty years after Samson's death, is one of the earliest and most informative of such chronicles. The writer consulted an aged monk at Samson's Cornish monastery who possessed written and oral information passed on from the saint's mother via a cousin. Samson's parents, Amon of Dyfed and Anna of Gwent, sent him aged five to be educated by St Illtud at Llantwit Major (Vale of Glamorgan) where he was soon ordained deacon, then priest, by St Dyfrig (Dubricius), the 'pope' (*papa*) of the area. Fearful that he would be made abbot over them, Illtud's jealous nephews attempted to kill Samson by poisoning his herbal tea. Samson went to Caldey Island as cellarer, becoming abbot after Piro, the founder, fell drunk into a well. At night St Samson indulged his mystical inclinations, slipping in and out of sleep propped against a wall waiting for visions.

After a visit to Ireland with a group of pilgrims returning from Rome, Samson set up a small monastery in a deserted fort with his father and two companions but lived mainly in a cave pursuing his austere regime of fasting and wakefulness. He was

Caldey is home to a Mediterranean-looking monastery built 1910–13 and an order of Reformed Cistercians who pray, and make perfume from the fragrant gorse. In the Old Priory church a sandstone slab bears an incised cross, an eighth-century Latin memorial to Catuoconus and an earlier ogham inscription referring to 'the (tonsured) servant of Dyfrig'. St Illtud is shown in the adjacent stained glass window in conversation with an angel.

St Sampson's Church and Well, Golant, Cornwall

St Cuby's Well, Duloe, Cornwall

called from these private devotions to become abbot of Llantwit, and made a bishop by Dyfrig. During a vigil 'a mighty man shining' told him that he was destined to become very great in the Church as a pilgrim beyond the sea. Collecting goods and companions Samson took ship for Cornwall, landing in the Camel estuary. The brethren of Lan Docco monastery, founded by an earlier Welsh missionary at or near modern St Kew, sent a spokesman to him to say that their community, having fallen from its former high standard, was undeserving of such a holy visitor. Loading books and sacred vessels into a wagon, and obtaining two horses to pull his small Irish 'car', Samson followed the ancient trade route south-eastwards across the peninsula to the Fowey estuary. Somewhere on Bodmin Moor he encountered a wild festival being held in honour of a wooden image below a hill-top standing stone. As Samson investigated the pagan revel, a boy fell from his horse and lay senseless. The saint revived him, unharmed, with a two-hour prayer, carved a cross on the monolith and persuaded the worshippers to destroy their wooden ancestor. Travelling on he overcame a troublesome serpent and occupied its cave while establishing a monastery.

Golant church with its spring is the traditional site of Samson's monastery but, as it appears not to be an ancient foundation, Fowey itself has been suggested as a better location (Thomas 1994) and a cave in Golant village identified as the serpent's lair (Olson 1989). Thanks to the twelfth-century chronicler Béroul, Golant church is also linked with the tragic love story of King Mark, Tristan and Iseult (Isolde). Samson is depicted in the chancel north window and on the pulpit as a bishop carrying a cross. Leaving his father to head the Cornish monastery, Samson continued his missionary work in Brittany, founding many churches with help from the Frankish royal family, including Dol where he was buried aged over 100. The *Life of St Teilo* describes Teilo escaping the 'yellow plague' in Britain by spending time at Dol helping St Samson lay out the monastic orchard.

St Cybi (Cuby, Kebius) is a fine example of a Celtic traveller, or *peregrinus*, with dedications charting his progress from

Cornwall to Anglesey (possibly via Ireland) against the tide of missionaries heading south. His churches and wells are within easy reach of the coast or such navigable rivers as the Fal, East Looe, Usk and Teifi. At Tregony – Cybi's other main Cornish foundation and rival for the honour of his birth – a sixth-century memorial set into the church wall commemorates three children of *Ercilingus:* two masculine names plus *Nonnita* identified as Nonna, mother of St David and reputed aunt to Cybi. The medieval well-house built of granite blocks at Duloe has an antechamber and seat. At the rear is a square pool inside a beehive cell whose corbelled roof is a nesting site for swallows. Water used to flow into a carved basin, removed in the nineteenth century. Cybi's medieval *Life* credits him with missionary travels in Ireland, pilgrimages to Jerusalem and to Rome, where he declined to become pope despite being chosen by the Holy Spirit in the form of a dove. He served under St Hilary, Bishop of Poitiers, before returning from France with ten disciples to evangelize Cornwall and Wales. A

standing stone near the River Usk, south-east of his church at Llangybi (Monmouthshire), is associated with a characteristically colourful incident. Having camped in the meadow with his followers, Cybi was confronted by an angry local ruler whose horse suddenly dropped dead while his retainers went blind; when Cybi's prayers undid the harm, land was granted for a church. At Llangybi near Lampeter (Ceredigion) there is a holy well known as Ffynnon-wen (white well) or Ffynnon Gybi. The saint is reputed to have lived nearby in a house called Llety Gybi, possibly the destroyed megalithic burial chamber formerly used in conjunction with his well for Ascension Eve cures (Jones 1992). At Llangybi in Llŷn (Gwynedd) another healing well credited to Cybi became a place of medieval pilgrimage and, in the eighteenth century, a spa resort curing the blind, lame, fever-ridden and warty.

In troubled times the Romans built a

St Cybi's Church (Eglwys y Bedd) and Caer Gybi Roman Fort, Holyhead, Anglesey

signal tower on Holyhead Mountain to watch over the seaways and by AD300 they had constructed three high stone walls to create a defended beaching point for their ships protecting the coastal waters from Irish raiders. It was some 200 years later that St Cybi founded a monastery inside the ruined fort after using his persuasive powers on the volatile Welsh king Maelgwn Gwynedd of Cunedda. The contemporary writer St Gildas denounces 'Maglocunus' in *The Ruin of Britain* as an evil debaucher, mighty in power and malice, profuse in giving but extravagant in sin. Maelgwn's death by the 'yellow plague' in 547 was prophesied by the bard Taliesin. St Cybi's relics were stolen from Holyhead in the sixteenth century by pirates who took them to Ireland. A modernized detached chapel (Eglwys y Bedd – Church of the Grave) stands on the traditional site of Cybi's burial close to the Roman wall and medieval church.

Cybi's great friend Seiriol is credited with heading the linked communities of Priestholm and Penmon. A twelfth-century tower with a pyramidal stone roof stands within an earlier monastic enclosure on the rocky island. The tower was built butting up to a small, square chapel which had a stone barrel-vault and high, steeply-pitched roof looking something like a small version of the twelfth-century Cormac's Chapel at Cashel (Co. Tipperary). It covered the burial of a tall, muscular man who had been squeezed into a rock-cut grave on his back with knees bent upwards. Other burials on a different alignment were made close by. A larger chancel later replaced the *cella memoriae* on the east side of the tower and a nave was constructed against the tower on the west. In 1188 Gerald of Wales described the island as the burial place of many saints, where women were never allowed to set foot. He also said it was the home of hermits who served God by labouring with their hands: if discord arose between the holy men, a species of small mice stole and spoiled their provisions but immediately disappeared when passions subsided. In 630 Cadwallon of Gwynedd was besieged at Priestholm by Edwin of Northumbria and forced into temporary exile in Ireland.

St Seiriol's Well, Penmon Priory, Anglesey

The monastery which grew on Seiriol's foundations was swept away by Viking raids in 968. Penmon 'the fairest spot in all Anglesey' was 'devastated', 1000 men were claimed killed and 2000 captives taken as slaves from Anglesey in 987. A carved stone cross standing in the south transept is one of the few survivals from the tenth century at

St Beuno's Church, Clynnog Fawr, Gwynedd

Penmon. The Romanesque church was built around 1160 during the reign of Owain Gwynedd. In the thirteenth century, when the Celtic monastery was reorganized as an Augustinian priory, a large chancel was added with other buildings around a cloister. The southern range contained cellars and the canons' dining room with dormitory above. A warming-room or private apartment was built on later, and a dovecote added to the complex after the priory had been dissolved. Circular footings and a well house north-east of the church are traditionally described as Seiriol's cell and chapel, but excavations have failed to link them to the early Christian period. The brickwork dates from around 1710, the stone pool, benches and slabbed floor may be earlier. The boulder circle is a puzzle but very unlikely to have been Seiriol's hut. Cures were claimed at the spring which still flows into the monastic fish-pond. Cybi lived in the west of Anglesey, Seiriol in the east:

St Beuno's Well, Clynnog Fawr, Gwynedd

they would walk to the middle of the island to converse at their wells at Pont Clorach (Llanerchymedd) where only the dilapidated Ffynnon Gybi (SH 449841) survives. Seiriol (the Fair) would set out and return with the sun at his back, tanned Cybi (the Tawny) with the sun in his eyes.

What is known of the 'Apostle of North Wales', St Beuno (d. *c.* 640), comes mainly from the brief summary made by an anchorite at Llanddewi-Brefi (Ceredigion) around 1350. Descended from the princes of Powys, Beuno was educated at the monastery of Caerwent (Monmouthshire) and established a church in Herefordshire before returning to Powys to tend his dying father. After burying him, and planting an oak tree reputed to kill Englishmen, he moved to Berriew where he was unsettled by hearing a Saxon hunting cry from across the River Severn. Moving on he spent time with St Tysilio at Meifod, then travelled north to the Clwyd valley area before settling at Clynnog (*Celynog*, 'the village in the holly trees'), on land given by a cousin of Cadwallon, king of Gwynedd. Beuno restored several people to life, including a princess of Gwent and his niece, Gwenfrewi of Holywell (Flintshire). He also cursed a few, notably Cadwallon himself and some princelings of Powys who demanded board and lodging of him, then complained that the food was bewitched. A *clas*, or mother church, with a college of canons developed around Beuno's tomb at Clynnog. By the twelfth century it was a major stopping place for Bardsey pilgrims, especially those travelling along the north-west coast from Holywell. Pilgrim donations paid for the extensive rebuilding of 1480–1530 which created the present spacious, light-filled structure. A detached chapel covers the site of Beuno's original shrine-chapel and part of the cemetery which grew up around the founder's grave. The sixteenth-century chapel was linked to the church tower in the seventeenth century by a deceptively ancient-looking stone-roofed passage, very similar to the arrangement at Llaneilian (Anglesey). A large natural boulder standing by the north transept door was discovered in 1928 buried near the centre of the crossing, its top level with the original floor. It is tempting to see this as a pagan stone incorporated as an omphalos (navel stone) within the church.

Beuno had a great reputation for healing, his well and chapel being used extensively for cures, especially of epileptic children. After bathing in the well a patient would spend the night in Capel Beuno lying on 'his' stone tomb or altar which survived until 1856. Sleep was made easier by a layer of rushes or, in one case seen by Thomas Pennant in 1776, a feather bed. Scrapings were taken from the stone pillars and mixed with spring water as a cure for sore eyes. Lambs or heifers born with Beuno's Mark – a hollow or split in the ear – were offered to the church, the sale money placed in Cyff Beuno, a padlocked wooden chest.

Beuno was assisted in his missionary work by numerous followers whose churches form dense groupings with his, especially on Llŷn and the west coast of Anglesey. SS Aelhaearn,

St Cwyfan's Church, Llangwyfan, Anglesey

Cwyfan, Edern and Twrog are among those named in Beuno's *Life*. St Cwfan's is a perfect Celtic location: a tidal island in a small sandy bay, not far from Beuno's church at Aberffraw and the palace of the kings of Gwynedd.

St Columba and twelve companions came to Iona in 563 to set up a monastery within the kingdom of Dalriada (Argyll) which had been established sixty years earlier by the ruling élite of a Gaelic-speaking tribe from Co. Antrim in Scotia (Ireland). Columba was born in 521 to a Co. Donegal noble family, a branch of the Uí Néill clan and kin to the

High Kings of Ireland. Fostered and trained by priests, he combined a pagan Celtic inheritance with the unquenchable fire of the love of God. There had been Christian communities in Ireland since the early fifth

St Mary's Abbey and Cladh an Disirt, Iona, Argyll

OPPOSITE: Sithean Mor, Iona, Argyll

century but the customs of earlier times often sat uneasily with Christian virtues. Columba's childhood name was Crimthann (fox), perhaps descriptive of his quick nature and temper. Having adopted the name Colum (Columba: dove) he was known affectionately as Columcille (church-dove).

Columba is credited with founding thirty-seven monasteries in Ireland, including Durrow, Kells and Derry, his first love whose dense oak woods he declared crowded with heaven's angels. In his early forties he distanced himself from the secular distractions and political intrigues of his kinfolk by moving to Scotland as 'a pilgrim for Christ'. Later stories speak of the hostility of other Irish saints, and of his enforced exile for provoking a battle against the High King in which 3000 perished. Choosing a sheltered site on the north-east coast of Iona overlooking the Ross of Mull, Columba's community created a twenty-acre, sub-rectangular monastic enclosure bounded by a high bank (*vallum*) and a ditch which, in places, had been cut through solid rock. Columba's buildings — sited in the same area as the later Benedictine abbey — were made of wattle and imported timber with roofs of reed-thatch. The monastery had a church and cemetery, sleeping cubicles, a communal building for cooking and eating, a guest-house, workshops, barns and a corn-drying kiln. Pollen samples from around the abbey reveal ash, birch, hazel, oak and willow, but no trace of the yew trees from which Iona (yewy island) is believed to derive its name. The monks grew culinary and medicinal herbs, vegetables, fruit, barley (bere) and oats, and ate red seaweed off the rocks. They kept cows, sheep, goats, and used a horse to pull the milk-wagon. Other more exotic products were brought to the island and seals on the islet of Soay were described by Columba as 'ours by right'. Leather goods were made, wooden bowls turned on pole-lathes, beeswax tablets employed for everyday writing and animal skins for manuscripts.

Columba slept on a rocky bed with a stone pillow which was later used to mark his grave. A water-worn boulder carved with a ring-cross (in the abbey museum) found in 1870 was optimistically christened 'Columba's Pillow', but its age and discovery location make this unlikely. Columba used to write in a wooden structure, possibly raised on piles or joists, on higher ground above the monastery with a view over Iona Sound to the shore of Mull. The rocky knoll (Tòrr an Aba) immediately west of the abbey may be the site of his cell. Nearby are the eighth-century high cross of St Martin, and St Mary's Chapel used by medieval pilgrims on their approach to the abbey.

The 'great mound of the fairies' lies beside the ancient route across Iona's narrow central plain to the western Bay at the Back of the Ocean. The fertile beach-land of the machair – where cereals grew and cattle still browse on seaweed – was a favourite haunt of Columba, who was taken to Sithean in a cart to announce his approaching death to monks working in the fields. The mound is also called 'Hill of the Angels' because Columba was observed here surrounded by a host of white-clad angels while he prayed with outstretched arms.

Angels and a marvellous monster were also seen on a rock in Iona Sound. Pilgrims and islanders would gather at Sithean on the feast of St Michael (29 September) in the hope of visions, and in the 1770s Thomas Pennant described horse races around the mound on the same day.

Urquhart Castle and Loch Ness, Inverness

Bede's claim that St Columba converted the Picts to the faith of Christ is an over-simplification. Columba made journeys into Pictland (to the north and east of Dalriada) in the company of other saints from Ireland to obtain King Bridei's (Bride, Brude) blessing for settlement and missionary work in his kingdom and the Gaelic (Irish) colony. After opening (with God's help) the barred gates to the king's stronghold – which may have been at Urquhart where signs of Pictish occupation have been found – and winning several magic contests with the druid Broichan, Columba gained Bridei's consent and respect but not his conversion. He did win over a few Pictish households and achieved the impressively novel feat of tacking up Loch Ness against a fierce wind and Broichan's incantations. He also cured the druid's illness with a white stone and used the sign of the Cross to scare off a man-killing monster about to swallow one of his monks in the River Ness.

Columba's biography was written around 690 by Adomnán, the ninth abbot of Iona, who used material on Columba's miracles recorded earlier. He describes Columba as having 'the face of an angel', an 'excellent nature', 'polished in speech, holy in deed, great in council', 'gladdened in his inmost heart by the joy of the Holy Spirit'. Columba's *Life* reveals fascinating contradictions, extremes of Celtic temperament and a strong yearning for things rejected in taking Christ as his 'druid': the call of birds, the harp, earthly success,

Castle Stalker and Lismore Island, Loch Linnhe, Argyll

married life and the Celtic fascination with luck or chance. He had the gifts of telepathy, prophecy, second sight and spiritual healing combined with practical skills of medicine, sailing and weather prediction. He was passionate and quick tempered, exchanging venomous curses with friend and foe. Proud of his royal blood, he was fiercely loyal to his people and preferred the Gaels to all other men of the world save two of his closest colleagues, who were Irish Picts. He is charged with burying his cousin alive on Iona to appease evil spirits, and with causing deaths by magic and in combat. He had visions of angels (one hit him with a scourge), killed with a word a charging wild boar on Skye, turned the Queen of Derry and her serving maid into cranes, ensured the nursing of an exhausted crane on Iona and was wept over by a white horse who sensed the saint's approaching death. These highly symbolic incidents demonstrate Columba's suitability to be Christ's warrior-apostle and shaman in a pagan world.

Lismore is a narrow, green dreamlike island reclining in Loch Linnhe north of Oban. Port Moluag on its eastern shore, just north of Tirefour Broch, is the traditional landing-place of the Irish 'Pict' St Moluag, a monk from Bangor (Co. Down) who founded a monastery on the island in 562. St Columba, newly arrived from Ireland and also looking for a suitable monastic site, wanted Lismore for himself. Seeing Moluag heading to claim it, Columba outsailed and overtook him; but Moluag cut off his little finger and hurled it ashore: 'my flesh and blood have first possession of this island, and I bless it in the name of the Lord'. Enraged, Columba issued spiteful curses including 'the edge of the rock be upwards'. The jagged folds of ice-scraped limestone running down the length of Lismore did not trouble Moluag, who replied 'the Lord will make it smooth for my feet'. A stream falls through a small ravine before running between alder trees on a grassy raised beach, and emptying onto the shingle where Moluag came ashore. He did not build his church there, being attracted inland to a fertile, sheltered area around Clachan, said to be the cremation-place of 'Pictish' kings.

Lismore's parish church is the much-restored choir remaining from the cathedral of the medieval diocese of Argyll. This is believed to be the site of Moluag's monastery. There are no early Christian remains, but field boundaries forming a wide circle around the church may preserve the shape of the enclosure. A rough boulder-cross stands in the field over the road from the churchyard. It marked an area of sanctuary once associated with a building known as the 'nunnery' which gave refuge to 'malefactors of every description'. The Bachuil Mor, Moluag's pastoral staff of blackthorn which used to be carried to war by the men of Lorne, remains on the island in the care of its hereditary keepers, the Livingstone family. It may be viewed by appointment in the drawing room (formerly used as a

St Moluag's Church, Lismore Island, Argyll

Baptist chapel) of Bachuil House. Until the sixteenth century Moluag's bell also survived on Lismore: an enshrined and broken iron bell (now in the National Museum of Antiquities, Edinburgh) found at Kilmichael Glassary on the mainland near Kilmartin (Argyll) in 1814 was claimed as the Lismore original.

Moluag 'of the hundred monasteries' – rather than Columba – was missionary to the Picts whose language he shared, some indication of his influence being given by the numerous Kilmaluag dedications throughout Pictland. He is invoked for cures of madness on Lewis, has churches on Skye and is associated with a chapel and Pictish symbol stones on Skye's satellite island of Raasay. He is believed to have died in 592 while working in eastern Scotland and may have been buried at his church on the Black Isle, although Curadán-Boniface later became the patron and pilgrim attraction at Rosemarkie. In 1010 King Malcolm II established a cathedral on the site of Moluag's foundation at Mortlach (Moray) in thanks for Moluag and St Mary interceding to give him victory over the Vikings in a battle fought nearby.

In common with Columba, St Maelrubha was descended from Niall of the Nine Hostages (founder of the Gaelic dynasty of Ulster kings) and emulated Moluag by leaving Bangor monastery to work in Scotland. He was also related to the family of the Irish Pict St Comgall who had helped Columba and Moluag negotiate with King Bridei in Pictland a

Applecross Bay, Wester Ross, Highland

century earlier. Maelrubha went as missionary to Gaelic Dalriada, but he is best known as an apostle to the Picts. In 673, after work in Argyll, he founded a monastery at the mouth of the Crossan river which became a sanctuary for fugitives for a six-mile radius around his church. Maelrubha chose a sheltered, gently sloping patch of land – made fertile by underlying limestone – at the back of the machair of Applecross Bay. On the north side of the river valley, it was warmed by the sun and gave magnificent views across the broad

landing-place to Raasay and Skye. Applecross was beautifully situated for journeys to his other foundations: seaward to Skye and the Outer Isles, and – via lochs and passes – north to Loch Maree and the east coast. Sailing due south Maelrubha would land at Ashaig ('ferry') – now the site of Skye's airstrip outside Broadford – where an ancient burial ground and holy well survive. He preached from 'the rock of the book' across the stream and his bell hanging in a tree automatically rang the hour of service on a Sunday. Little survives of Maelrubha's monastery which seems to have failed in the Viking raids of 790–800. An incised sandstone cross-slab at the cemetery gate traditionally commemorates the second (and last) abbot, Ruairidh MacCaoigen, who escaped to the Irish mother-house of Bangor, but whose body was brought back for burial around 801. Other early decorated fragments are on display in the nineteenth-century church. Maelrubha died in 722 aged eighty. His traditional burial place is marked by two small stones close to the ruined fifteenth-century chapel. A pinch of earth taken from his mound (Cloadh Maree) would ensure a safe return to Applecross from any travels. John Dixon (Dixon 1886) documents from various sources the cult of Maelrubha (Maree) in the Gairloch and Lochcarron area. In the seventeenth century and beyond bulls were sacrificed and cures for lunacy sought at the saint's chapel and well on Isle Maree (Loch Maree) which, according to Pennant, was 'of power unspeakable in cases of lunacy'. Maelrubha was referred to as the 'god Mourie', and at Applecross bulls were sacrificed in his name, ruined chapels processed around, wells and standing stones 'adored'. St Maelrubha seems to have allowed his converts considerable ritual freedom and took over some of the functions of their ancient deity. Maelrubha was canonized by Rome in 1898.

An Irish-born monk of Iona, St Aidan brought Columban Christianity to the north-east of England. In 635, Oswald – the new king of Northumbria, who had become a Christian while in exile on Iona – requested a missionary. Iona first sent Corman, a severe unbending monk who returned complaining that he could make nothing of the untamable Angles who were savage, stubborn and barbarous. Advocating a gentler approach, Aidan was chosen to lead a new party of twelve missionaries. He set up his monastery on the tidal island of Lindisfarne – in sight of Oswald's capital at Bamburgh – as an eastern mirror of Columba's isle. With Oswald's enthusiastic support as interpreter, Aidan founded churches and made many converts. He ransomed Saxon slaves – educating in Christ twelve youths at a time – some of whom became missionaries to other Anglo-Saxon regions. Aidan and his disciples were greatly respected because they 'lived as they taught'. Bede wrote disapprovingly of Aidan spreading the Celtic calculation of Easter (in Ireland at this time the Roman Easter had been accepted by all but the Columban monasteries) but could not fault either his personal qualities or love of God. Despite his gentle humility, Aidan had some influence over the elements and prepared an oil which calmed a brewing storm when poured onto the sea. From the island of Inner Farne he saw Penda, the pagan king of Mercia, lighting bonfires against the landward walls of Bamburgh, the western wind carrying smoke and flames to the town. Aidan's mild and tearful prayer 'Lord, see what evil Penda does' immediately turned the wind, driving the flames back against the attackers.

OPPOSITE: Bamburgh Castle, Northumberland

Oswald was killed by Penda in 642 but Aidan's work continued with the friendship of Oswin who took over Deira, the southern part of Oswald's united Northumbria, while his cousin Oswy (Oswald's brother) ruled in Bernicia to the north. Aidan and his monks insisted on walking everywhere like Anglo-Saxon peasants. Oswin presented him with a fine horse but Aidan gave it away to a beggar; when reproved he asked the king if the child of a mare was more to him than a child of God. Aidan died eleven days after 'his beloved king' had been murdered on the order of Oswy who wished to rule all of Northumbria. When Aidan fell ill he was sheltered by a tent hastily erected against a church whose western buttress supported him as he died. The church burnt down twice; the wooden beam survived and was set up in the third church as a memorial. Bede does not precisely locate the building, but a shrine in Bamburgh Church is believed to mark the spot where Aidan died, and an ancient beam of no apparent structural use can be seen in the baptistery high above the font. Aidan was buried in the cemetery on Lindisfarne and later his relics were placed in the church there. Some of them were taken to Ireland by Colman, but others may have been displayed to medieval pilgrims in the crypt beneath the chancel at Bamburgh, along with the right arm and hand of St Oswald. Although St Augustine usually receives the credit for bringing Christianity to the Anglo-Saxons, Aidan was a more influential and effective 'Apostle to the English'.

*Pickering Church, North Yorkshire:
St George and the Dragon*

3.
Virtues, Vices and Virgins
Anglo-Saxons & Beyond

The non-Celtic peoples of northern Europe (Angles, Jutes, Saxons) who came into Britain to become the 'English', and the Continental missionaries sent to convert them, are included here along with the Danes (Vikings) and Normans. The location is 'England', the time scale from the end of the sixth century through to the twelfth, and much of the early detail comes from A History of the English Church and People *written in 731 by an Anglo-Saxon scholar-monk, the Venerable Bede. The collapse of Roman rule, bubonic plague and the influx of pagans had shattered the Romano-British Church in the South and East, and Britons in the West (who were becoming the 'Welsh') refused to spread the Gospel among their English enemies who practised Wodenism (Odin) and nature-worship. Some Anglo-Saxon kings earnestly adopted Christianity but others – only wanting supernatural help in battle, or the 'fine white bread' of the Host without the commitment of baptism – soon lost interest or hedged their bets by following both religions. Most Anglo-Saxon saints were members of the many regional royal families for whom founding a monastery was often a pragmatic public act of conscience after achieving their aims by violence and treachery. King Oswy funded a monastery at Gilling West (North Yorkshire) after having his cousin King Oswin killed, and King Egbert gave land to establish Minster-in-Thanet (Kent) in compensation for the murder of his two nephews. Bede, critical of the large numbers of men and women entering double monasteries (which accommodated both sexes) to evade public duty and military service, advocated the suppression of 'wicked' houses where prayer, fasting and penance were neglected in favour of such 'amusements' as drinking, feasting, gossiping and 'weaving fine clothes'. Nunneries sheltered princesses avoiding unwelcome arranged marriages, as* well as truly religious virgins wedded only to Christ. St Edgar, generally considered to be an excellent king, had a weakness for nuns: St Edith was his illegitimate daughter by the novice Wulfthryth, and St Wulfhilda had to escape his sexual advances by crawling through a sewer. From 793, when Lindisfarne was raided, the Saxon monasteries had the seagoing Vikings or 'black pagans' to fear. As Danes attacked the nunnery on Kirk Hill (St Abb's Head), abbess St Ebbe the Younger slashed open her lips and nose with a razor, and her nuns, hoping to preserve their virginity, followed suit. The Vikings were initially repelled, but soon committed them to the flames: 'spotless victims to their heavenly spouse'. Several royal Anglo-Saxons became saints through martyrdom in battle against pagans or murder by fellow Christians out of sexual or political jealousy. In time the Danes came to be Christians and to rule England. King Cnut (1016–35) was converted by the story of St Wendreda after capturing her relics while defeating King Edmund Ironside. One of Cnut's new laws ran thus: 'We earnestly forbid all heathendom. Heathendom is that men worship idols; that is, they worship the sun, or the moon, rivers, water-wells or stones, or great trees of any kind'.

After their victory over the English at the battle of Hastings in 1066, the Norman rulers and their new bishops were extremely sceptical of Anglo-Saxon saints. Lanfranc, the Italian Archbishop of Canterbury appointed by William the Conqueror, put some of their relics to trial by ordeal: it was reported at Evesham in 1077 that the relics of St Credan and other local saints had shone like gold after emerging unscathed from the testing fire. Ireland's patron, St Patrick (c. 390–461), originally came from a part of Britain which is now England, while St Margaret (1046–93), the official patron of Scotland since 1673, was

one of the last members of the Anglo-Saxon royal family. She still enjoys a universal cult but England's best known patron, St George, was demoted to a local hero in Pope Paul VI's 1969 reform of the Roman Calendar. It seems strange that a Palestinian soldier-saint martyred by the Romans around 303 should have taken over from SS Edward the Confessor and Edmund of East Anglia; but his legendary rescue of a beautiful princess from a dragon in exchange for the baptism of her people made him the epitome of military prowess and Christian chivalry. He appeared to Crusaders before their defeat of the Saracens at Antioch, and was famously invoked by King Henry V at the siege of Harfleur: 'Follow your spirit; and upon this charge Cry – God for Harry! England and Saint George!'

St Martin's Church, Canterbury, Kent: the Saxon font

St Ethelbert of Kent was the first Saxon king in England to become a Christian. With relish and gratitude Bede tells how Pope Gregory I brought the English nation from 'the bondage of Satan'. The former Roman prefect and monk had noticed fair-haired slave-boys from Deira on sale in the market in Rome. On being told that they were pagan Angles from the island of Britain he called them angels, musing aloud on the pity of such attractive folk not knowing God. As Pope in 596, Gregory was able to do something about it. He chose Augustine, the Italian head of a monastery in Rome, to lead forty monks to Kent whose pagan king was married to a Frankish Christian princess (Bertha, daughter of King Charibert of Paris). Augustine's party did not share their superior's enthusiasm for reintroducing the Faith to the heel of Britain. Part way into the Continental journey they requested to be recalled from their dangerous task. Gregory dispatched an encouraging letter; his missionaries continued to England, landing at Pegwell Bay on the Isle of Thanet in 597. Through Frankish interpreters they sent a message to Ethelbert who, fearing that their magical arts would have greater power over him inside a building, agreed to meet them on the island in the open air. Carrying a silver cross and a painted icon of Jesus, the monks prayed, sang and preached to the king. Not wishing to abandon his age-old beliefs but impressed by their sincerity, he granted them a dwelling in Canterbury and freedom to worship and win converts by persuasion. A cross erected at Ebbsfleet in 1884 marks the traditional site of this historic meeting. Approaching Canterbury from the east along the Roman road (now the A257) from Richborough fort, Augustine viewed Ethelbert's palace and the Roman city walls from beside a Romano-British church on St Martin's Hill. The chancel – whose walls still contain Roman bricks – had been repaired for the use of Queen Bertha and her chaplain Bishop Liudhard. It was further modified by Augustine's monks and was probably used for Ethelbert's baptism after Augustine's miracles and the example and 'gladdening promises' of the missionaries had won him over. The unusual Saxon font may have been converted from a 'foot-bath' used in adult baptisms to a taller font for infants by inserting an extra ring of decorated stone.

Augustine was granted land between St Martin's and the town in order to found a monastery: its regime was based on the *Rule* of St Benedict, its first six abbots Italian. Four separate chapels were built in a line, west to east: a small chapel, the church of SS Peter and Paul which became the main monastic church, burial place of Augustine and the Kentish royalty, a chapel to St Mary and St Pancras' Church. St Mary's Chapel and the monastic church were joined together around 1050 by Abbot Wulfric's octagonal tower and the whole complex was massively rebuilt by the Normans as a standard medieval Benedictine abbey. The Saxon part of St Pancras' – west porch, eastern apse, central nave with small chapels north and south – was built of reused Roman bricks and four stone columns. It was believed by the fourteenth-century monks to have been Ethelbert's pagan temple, its southern (right) chapel the scene of Augustine's first Mass. Pope Gregory

St Pancras' Church, St Augustine's Abbey, Canterbury, Kent

counselled that pagan idols must be destroyed but the temples could be cleansed with holy water and furnished with altars and relics. He also warned Augustine not to boast about his miracles: good advice, as Augustine was conceited and had alienated a group of British bishops by his haughty, disrespectful behaviour.

In 601, after Augustine's initial conversions in Kent, Pope Gregory sent him a second party of monks including Mellitus who became Bishop of London, and Paulinus, chosen as Bishop of York. Ethelbert's daughter was married to King Edwin of Northumbria on the understanding that he would allow her freedom to practise Christianity while considering the new religion for himself. Paulinus was consecrated bishop and went north as Ethelburga's chaplain. Pope Boniface wrote to Edwin urging him to accept the Faith, pointing out that as men created idols it was foolish to worship them. Boniface also wrote to chide Ethelburga for not achieving her husband's conversion, saying that their marriage was not a true union while he continued to serve 'abominable idols'. Paulinus reminded the king of his meeting with an angel while a youth in exile, and Edwin's chief priest, Coifi, confessed that their own religion seemed without value or power. Another of

Edwin's advisers welcomed the certainty of the Christian afterlife, likening human life to a sparrow's brief flight through a comfortable feasting hall on a hard winter's day. Coifi then rode to his temple and threw a spear into it, ordering that the enclosure be destroyed, the building set on fire. Edwin was baptized in 627 by Paulinus in a hastily erected wooden church on the site of the Roman headquarters building at York. This was replaced by a stone 'basilica' which grew into the present Minster. A Roman column from under the south transept was re-erected in 1971 to celebrate the founding of Roman York in AD71. Medieval pilgrims visited the shrine of St William of York (who still lies buried in the Minster) and to venerate many relics, including the head of St Edwin, kept in the crypt which has an ancient holy well.

Paulinus went on to preach in the modern counties of Yorkshire, Northumberland and Lincolnshire, baptizing prodigious numbers of people in the rivers Swale, Glen and Trent. He gave open-air sermons beside Edwin's great timber palace at Yeavering (Northumberland) and used Lady's Well (Holystone) for baptism as had the Romano-British bishop St Ninian. The Christian advance in Northumbria came to an abrupt halt in 633 when Edwin was killed at the battle of Hatfield Chase by the kings of Gwynedd and Mercia in retaliation for Northumbrian expansion into their territories. Paulinus and Ethelburga withdrew by sea to Kent where Paulinus ended his days as Bishop of Rochester. The Italian mission also suffered setbacks among the South and East Saxons, where it fell to others to finish their work. Edwin's successors were killed in battle by Cadwallon and Penda whose alliance in Northumbria was finally broken by Oswald. James the Deacon remained in York, but it was Oswald and St Aidan who secured the Faith in Northumbria. Dying as a Christian king in battle, St Edwin was regarded as a martyr and tribal hero. His head was enshrined at York, his body – discovered later by divine revelation at Hatfield – taken to Whitby Abbey.

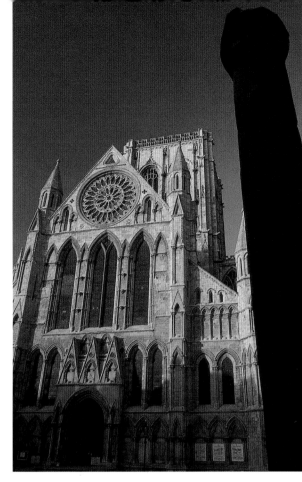

York Minster, North Yorkshire

Hatfield Chase, South Yorkshire

All Saints Churchyard, Dunwich, Suffolk

Old gods regained their ascendancy in south-east England as Christian kings were murdered, succeeded by pagan offspring or, like Radwald of East Anglia, worshipped both Christ and Odin. More determined Christian rulers and a new influx of missionaries tipped the scales. In 640 Eorconbert of Kent imposed a total ban on the worship of idols and made Lenten fasting compulsory. A few years earlier Sigebert, who had become a Christian while in exile in Gaul, returned to rule East Anglia, and the Archbishop of Canterbury sent St Felix of Burgundy to be his bishop with a seat and school at Dunwich. Sigebert also granted land for a monastery and mission centre to St Fursey and his monks, 'wandering for God' in voluntary exile from Ireland. Sigebert retired to a monastery but he was forced to attend a battle against Penda's invading Mercians and was killed for refusing to fight. Roman in origin, Dunwich grew into a flourishing medieval port with a friary and nine churches. The great storm of 1326 destroyed over 400 houses and washed away three of the churches. As erosion continues all that remains of the churches are foundations beneath the sea and a few headstones near the cliff edge.

St Birinus arrived in England from Italy having promised Pope Honorius that he would preach in the most remote regions unvisited by other teachers. Finding the West Saxons 'completely heathen' he baptized Cynegils, their king, in 635, and became Bishop of Wessex based at the former Romano-British town of Dorchester-on-Thames. Wet from the font, Cynegils was met by his godfather, Oswald of Northumbria, offering an alliance through marriage to Cynegils' daughter: the offer was not refused. Birinus also established Winchester which took over as the ecclesiastical centre of Wessex: his relics were translated there by Bishop Hedda around 690. Dorchester later became the seat of a Mercian see but this was moved to Lincoln in the 1070s. In 1225, after being refounded as an Augustinian abbey, Dorchester claimed to have the true relics of Birinus by producing the body of a bishop. Miracles and visions accumulated during the following century, the resulting pilgrim revenues being used to rebuild the church and construct a carved marble shrine. The 1960s memorial in the Lady Chapel is inspired by the medieval shrine destroyed at the Dissolution.

Oswy of Northumbria sent Cedd, a young English trainee of St Aidan, to help reconvert the East Saxons who, in 616, had expelled Augustine's missionary bishop Mellitus. Carrying Celtic Christianity south, St Cedd arrived by sea at the village and ruined Roman

OPPOSITE: Dorchester Abbey, Oxfordshire

fort of Othona. He was consecrated bishop in 654, his chapel becoming the cathedral of Essex. The initial timber church was quickly replaced by a Continental-style one built of reused Roman materials and sited on the fort's western gate. Cedd ordained priests and established other churches including one at Tilbury beside the Thames. Raided by Danes and absorbed into the diocese of London, St Peter's continued as a parish church until a new one was built inland at Bradwell in the late fourteenth century. It became a chapel of ease; the tower was used as a beacon, the chancel was pulled down and the nave became

St Peter's Chapel, Bradwell-on-Sea, Essex

a barn. Reconsecrated in 1920, the nave is now the scene of lively worship by the Othona Community, and destination of the Chelmsford Diocesan pilgrimage held on the nearest Saturday to St Peter's Day (29 July). The ground plan of the original seventh-century church with eastern apse, north and south *porticus*, and western porch is laid out in the grass. Inside the eloquently simple nave a modern altar contains stones from the three other places in St Cedd's life: Iona, Lindisfarne and Lastingham.

Regularly returning to his home province, St Cedd was granted land to found a monastery by Oswald's son. According to Bede, Cedd's chosen site among remote hills at Lastingham was 'more suitable for the dens of robbers and haunts of wild beasts than for human habitation'. Before laying the foundations he purified the site during Lent with fasting and prayer. In 664 Cedd attended the Synod of Whitby and accepted the Roman calculation of Easter. On a visit to Lastingham later in the same year he caught the plague and died.

Initially buried outside, Cedd's body was entombed beside the altar as a stone church replaced his timber one. When the Norman church was built *c.* 1080 his relics were transferred to the crypt, a complete church in itself. Pillar bases and many decorated fragments survive from the Saxon building. St Chad, one of Cedd's three brothers, took over at Lastingham. When news of Cedd's death reached his Bradwell monks, about thirty of them travelled from Essex requesting permission to live or die beside their founder: all died of the plague except for one unbaptized little boy.

After Oswald was killed by the Mercian Penda in 642, Northumbria split again into the provinces of Bernicia and Deira. Oswald's brother Oswy ruled in the north, his cousin Oswin in Deira. St Aidan had predicted an early death for the devout, courteous Oswin. Oswy invaded Deira but Oswin, wishing to avoid the slaughter of his outnumbered forces,

St Mary's Church, Lastingham, North Yorkshire

withdrew to the house of a trusted friend. The trusted friend betrayed Oswin, who was executed at Gilling West (North Yorkshire) where Oswy built a monastery in atonement. Oswin's relics were venerated at Tynemouth Priory (Tyne & Wear) as those of a martyr because he died 'for the justice of Christ'. Having reunited Northumbria, Oswy avenged his brother in 655 by killing Penda at a battle near Leeds, many fleeing Mercians perishing in floodwaters of the River Winwaed. Before the campaign, Oswy had vowed to found twelve monasteries and pledged his infant daughter Elfleda as a perpetual virgin to God in return for victory. Elfleda was sent to Abbess Hilda at Hartlepool, then moved to Whitby where Hilda created a double monastery of monks and nuns. Elfleda, who succeeded her mother Enfleda as abbess of Whitby, was friend to St Cuthbert whose girdle cured her of

paralysis. Whitby became a monument and shrine to the Northumbrian royal family, home to the first poet and hymnist in the Anglo-Saxon tongue. St Caedmon, a herdsman, discovered his gift of improvising vernacular verses about the Scriptures on being divinely

Whitby Abbey,
North Yorkshire

instructed in a dream to sing the Creation: '... How he the Lord of Glory everlasting,/ Wrought first for the race of men Heaven as a roof-tree,/ Then made he Middle Earth to be their mansion'.

A political centre and famous school, Whitby was the venue for a synod called by Oswy in 664 to settle the differences between Celtic and Roman religious practices. The most contentious issue was the timing of Easter, celebrated by the Celts while the Romans were still fasting for Lent. Oswy settled for Rome on being persuaded that St Peter, rather than Columba, held the keys to Heaven. Refusing to accept the decision, Abbot Colman of Lindisfarne retired to Iona taking with him a few of St Aidan's bones. Iona accepted the 'universal' practices in 716.

At Whitby the main speaker against 'Irish' practices was St Wilfrid, an Anglian boy educated at Lindisfarne. He went to Canterbury, Lyon, then Rome, falling under the spell of that city's customs and culture. Returning to England, he was granted a monastery at Ripon vacated by Scots clergy unwilling to amend their ways. The Lindisfarne monks gave away offerings and refused grants of land, but Wilfrid desired wealth and property for his monasteries to advance a lofty vision of the Church. Before becoming Bishop of York he arranged to be consecrated in Gaul – with considerable pomp and splendour – by Frankish bishops whose lavish lifestyle and system of patronage he emulated. Shortly before his death Wilfrid ordered that one quarter of the silver, gold and jewels in his Ripon treasury should be used 'to buy the friendship of kings'. He also introduced use of the strict and

The crypt of Hexham Abbey, Northumberland

orderly Rule of St Benedict to his monasteries. Disliked by the Columbans in Northumbria he was involved in disputes, twice appealing to Rome when unfairly deposed as Bishop of York. In exile he continued to found monasteries, going on missionary wanderings in the Netherlands, central England and Sussex where he made converts after ending a severe drought and famine. He died aged seventy-six on a visit to Northamptonshire in 709 and was buried in the crypt at Ripon where recent excavations have revealed the grand scale of his transport and reuse of Roman masonry.

Inspired by the buildings he saw in Rome, especially the relic crypt beneath the apse of St Peter's, Wilfrid prized highly the legionary legacy of stone columns and blocks. In St Andrew's Church, Corbridge (Northumberland) a complete Roman gateway was re-erected between the nave and west porch, while at nearby Hexham, founded in 674, Wilfrid employed Roman materials and techniques to construct a crypt similar in layout to the one at Ripon. A central room and antechamber with barrel vaults, ventilation shaft and flanking passages were constructed, using tooled blocks, inscribed slabs and an altar bearing the name of Emperor Geta (AD208). The main chamber displayed relics – possibly of St Andrew brought from Rome – to pilgrims who pressed against a grill after entering the antechamber via the northern passage. The southern passage, leading directly into the relic chamber, was used by guardian monks moving in the glow of cresset lamps. Both passages have been filled in and a later, western, entrance is the only access. The crypt was originally part of St Andrew's Church, one of a row of three built by Wilfrid at Hexham, later encompassed by the Augustinian priory. As one of the earliest English churches to be built in stone, Wilfrid's biographer said of St Andrew's 'We have never heard of its like this side of the Alps.'

Wilfrid was granted the right of sanctuary for fugitives within a mile of his cathedral monastery at Hexham. This early *cathedra* (bishop's seat) may have been used by Wilfrid himself. Standing in the choir of the priory church it overlies its original location in the Saxon apse. Another stone sanctuary seat or Frith Stool (Fridstol, 'peace chair') survives in Beverley Minster (East Yorkshire).

The crypt's western entrance

Cathedra

St Aldhelm's Well, Doulting, Somerset

Born in Wessex, Aldhelm was initially educated in a monastic community at Malmesbury (Wiltshire) set up by an Irish hermit called Maeldubh. He was 'polished' at Canterbury, returning to Wessex to build churches at Bradford-on-Avon and Frome, and became abbot of Malmesbury and Bishop of Sherborne. Sometimes described as the first English librarian, he knew Greek, Latin and Hebrew as well as his native Anglo-Saxon. King Alfred praised his vernacular poems and his ballads were said by his biographer William of Malmesbury to be still popular in the twelfth century. He attracted and entertained crowds with music, singing and clowning interspersed by preaching: his staff took root during one particularly wordy sermon. Although his writings were respected, their style was considered impenetrably convoluted: Aldhelm was intoxicated by Latin, in love with word-plays, acrostics and riddles. He wrote a letter to King Geraint of Devon and Cornwall explaining the errors of the British clergy, and composed the treatise *On Virginity* for the nuns of Barking (Essex). He died in 709 – 'laying aside the garment of the flesh' as William of Malmesbury put it – after requesting to be carried inside a wooden church. This was probably at Doulting where local tradition says he used to sit in the holy well during his last illness. The hillside spring flows into a stone channel where medieval pilgrims used to bathe sheltered by a roof. Aldhelm's body was taken to be enshrined at Malmesbury, the stopping-places on the way later marked by stone crosses at approximately seven-mile intervals.

The Saxon font recovered from SS Peter and Paul's churchyard in 1923 is associated with the baptism of the infant prodigy St Rumbold. Born at Sutton around 662, and reputedly a grandson of Penda of Mercia, the child declared himself a Christian, professed his belief in the Trinity and requested baptism and Holy Communion.

St Rumbold's Font, King's Sutton, Northamptonshire

This accomplished, he preached a sermon, quoted scripture, announced his imminent death and expired, aged three days. He was venerated in Kent – Boxley Cistercian abbey had a statue of him which could not be moved by the 'unchaste' – and is patron of Buckingham where he was buried. His unofficial cult was as popular and persistent as his legend is inexplicable. A spa well (in the grounds of Astrop House, east of King's Sutton) was associated with Rumbold's cult, attracting many pilgrims seeking cures. To divert these tiresome visitors a replica was constructed beside the public road, to which I was directed in 1993 by the lady of the house because the original needed 'weeding'.

St Benedict Biscop and the Venerable Bede walked past the watchful eyes of these bird-headed serpents at the threshold of St Peter's Church. Founding Wearmouth monastery in 674 with the help of King Egfrith, Benedict imported Frankish masons, glaziers and other craftsmen to build a Romanesque church, the porch and west wall of which survive.

Monkwearmouth, Sunderland, Tyne & Wear

A large standing figure of Christ in Majesty (or St Peter) marks the apex of the original porch to which a tower was added in the eleventh century after Viking raids. Biscop Baducing, who adopted the name Benedict, was a Northumbrian noble in the service of King Oswy before becoming a monk and visiting Rome with St Wilfrid. Benedict went on to found the twin monasteries of Wearmouth and Jarrow, filling them with books, ecclesiastical art and other church treasures gathered on his six journeys to Rome. Bede started his training here as a boy of seven, then moved to Jarrow where Biscop's library helped him to become a renowned biblical scholar and the first historian of the English Church.

At Jarrow the parish church of St Paul occupies the site of a monastic chapel and separate basilica founded by Benedict Biscop in 681. The chancel retains the

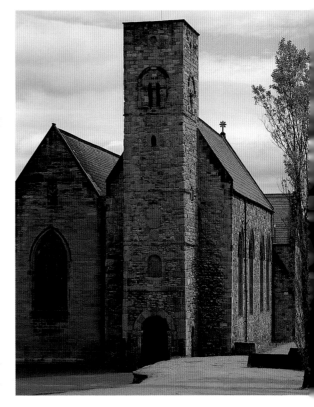

St Peter's Church, Monkwearmouth

reused Roman masonry of the Saxon chapel, but the nave on the site of the basilica is Victorian. To the south are Norman Benedictine buildings which replaced the earlier monastery burned by Vikings. Bede spent most of his life at Jarrow where he devoted himself to study of the Scriptures, both for his own benefit and that of his brethren. He observed the regular discipline, sang the choir offices daily in church, but his 'chief delight' was always 'in study, teaching and writing'. Shortly after Jarrow had been founded with monks and novices from Wearmouth, a plague killed most of the choir monks: Abbot Ceolfrith and the boy Bede were left to sing the services until replacements were trained in the Roman-style chant favoured by Biscop. Bede knew 'that the angels are present at the

canonical Hours'. He died on Ascension Day eve (25 May) 735. A contemporary account of the two weeks approaching his 'heavenly birthday' describes him as weak, breathing with great difficulty, but never ceasing to pray, sing, give lessons and dictation, cheerfully urging his monks to 'learn quickly ... for my Lord may call me in a short while'.

Bede was buried with honour in the church at Jarrow. In 1022 his relics were stolen by a monk from Durham who placed them in the tomb of St Cuthbert. Around 1370 they were translated to the Galilee Chapel enshrined in a gold and silver casket which, when not being carried in procession, sat on a marble base supported by pillars. The present tomb is believed to hold his bones, hidden at the Dissolution when the shrine was

Jarrow Monastery,
South Shields, Tyne & Wear

destroyed. In 1899 the Pope awarded Bede, for saintliness and outstanding theological merit, the title Doctor of the Church.

Bede says that he was ordained deacon and priest 'at the hands of the most reverend Bishop John'. St John of Beverley was born *c.* 640 at Harpham (south-west of Bridlington) where an annual procession and dressing of his well (east of the village) mark his feast day (7 May). Educated at Canterbury he returned to become a monk at Whitby, was ordained Bishop of Hexham in 687, then Bishop of York in 705 when the aged Wilfrid was reinstated at Hexham. John founded his monastery in a wooded swamp at Beverley where he retired in 718 to spend the last four years of his life. The present Minster dates mainly from 1220 to 1400 with major restorations of the eighteenth and nineteenth centuries. Beverley was an important pilgrimage centre with wealth, status and the right of sanctuary for a two-mile radius around the town: the stone Frith Stool or 'Peace of St John' stands beside the altar.

Beverley Minster, East Yorkshire

John travelled about his diocese with a group of young men in training, retiring with them for periods of quiet retreat, especially at Lent. He sought to help the poor and infirm, and worked miracles of healing. He is patron of the deaf and dumb for his unlocking of a silent youth's tongue by tracing the sign of the Cross upon it, then teaching him to speak by the constant repetition of sounds. John was asked to assist a nun in terrible pain and likely to die, whose arm had swollen to a great size after being bled. He refused, saying that it had been foolish to let blood on the moon's fourth day when its light and the pull of the tide were increasing. As the abbess insisted, he reluctantly blessed her daughter who immediately improved. Using holy water he raised a thegn's wife from three week's illness in bed, and retrieved a serving-lad from the point of death (his coffin had been brought into the room) with a cup of blessed wine and the words 'hurry up and get well'. Heribald, one of John's youthful clerics, fell while horse racing during a journey, breaking his head and thumb; according to his own account he lay speechless in bed all night, vomiting blood while John did vigil praying for him. Discovering in the morning that he had been incompetently baptized, John

OPPOSITE: Galilee Chapel and Bede's Tomb, Durham Cathedral

catechized him, breathed on his face, blessed him, had his head bound and later baptized him correctly. John's servant Sigga once spied on him in the chapel of St Martin in York, kneeling at the altar attended by the Holy Spirit in the form of a dove. The intensity of heat and light was such that Sigga was blinded, his face 'crazed' until healed by his compassionate master.

John was canonized in 1037 and his relics were translated to a costly new shrine later destroyed by fire. Around 1300 the relics were transferred to the reredos behind the high altar, then hidden when that shrine was dismantled at the Reformation. They were rediscovered in 1736 when the nave floor was renewed, and now lie at the site of his original tomb, in the east of the nave beneath a black marble slab annually decorated with primroses brought from Harpham. Pilgrims to Beverley included William the Conqueror who saw a vision of John above the shrine, and King Athelstan who believed that the saint had aided his emphatic victory over the Scots and Norse at the battle of Brunanburh in 937. Monarchs, including Edward I, took the banner of St John on their campaigns, Henry V ascribing his triumph at Agincourt (25 October 1415) partly to it being the feast of St John's translation.

St Edith's Well, Kemsing, Kent

St Edith was born at Kemsing in 961, making this well holy by her presence. Edith's father was Edgar the Peaceful, king of all England from the age of sixteen; her mother, a nun named Wulfthryth, was his concubine. Wulfthryth quickly returned with Edith to her monastery at Wilton (Wilton House, Wiltshire). Refusing offers to run three other monasteries, Edith stayed with her mother who became abbess. Preferring to commune with nature and the poor, Edith is reputed to have refused the crown, offered after the murder of her half-brother Edmund the Martyr. She built an oratory to the martyr St Denys, at the dedication of which St Dunstan accurately prophesied that Edith's thumb would not decay after her approaching demise. Death at twenty-three, and miracles around her tomb, ensured the spread of St Edith's cult despite the circumstances of her birth.

King Edgar obviously admired the Wilton novices: before Wulfthryth, he had offered marriage to a young nun named Wulfhilda. She refused but was lured by the abbess to Wherwell monastery where Edgar tried seduction. Making a dramatic escape through the drains, Wulfhilda was pursued to the Wilton cloisters where she resisted the King's further advances before taking refuge in the sanctuary. Finally getting the message, Edgar made her abbess of Barking (Essex).

Wulfhilda must have had something special: on one occasion she entertained Edgar and a party of sailors at Barking by miraculously multiplying the drinks.

Despite his early weakness for nuns, Edgar was widely considered an admirable monarch. Under the influence of St Dunstan (Archbishop of Canterbury) he instigated a reform of the Church, recovered monastic properties lost to local landlords and put an end to lax practices. Benedictine monasticism was revived with its strict daily regime and insistence on celibacy for the secular canons. On Edgar's death, the supporters of his young children vied for the throne. Edward, son by his first wife Athelfled, was voted king by the witan (council) but murdered at Corfe Castle (Dorset) at the instigation of his stepmother, Alfthryth, who wanted her son Ethelred to become ruler. Edward was stabbed in the stomach by a servant while being treacherously welcomed at the door by his stepmother; he spurred his horse away but fell dead with his bowels ripped open. His body, thrown into a deep marsh, was revealed by a pillar of light. When miracles occurred at Edward's tomb at Wareham, Dunstan enshrined his entire body at Shaftesbury Abbey (Wiltshire). In a mixture of genuine regret and political self-preservation, Ethelred declared him a saint and martyr and ordered that his feast be observed throughout England. Alfthryth retired to a nunnery, 'that she might repent in ashes the wickedness she had done'.

St Mary the Virgin, Hawkesbury, Gloucestershire

Born of Anglo-Saxon parents, Wulstan (Wulfstan) was educated at Evesham and Peterborough, later employed in the household of the Bishop of Worcester, then sent to serve at the minster church at Hawkesbury (1033–8). While saying Mass there one day he was overwhelmed by the smell of a goose being cooked for his dinner. Realizing that his senses had caused him to fail in his duty to God, he vowed never again to eat meat. In his youth Wulstan was so touched with 'wanton love' on seeing a young woman dance that he withdrew to a thicket and 'bewailed his fault before God'. Preferring to be a monk rather than a parish priest, Wulstan entered the cathedral priory at Worcester, becoming its prior in 1050. He improved monastic discipline, reclaimed lost land, attracted new monks, and sought patronage including that of Lady Godiva and her husband Earl Leofric. He became Bishop of Worcester in 1062, building a hospital in Worcester, establishing churches on his own manors and consecrating the personal churches built by local landowners. At Longney (Gloucestershire) he was invited by Ailsi to dedicate his new church, but Wulstan said that a nut tree in the cemetery must be cut down as it deprived the church of light. The thegn chose to forego the consecration rather than harm the tree in whose shade he used to game and feast. With a curse Wulstan killed the tree so that Ailsi had to cut it down, ruefully admitting 'that there was nothing more bitter than Wulfstan's curse, nothing sweeter than Wulfstan's blessing'.

Wulstan managed to retain high office after the Norman Conquest. When Edward the Confessor died, Harold Godwinson sent Wulstan to reconcile the people north of the Humber to their new king, to warn of the perils of disunity. The mission failed, forcing Harold to defeat a combined Northumbrian and Norwegian army before marching 250 miles south again to meet his fate at Hastings. Wulstan quickly pledged his allegiance to William the Conqueror, supporting the continental reforms undertaken by the new Archbishop of Canterbury, Lanfranc. Together they worked to halt the trade in slaves from Bristol to Viking Ireland, and persuaded married clergy to renounce either their wives or their churches.

Wulstan undertook the destruction and rebuilding of the Saxon priory founded by Bishop Oswald in 938. He may have done this on Norman orders; his biography describes him weeping while watching the demolition of 'the work of our saints'. The new church included a magnificent crypt and a curious circular chapter house designed to retain the shape of Oswald's Saxon rotunda. Wulstan transferred Oswald's relics, and those of other saints previously brought from Ripon, to a fabulously rich silver shrine at the high altar, and when he himself

The tomb of King John in Worcester Cathedral

died in 1095 he was placed in a tomb with a stone canopy protected by an iron grill. By the time of his canonization in 1203 his relics had been performing daily miracles for pilgrims, and in 1216 King John was at his own request buried between the two shrines: an effigy of Purbeck marble, originally gilded and coloured red and green was added *c.* 1230. Two episcopal figures at his head – formerly in blue and white with golden crowns – representing a death bed scene may be Oswald and Wulstan.

Wulstan's shrine was stripped to pay a levy demanded by the Prince of France, but in 1218 the church was rededicated in the presence of Henry III and the relics translated to a new shrine. (Attending abbots were given a share of the bones, St Alban's carrying off in procession a rib in a case of gold.) Pilgrims flocked to the shrines and lay on mats day and night awaiting a miracle or cure which would be recorded in a book. As well as its reputation for cures, Worcester had a wonder-working image of the Virgin Mary which became popular with pilgrims in the later Middle Ages. Visitors were lodged in the Guesten Hall, one red-stoned wall of which remains standing south of the choir. By 1540 the monastery had been dissolved, the shrines and images destroyed, the relics hidden, still to be located.

England's only religious order (the Gilbertines) was created by Gilbert of Sempringham, the son of Jocelin, a Norman knight. During her pregnancy, his Anglo-Saxon mother dreamed that the moon lay in her lap, presaging her coming child's greatness. Gilbert was, however, born deformed, initially so dull and lazy that even the household servants made fun of him. Sent to be educated in France, he returned a 'Master' in Liberal and Spiritual Studies. He started a coeducational school and worked as clerk for the Bishop of Lincoln who ordained him priest. By 1132 Gilbert was vicar and squire at Sempringham where he set up a community based on the Rule of St Benedict, at the request of seven of his young female parishioners. Lay sisters and brothers were added and, later, canons under the Rule of St Augustine.

The Norman church with its Victorian apse, is the

St Andrew's Church, Sempringham, Lincolnshire

remaining portion of Jocelin's cruciform building of *c.* 1100. Gilbert founded his monastery to its south in 1139, in the shallow valley where crops now grow. He built twelve more monasteries, most of them double, and founded leper-hospitals and orphanages. He wore a hair shirt, ate chiefly roots and pulses and spent his nights in prayer, but his austere life was not without controversy. Henry II was angry with the Gilbertines for helping Thomas Becket escape to France and in his nineties the now-blind Gilbert faced a rebellion of lay brothers over too much work for too little food. On canonization in 1202, Gilbert's shrine was built into the wall between his monks and nuns at Sempringham, enabling them to share him. Some of his relics were taken to Toulouse (France), the rest may still be buried at Sempringham.

Gwenllian, the daughter of Eleanor and Prince Llywelyn, spent a lifetime of exile at the nunnery from 1282, when her mother died at her birth and her father was killed leading the Welsh against Edward I. Her plaque beside the monastery site is a focus for offerings and national sentiments. There is a modern memorial to the Gilbertines in Lincoln Cathedral's Angel Choir.

An Anglo-Saxon born in Devon around 680, Boniface was christened Winfrith but given a new name in Rome. Educated as a monk, Boniface worked as a teacher and preacher before being ordained priest aged thirty. He went to Rome in 718 seeking direction from Pope Gregory II, working afterwards at conversion in the Netherlands, Germany and France. An interesting example of an English missionary taking the Christian message to pagan Saxons on the Continent, he wrote from Germany to the English people requesting their prayers and material aid in the conversion of those who 'are of one blood and bone with you'. He is remembered for teaching, church organization, and for making alliances between popes and emperors. With a band of male and female followers from England he created bishoprics, monasteries and mission stations as they travelled, eventually setting up his own see at Mainz near Frankfurt (Germany). He won many converts at Geismar after felling an oak tree sacred to pagan gods without being harmed. Returning in his seventies to have another go at the particularly stubborn heathens in

St Boniface Statue, Crediton, Devon

Frisia (Friesland, Netherlands) he and his companions were killed while camped beside the river at Dokkum. His symbol of a Gospel book pierced by a sword recalls that he was attacked while reading in his tent and used the book to defend himself. His body was taken to his abbey at Fulda (north-east of Frankfurt) where it is still venerated. A human larynx bone in Brixworth Church (Northamptonshire) may be a relic of Boniface; it was formerly displayed to pilgrims in a partly-sunken ring-crypt of the Saxon church built, or enlarged, in honour of the saint *c.* 750 by King Ethelbald of Mercia. Boniface, along with other bishops, had written to Ethelbald in 747 deploring his scandalous behaviour, which included misappropriating church revenues and debauching nuns.

Anchor Church, Ingleby,
Derbyshire

4.
Solitary Spirits
Hermits and Visionaries

A number of caves which I used to visit in the Derby area are traditionally associated
with hermits. At Anchor Church I was thrilled by the idea of a succession of hardy
medieval anchorites living in austere solitude, thinking holy thoughts while carving out
the rock with their fingernails. But the 'church' has no proven connection with hermits:
its doorway and windows date from the 1720s when the cave was used for summer
entertainments, being a feature in the landscape of Foremark Hall. Unwelcome facts
about medieval hermits being attached to monasteries, receiving daily visitors, having
servants, collecting tolls and being paid to act as guides, ferrymen and hosts to travellers
further dented my fantasy. I was responding to the eighteenth-century romanticization of
the Middle Ages: the hermits I longed for had existed, I was just looking in the wrong
place for those who sought God in solitude, saw visions, wrestled with demons and were
sustained by angels. Their inspiration came from the early ascetics of Egypt (Desert
Fathers) who spurned the corrupting distractions of everyday urban life in the Roman
world. The most commonly illustrated desert story is the meeting of St Anthony of Egypt
(251–356) with 'the first Christian hermit', St Paul of Thebes (d. c. 345), as related by St
Jerome (c. 341–420) in his Life of St Paul, *which was based on an earlier version in Greek.*
A raven dropped a loaf of bread for them to share and later, as Paul lay dying, two lions
dug a grave enabling Anthony to bury him. In his book From the Holy Mountain
(HarperCollins 1997) William Dalrymple describes visiting the candle-lit cave chapel and
lean-to shelter of 'the last hermit in Lebanon'. The hermit described his daily routine of
prayer and spiritual reading (with breaks to tend olives and grapes) and outlined the
'vocation' of solitude: to clear the troubled waters of the soul of 'alien thoughts and

distractions' in order to obtain the 'light and heat' of prayer to God – as the goal draws nearer 'your enemy attacks you more'. The enemy is not always spectral, for many hermits in Britain were robbed of their meagre possessions and murdered. Not every man or woman who became a solitary initially did so with high spiritual motives: cowardice, guilt, the prospect of marriage or the unhappiness of ill-fated love drove some to contemplation. St Credan of Cornwall 'abandoned the world' after the misfortune of killing his own father. Most descriptions of genuine solitaries include episodes of extreme deprivation, physical distress, demonic attack, lascivious visions, self-disgust, despair, heavenly helpers, blissful reveries and an intense feeling of 'oneness'. 'Religious' experiences can be artificially provoked and the body's own chemicals respond strangely to a lack of food or sensory input: ergotism (raphania), the condition caused by eating rye flour contaminated by the pathogenic fungus Claviceps purpurea, *was known as 'holy fire' or 'St Anthony's fire'. Symptoms included numbness, gangrene, a feeling of ants running under the skin (formication), burning sensations, convulsions and hallucinations; alkaloids of ergot were originally used to create the hallucinogenic drug LSD. The disease was widespread in medieval Europe where monks of the order of St Anthony were dedicated to its treatment. Psychotropic plants such as henbane and other 'Saturnian herbs' were used to create sensations of flying and shamanistic spirit-journeys. Nevertheless, it is the business of contemplatives to still clamorous egos, thus enabling them to hear the eternal music in forms shaped by their personal beliefs, temperament and social milieu.*

Archangel Michael, the great purger of evil and haunter of high places, is patron of Roche Rock, a brooding outcrop of granite in Cornwall. St Michael's Chapel was built around 1409 over an earlier rock-cut hermitage. The site is an ancient one for hermits, the earliest-recorded being the tenth-century St Conan who lived here before moving to St Germans, near Saltash, to become Bishop of Cornwall under the Saxon King Athelstan. The nearby parish church is dedicated to St Gonand who may be 'Conan' or another medieval solitary. A leper and his daughter later occupied the rock, drawing water from a now vanished well. Roche is the feminine form of the French word for rock and St Roch was born in Montpellier in southern France around 1350. He was a hermit, pilgrim and miraculous healer of the plague-stricken. When Roch himself caught the pestilence he was – in an echo of Romano-Celtic healing practices – tended by a dog who licked his sores. On returning home from pilgrimage in Italy he was imprisoned as an impostor, his relatives being unable to recognize him. There is a village called Rock ten miles to the north of Roche but no direct connection has yet been made with the French saint although he was popular throughout medieval Britain.

About two miles off the Northumberland coast, the largest of the Farne Islands was

Roche Rock, St Michael's Chapel, Cornwall

used as a place of retreat by various saintly hermits. Aidan used to retire to Inner Farne for prayer and penance during Lent, and it was from this vantage point that he saved Bamburgh by turning wind and flames against Penda. Cuthbert was prior of Lindisfarne up to 676 when he retired to Inner Farne for a life of silent contemplation and 'the secrecy of solitude'. Unfortunately his reputation for holiness, prophecy and healing ensured a constant stream of visitors and distracting responsibilities. Cuthbert first drove evil spirits from the isle, then built a combined oratory and hut surrounded by such a high bank that he could see only sky. He dug two stony hollows which filled with water; the surviving well is now a stagnant depression surrounded by the nests of arctic terns, and the bird wardens bring water from the mainland or collect rainwater from the roofs. Wheat would not grow in the soil but Cuthbert was successful with barley. He had an affinity with animals and protected the eider ducks who nested at the foot of his altar. Cuthbert practised austerities including spending the night in prayer up to his neck in the sea. Once, when staying at the monastery at Coldingham (Kirk Hill, St Abb's Head) he was observed coming out of the surf at dawn to have his feet dried and warmed by a pair of otters. Cuthbert reluctantly agreed to become a bishop and was based at Lindisfarne for two years before returning in 687 to die on Inner Farne. Ethilwald took Cuthbert's place as resident hermit, and once by his prayers saved a boat of visitors from being wrecked in a sudden storm. When Bede was writing in 721 the seventy-year-old Felgild was being an 'athlete of Christ' on Farne. Other hermits followed: the most notable, Bartholomew of Farne, spent forty-two years on the island cheerfully experiencing an exposed, stormy life of penance and privation. He fished, milked a cow, tended his crops, kept a pet bird and paced his tiny kingdom singing psalms. When a woman friend from his earlier life tried to gain entry to his chapel she was hurled backwards by a whirlwind. Bartholomew experienced visions and carved a stone coffin for himself as death

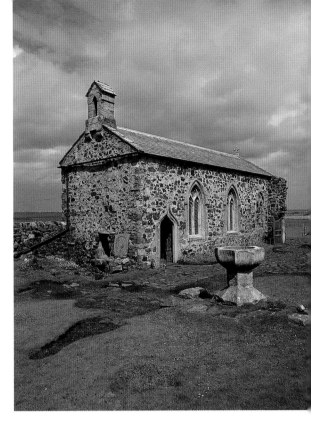

St Cuthbert's Chapel, Inner Farne, Northumberland

approached. Miracles were later reported at his tomb on Farne. The last true hermit was Thomas de Melsonby, prior of Durham, who died on the island in 1246. By 1255 Durham had formed a small Benedictine monastery (the House of Farne) which remained in use until 1536. The monks and their servants grew barley, kept a variety of animals, ate sea-birds and their eggs as well as seals and porpoises. The island is now a nature reserve, the National Trust wardens – in the tradition of Cuthbert – dedicated to studying and preserving the wildlife rather than eating it.

Cuthbert's great friend was 'Herebert', a solitary priest who lived on an island in Derwentwater, now known as St Herbert's Isle. Each year the hermit went to see Cuthbert on Lindisfarne, but in 686 they met instead at Carlisle. Aware of his coming death, Cuthbert warned Herebert that they would not meet again on this earth. Appalled at the thought of losing his spiritual guide, Herebert begged that, as they had served God together, they might be allowed to 'pass away together to the vision of heavenly grace'. After praying for this end, Cuthbert predicted that it would be so, and both died on 20 March of the following year. In the late fourteenth century, forty days' indulgence were granted to those who visited the island on St Herebert's feast.

St Herbert's Isle, Derwentwater, Cumbria

A grave-slab set into the west end of the modern church of St Molios at Shiskine represents a bishop holding a chalice and crozier who may be St Laserian (Molaise). He was born into the royal family of Dalriada, the kingdom combining parts of Ireland and Scotland. He was an abbot in Co. Carlow, but the centre of his present-day cult is at his Co. Sligo foundation of Inishmurray. His *Life* claims that he was sent to Rome to be consecrated bishop and investigate the Roman calculation of Easter on behalf of Irish monastics. On his return in 633 the Celtic method was abandoned in Ireland except by the monasteries of Columba.

St Molios' Church, Shiskine, Arran

Laserian traditionally spent time as a hermit in a cave on Holy Island off the east coast of Arran. The belief that he voluntarily accepted illness from thirty diseases at once to cancel out his sins, thus avoiding the punishments of purgatory on the way to heaven, ensured that his cave hermitage became a popular destination for medieval pilgrims. A monastery was founded on the north-west of the island, near the present pier and farm, to act as a hospice for visitors. Since 1990 the island has been owned by Buddhists from Samyê-Ling Tibetan Centre in Eskdalemuir (Dumfries-shire). The rock shelter is a shrine treated with love and respect, swept clean and furnished with offerings. Paintings of Buddhist teachers can be seen on rocks beside the pathway: enlightened, compassionate, holy men whose ways share many similarities with those of Christian mystics and visionaries. Retreats are held at the lighthouse buildings on the south-west coast;

St Molaise's Cave
Holy Island, off Arran

Burgh Castle, Norfolk

volunteers may help with environmental tasks and work is in progress to build an eco-friendly religious complex on the hill facing the sun.

Around 633 King Sigebert gave land for a monastery at Burgh in Norfolk to a group of Irish clergy who had taken the 'white martyrdom' of 'exile for Christ'. Using the Roman Saxon Shore fort as a base, St Fursey and his companions did missionary work among the

St Decuman's Well, Watchet, Somerset

East Saxons. Bede describes a series of remarkable visions which Fursey experienced at a time of illness. Initially he left his body for a night and was able to see choirs of angels, hearing them sing such things as 'the saints shall go from strength to strength'. On a second occasion he saw greater joys but his journey to heaven was impeded by devils using the events of his life to harry and accuse him. With angelic help he reached his goal where he learned of the extremes of joy and sorrow from saints who appeared among the angels. Looking back at gloomy Earth far below, he saw the fires which would consume the world: cruelty, covetousness, discord, falsehood. They joined and came towards him but Fursey, having been assured that the fire would harm only those who lit it, passed through while devils stirred up the flames with false accusations and good spirits spoke in his defence. Returning from his beatific vision, angels again parted the fire, but this time Fursey was scorched by devils pushing a burning man against him. The man had died in his sin and Fursey had to share his punishment for accepting some of the man's clothing. The angels instructed Fursey on what should be done to gain salvation for those sinners who repented on their death-bed. Fursey's ordeal left him with a scarred jaw and shoulder, and sweats whenever he recollected the terror of the burning man.

St Decuman's Well in Watchet, Somerset, commemorates a sixth-century Welsh monk from Pembrokeshire who came to north Somerset as a missionary hermit. According to legend, he and his cow crossed the Bristol Channel on a cloak or hurdle. After years of solitary devotion he was beheaded at prayer by those opposed to his missionary work. Decuman picked up his head, carried it to a spring west of the church, washed it in the cleansing waters, replaced it and continued his mission. Decapitating enemies, collecting, washing, preserving heads and belief in their magical properties are recurring images in the lives, myths and folk tales of the pre-Christian Celts. A number of early saints were able to demonstrate their spiritual power to pagan adversaries by carrying heads away and, sometimes, successfully replacing them. Churches in Wales and throughout the south-west are dedicated to Decuman thanks to his followers and disciples. His cult was celebrated in Somerset at Watchet, Muchelney, and Wells Cathedral where pre-Christian sacred springs flow; around 400 figures of saints and monarchs grace the magnificent west front.

Another saint credited with carrying his decapitated head is Nectan, mentioned briefly in the account of his 'father', St Brychan. According to the twelfth-century Hartland version of his life, Nectan was a sixth-century missionary from Wales who crossed the Bristol Channel to lead a hermit's life in a beautifully remote, densely wooded valley. From across Devon and Cornwall Brychan's saintly children would gather at Nectan's hermitage each year-end to acknowledge him as senior brother and 'talk of God'. His eremitic idyll did not last. After helping a swineherd locate lost pigs, Nectan was rewarded with the gift of two very good milking cows which were soon stolen from him, and he was beheaded by the robbers while attempting the tricky combination of property reclamation and Christian conversion. Undaunted, the saint carried his head over half a mile back to his well and hut, inside which he was buried. His well remains in Hartland (Stoke), Devon, where St Nectan's Church was built in his honour.

A British monastic community probably first guarded the shrine at Stoke and may have translated Brychan/Nectan's body from Lundy Island (Thomas 1994). By the tenth century English priests were in charge and, following instructions in a dream, dug up Nectan's body, in a stone sarcophagus with decorated lid. King Harold's mother, Gytha, is recorded as patron of the minster in the 1050s. During the following century Hartland Abbey was founded to the north-east, and the restored shrine and church at Stoke came under the care of Norman Augustinians who commissioned a self-promoting *Life of St*

St Mary the Virgin, Oare, Somerset. Pilgrims would use a scallop shell to remove holy water from the piscina to make the sign of the Cross. The carved basin in the chancel wall, close to where the altar used to stand, represents a stoical St Decuman carrying his head.

St Nectan's Well, Hartland (Stoke), Devon

St Nectan's Church, Hartland (Stoke), Devon

St Levan's Well, Land's End, Cornwall

St Levan's Church, Cornwall

Nectan. The shrine was undoubtedly a place of medieval pilgrimage: relics, including a staff decorated with precious metals and jewels, were taken around the neighbourhood and miracles were recorded, one knight being cured of a paralysed arm simply by looking at the church from a distance.

St Selevan was a member of the royal family of St Constantine, king of West Cornwall, which came from Ireland via Wales. He was grandson of St Geraint and great-nephew of his namesake St Solomon (Selevan is a Celtic version of the Hebrew name meaning peaceable). He was father of St Cuby and brother to SS Just and Silwen (Sennen). He built a two-roomed chapel-oratory on a platform cut into the cliff face overlooking Porth Chapel. Above the slight remains of his chapel, and linked to it by around fifty stone steps, are his well and baptistery built over the spring. Its water was recommended for toothache, sore eyes and used in church for baptisms. Cures were obtained under the healing influence of Selevan by sleeping on the stone slab over his well.

The saint's favourite occupation was fishing from the western rocks of Porth Chapel beach. Once he passed a woman called Jonah picking vegetables who criticized him for going fishing on a Sunday. He replied that there was no more harm in his gathering of dinner than in hers, and if another was ever christened Jonah at his church or well she would be an even bigger fool than the woman herself. The most famous story of Selevan's fishing is commemorated on a fifteenth-century bench-end inside his church (St Levan's). Selevan repeatedly caught the same two chad or sea bream which he rejected as too bony. He eventually took them home and fed them to his hungry nieces who had come on a surprise visit with his sister Silwen. The children greedily swallowed the fish, choked on the bones and died. Several moral twists are given to this story, blaming Selevan for initially rejecting the God-given fish, and the children for complaining or being greedy. A large granite boulder split in two lies in the churchyard. Legend describes Selevan breaking it with his staff, prophesying that the world would end when the crack was wide enough to allow the passage of a donkey bearing panniers. With its obvious fertility associations, it is most likely that the split stone was an object of pre-Christian worship, the church and crosses erected here to cancel out the pagan energies. The gap is growing discernibly wider.

St Cenydd's Church, Llangennith, Gower

Scenes from St Cenydd's (Kyned) legendary life are illustrated on the gates to his churchyard at Llangennith, Gower: the sixth-century hermit does seem to have existed, but his details are as fabulous as they are contradictory. One version of his legend makes him a son of the scholar-monk St Gildas, while another claims he was the illegitimate son of a knight of King Arthur, born with a deformed leg as a punishment on his parents. Most versions agree that he was set adrift in a cradle, rescued by birds, then looked after by angels who gave him Christian instruction. The swearing of oaths on a breast-shaped bell features prominently in the legend, and St David cured his deformity but Kyned angrily demanded its return. He became a hermit with a servant 'among the rocks of Gower', probably on the nearby tidal island of Burry Holms where St Caradoc used the ruined church as a hermitage in the twelfth century. Kyned also founded a monastery on the site of Llangennith (Llangenydd) church in which he is reputed to be buried. Vikings destroyed his priory in 986. The present church with its saddleback tower dates mainly from the thirteenth century and some of the former monastic structures now serve as farm buildings. Outside the church gate is an ancient well whose capstone bears an incised cross.

The long and varied life of St Godric is commemorated in the beautiful remains of a Benedictine priory standing on the site of his hermitage beside the curving River Wear at Finchale, north of Durham. Here, from *c.* 1115 until 1170, Godric lived a mystical life of 'fearful austerity', apparently haunted by the sins and spiritual shortcomings of his adventurous early years. An Anglo-Saxon born in Norfolk, he first became a pedlar travelling the Fens, then went to Rome as a pilgrim. On his return he worked as a sailor on trading vessels, eventually becoming a ship-owning merchant-adventurer. He went on pilgrimage to Jerusalem and may have been the 'pirate from the kingdom of England' who ferried King Baldwin I of Jerusalem around the Holy Land in 1102. Godric travelled home through Spain, making a pilgrimage to the shrine of St James at Compostela. He was bailiff for a Norman lord but, feeling guilt for participating in mistreatment of Saxon tenants, he again went on pilgrimage to Rome and the shrine of St Giles (Saint-Gilles) in Provence. On a third trip to Rome in his mid-thirties, he took his elderly mother who walked barefoot. They were accompanied by a divinely beautiful young woman, visible only to mother and son, who washed and kissed their feet. Inspired by the example of St Cuthbert on Inner Farne, Godric sold his possessions to live in forests near Carlisle, and with another hermit at Wulsingham, near Durham. Nursing his dying companion, Godric believed that he had 'seen' Elric's spirit depart from his mouth. He then went on a penitential pilgrimage to the Holy Land, living with hermits in the desert and working in a hospital, before returning to England to become a pedlar again. Godric lived as a hermit near Whitby, finally being

OPPOSITE: Finchale Priory, County Durham

drawn to Cuthbert's shrine at Durham by a vision in which the saint promised to find a place for him. At Durham he became a sexton, attended school with the choirboys, was made an honorary monk, and granted permission to settle on the bishop's land at Finchale. Initially, Godric lived north of the priory site in a hollow roofed over with turf, sharing his fire at night with countless snakes who twined around him. Becoming annoyed by their increasing boldness, he suddenly banned them. Existing on roots, berries, flowers and leaves, he was given gifts of food by local people, but fed them to the birds. Moving to the present site he built a wooden hut and an oratory dedicated to St Mary, where he would sit for long periods immersed in cold water in a sunken bath. He also sat in a rock pool in the Wear and was once nearly drowned by the flooding river. Godric wore a hair-shirt and a metal breastplate. He grew vegetables and barley, which he milled to bake bread, but he would not eat food until it was starting to decay. In the snow and ice of winter he revived frozen rabbits and field-mice at his fire. His sister, Burchwen, came to live with him for a while before becoming a nurse in Durham. They kept a cow but this was killed by Scots soldiers who severely beat the saint while searching for buried treasure. Godric wrote English verse, setting some of it to music including an air sung by his sister and angels, heard during a vision. Remembering his time in the desert, Godric added a chapel of St John the Baptist to his hermitage, connecting it to St Mary's by a cloister of wattle and daub. His reputation for holiness, supernatural gifts, clairvoyance and prophecy attracted admiring visitors and correspondents, including Thomas of Canterbury, Abbot Ailred of Rievaulx and Reginald of Durham who became Godric's biographer. The 'holy tramp' was very reluctant to discuss his former exploits with Reginald, other than to describe himself angrily as an unclean liver, a cheat, a hypocrite, greedy, negligent, cruel to those who served him and a lecher addicted to 'seaman's vices'. Eventually relenting, Godric provided details for the exceptionally full *Life* written by Reginald. Contemporaries described him as having a broad forehead, black hair, bushy beard and eyebrows, a hooked nose and flashing grey eyes. He was very small of stature but agile, strong and impressive. Towards the end of his life Godric was increasingly troubled by supernatural phenomena, including diabolic spirits and poltergeists. He died in 1170, aged over 100, after being tended in his long illness by the monks of Durham. His venerable body was not enshrined, but buried in his hermitage around which the priory grew. Godric's tomb lies in the central part of the chancel built over his chapel of St John. Finchale continued as a hermitage for Durham monks who decided to start building a priory in 1196: the present stone buildings date mainly from around 1237. In the fourteenth century Finchale was run by a prior and four monks as a rest-house for their Durham brothers, who, in groups of four, spent three weeks each year on 'holiday'. This rather indulgent arrangement was ended at the Dissolution in 1538.

St Govan's Chapel, Bosherston, Pembrokeshire

A chapel and a headland (St Govan's Head) on the coast south of Bosherston in Pembrokeshire are dedicated to St Govan, who was probably St Gobhan (smith), an abbot from Co. Wexford who, as a boy in Ireland, became a disciple of the Pembrokeshire missionary St Ailbe. Late in life, drawn to the south coast of Ailbe's county, Govan was pursued by Lundy Island pirates and sought the refuge of a rocky inlet. Part of the cliff miraculously enfolded him, opening again when his frustrated pursuers had withdrawn. Govan used the fissure as a cell, building his chapel where a later one now stands. Around seventy-four (they are traditionally difficult to count accurately) stone steps lead down the cliff, with more below the chapel to a well, now dry but formerly valued for granting wishes and cures. Pirates continued to be troublesome, on one occasion stealing St Govan's silver bell, but their ship sank in a storm. In answer to his prayers, angels

retrieved Govan's hand bell, placing it inside a large boulder which rang like a Tom when struck by the saint. Govan stayed here 'worshipping, preaching and teaching' until his death in 586. The eleventh-century chapel with a later stone roof is built around an earlier altar said to be St Govan's tomb. An adjacent doorway leads to Govan's cell where the imprints of his ribs can be seen in the rock cleft. Stone benches line two opposing walls and two splayed openings light the altar and piscina. Water from a shallow well beside the north door – collected in drops with a small spoon or limpet shell – was considered good for failing eyesight, lameness and rheumatism: crutches were still being abandoned on the altar in the nineteenth century. Patients also had poultices of red clay applied to their limbs and eyes before sunbathing for several hours. William of Malmesbury claimed that in William the Conqueror's time the body of one of King Arthur's knights was found near St Govan's Head and buried inside his chapel. Did Sir Gawain (Govan?) become a hermit here, or was a piece of Arthurian romance dropped into a suitably evocative location with a helpful name?

The legend of St Neot is illustrated in a stained-glass window in St Anietus' Church, Cornwall, paid for by the young men of the parish in 1528. Starting top left Neot gives his crown to a younger brother, takes vows as a monk and reads from a psalter with his feet in water. An angel gives him three everlasting fish for his well but only one must be eaten each day. Neot becomes ill, asks his servant for a fish, the servant serves two as treat but Neot orders that the cooked fish be returned to the well where they recover. A robber steals Neot's oxen, stags volunteer to be yoked to the plough and the oxen are returned. The final panel, bottom right shows St Neot in Rome receiving a blessing from the pope. Although Neot's story has many Celtic elements, his *Life* describes him as an Anglo-Saxon monk at Glastonbury who became a hermit in Cornwall. He may have been a relative of King Alfred the Great (871–99) who valued his council and was encouraged in his long struggle with the Danes by a vision of St Neot. According to his friend and biographer Bishop Asser, Alfred was cured of an infirmity at the shrine of St Gueryr, an obscure Celtic saint superseded by Neot. In the eleventh century the village was known as St Anietus and contained a small house of monks. By that time St Neot's relics, except for an arm, had been transferred to a monastery at Eynesbury (now

St Neot's Well, Cornwall

OPPOSITE: St Anietus' Church, St Neot, Cornwall

St Neots, Cambridgeshire) from whence a cheekbone was sent to the mother house of Bec (Normandy). At St Neot's shrine in the 1540s John Leland saw the saint's tunic and a comb made from finger bones and fishes' teeth.

St Neot was so small that he stood on an iron stool at the altar to say Mass, but his spirit was invincible. He rescued a hunted doe from pursuing hounds and spent hours submerged in his well reading the psalter. The well house was restored in 1852 and again in 1996. An arch of stones supporting a large oak tree formerly covered the well which was used for cures of 'weakly children'. Animals rub against the wooden door which opens on to descending steps and a rectangular pool of clear, chilly water where coins glint among stones. On my most recent visit, hazel nuts lay in a niche, a sooty spiral had been marked on the roof slab with a candle flame.

St Andrew's Church, Steyning, West Sussex

St Cuthman was a shepherd boy, originally from Dorset or the Chichester area of West Sussex. He drew a line around his sheep to stop them straying while he was away, or watched them from a boulder which later inherited his power to heal. After the death of his father, Cuthman built a wheeled couch for his paralysed mother and they headed eastwards as mendicant hermits. One day, the rope yoke of the barrow snapped, much to the amusement of nearby mowers who were immediately soaked by a heavy shower of rain. When a new yoke of hedgerow whips broke at Steyning, Cuthman took it as a sign from God to cease travelling. He made a place to live and constructed a timber church on a bramble patch beside a wooded hill enclosed by two streams. At a particularly difficult point in building the church, Christ appeared in the guise of a stranger to lend a hand. When Cuthman's straying oxen were impounded by a local woman called Fippa, the saint yoked her two sons to his cart as replacements; Fippa issued a curse but was hurled to the sky, disappearing beneath the earth on landing. Stories of resistance to Cuthman's missionary work fit in with the possibility that he took over a pagan sanctuary. In 1938 a step at the eastern churchyard gate was found to be six feet long with geometric carvings on its concealed face. It may have been a totem stone set up on the hill by the Saxon Stenningas or 'People of the Stone'. The enigmatic carving is in the church porch, in company with a grave-slab bearing two crosses.

Scott's View, Melrose, Scottish Borders

Cuthman was enshrined in his timber church which became a place of pilgrimage and marvellous cures. Edward the Confessor gave Steyning to the Benedictines of Fécamp (France) in return for Norman hospitality while he was in exile. After the Conquest a new monastery was built at Steyning using Caen (Normandy) stone and Cuthman's relics were transferred to the mother house at Fécamp. The former monastic church of St Andrew has a magnificent Romanesque nave with superb arches and carvings. Steyning was formerly a Saxon royal estate, a significant location as sea-going ships could navigate the River Adur to the port at Bramber within a mile of Cuthman's church. In July 1983 the south aisle chapel was dedicated to St Cuthman whose brightly coloured image fills the eastern window.

Scott's View, Melrose (Scottish Borders) was the favourite view of Sir Walter Scott, whose horses stopped here out of habit even when drawing his coffin to Dryburgh Abbey. The Eildon Hills rise in the distance while a bend of the river Tweed enfolds the former site of Old Melrose monastery. St Cuthbert trained at Old Melrose and here lived the

hermit St Drithelm, set apart from other monks to enable his regime of almost continuous prayer mixed with spiritual and physical penance. Drithelm was a layman, head of a devout household in Ayrshire. He became ill, dying in the early hours of the night but suddenly coming alive again at daybreak, scaring away all the weeping mourners except for his wife to whom he admitted that he had returned from the grasp of death and must change his life. Dividing wealth and possessions equally between his wife, his sons and the poor, Drithelm retired to Melrose where he often submerged himself in the Tweed, standing up to his neck in water for long periods reciting psalms and prayers. He occasionally discussed his out of body experiences with others, including King Aldfrith of Northumbria. Bede relates his story based on the testimony of a fellow monk. Guided by a handsome man in a shining robe Drithelm came to a valley – with burning flames to the left, raging hail and snow to the right – where tormented souls leapt between the unbearable extremes of heat and chill. These were those who repented only on death, waiting until the day of judgment for admission to heaven. A dark place followed where jets of flame and smoke issued from a burning chasm into which souls never to be freed were thrown by mocking devils with glowing tongs. A fragrant meadow behind an infinite wall came next, inhabited by white-robed, happy people, good but imperfect souls waiting for eventual admission to heaven. Finally they approached a place of exquisite beauty whose light, perfume and music made all else seem shoddy: this was heaven itself to which those perfect in word, thought and deed gained instant admission. Quickly taken on the return journey, Drithelm was promised the flowery meadow if he could keep to virtuous and simple ways. While smashing ice to plunge into the freezing river, or drying clothes on his body, Drithelm was often asked how he bore the cold and severe discipline: he replied that he had known it colder and seen greater suffering.

Croyland Abbey (Lincolnshire) stands on a former marsh at Crowland where St Guthlac overcame an environment hostile to body and soul. Son of a nobleman related to Ethelred, king of Mercia, Guthlac became a professional soldier at fifteen, delighting in raids and destruction. Overcome with conscience by the age of twenty-four he entered the double monastery of Repton (Derbyshire). His teetotal ways made him unpopular and he felt

OPPOSITE: *Croyland Abbey, Crowland, Lincolnshire.*
Thirteenth-century sculptures in a quatrefoil over the west face of the ruined nave illustrate scenes from the Life of St Guthlac.
BOTTOM: *Guthlac arrives by boat to find a sow suckling her piglets — a reference to Virgil's description of the founding of Rome.*
TOP: *Devils carry Guthlac to the jaws of hell, but Bartholomew intervenes.*
CENTRE: *Guthlac uses his whip to scare away demons.*
RIGHT: *Guthlac drives an evil spirit from the body of a sick nobleman.*
LEFT: *Guthlac in his oratory with altar and chalice, prophesying to Prince Ethelbald that he will become king.*

stifled by life in the abbey. After two years he was granted permission to become a hermit among the 'immense marshes, black pools, and foul running channels' of the Fens. He went first to the former island on which Thorney Abbey (Cambridgeshire) stands, but found it already occupied by Anchorites. A hermit-boatman named Tatwin offered to show him a very remote island of mud and, with a servant, they set up huts and an oratory in the midst of reed, sedge and the reek of decay. Skins were their clothes, their daily rations a little barley bread and muddy water: agues and marsh fever were prevalent, washing was not a priority. Britons taking refuge on the island did everything they could to intimidate Guthlac and drive him away. Real attacks merged with the violent torments of devils and consoling visions of angels. Guthlac's biographer, a monk named Felix, describes the demons as having horses' teeth, twisted jaws, shaggy ears, crooked legs and flames vomiting from their throats. He was rescued by his patron, Bartholomew the Apostle, who gave him a three-lashed whip to fight off the assailants – Bartholomew may have been chosen because he was a martyr flayed alive with knives. Sought out for his wisdom and prophesy, Guthlac once made ravens apologize for stealing his visitors' gloves. When envy tempted the servant to cut Guthlac's throat while shaving him Guthlac sensed the danger, made the man confess and forgave him. In 714 he realised that death was near and sent for his sister Pega, an anchoress at Peakirk (Cambridgeshire) to the south-west. She sailed down the Welland to help Guthlac's disciples bury him, and inherited his scourge and psalter which she later gave to his shrine. Pega went on pilgrimage to Rome where she died c. 719. (A small chapel and the modern house of a contemplative community occupy the site of her hermitage beside the B1443, east of Peakirk church.) After a year Guthlac's body was found to be incorrupt, possibly thanks to a shroud and the coffin of Wirksworth lead supplied by Edburga, abbess of Repton. On St Bartholomew's Day (24 August) 716, two years after his death, King Ethelbald laid the foundation stone to the first abbey at Crowland built on the site of the saint's hermitage. His cult began and by the twelfth century the shrine created at Crowland was embellished with marble, precious metals and jewels. Croyland also possessed the preserved body of St Waltheof (Waldef), an Anglo-Saxon earl executed for rebellion by the Norman King William, but considered a martyr and miraculous healer by the English. The first abbey, built on oak-piles and imported soil, was despoiled in 870 by Danes searching for treasure, who broke open tombs, killed the abbot, most of his monks and burned the bodies with the combustible buildings. The second abbey was burned accidentally, the third partly destroyed by an earthquake and then another fire. The buildings of the fourth abbey were surrendered to Henry VIII in 1539, the surviving northern aisle of the Benedictines becoming Crowland parish church.

A small island off the mouth of the River Coquet was home to a community of monks

OPPOSITE: Coquet Island, Amble, Northumberland

in the time of Bede and a meeting place for St Cuthbert and Elfleda, the saintly abbess of Whitby and daughter of King Oswy. In 684 Cuthbert prophesied that her brother King Egfrith would die within the year to be succeeded by their exiled half-brother Aldfrith. In the late eleventh century a pious Dane named Henry decided to become a religious abroad rather than be forced to marry at home. He lived as a hermit on Coquet under the patronage of Tynemouth Priory. He was resented by the monk who looked after the island but managed to grow food in a garden and make a holy life based on austere practices. A group of his fellow countrymen arrived one day to tempt him home but, after a night of prayer during which the figure of Christ crucified spoke to him, Henry decided to stay. Visitors were attracted by his growing reputation for prophecy, his ability to move objects at a distance and read the 'secrets of hearts'. He once punished a man who had refused his wife sexual intercourse during Lent. Henry became ill in 1127, enduring in solitude until the final moments when he rang his bell for assistance: the monk arrived to find him dead, hands grasping a candle and the bell-rope. Against the wishes of the island's other inhabitants Henry's body was taken to Tynemouth to be buried near King Oswin, the priory's patron. Coquet Island was occupied by a Royalist garrison of 200 men during the Civil War, and surrendered to the Scots in 1643. The lighthouse of 1841 was built on top of a much earlier light-tower on the site of Tynemouth's satellite Benedictine house. The RSPB now runs the island as a reserve which is home to many species of birds especially puffins, terns and eider or Cuddy's (Cuthbert's) ducks.

St Robert's Cave, Knaresborough, North Yorkshire

A cave and platform cut in a limestone cliff beside the River Nidd was occupied by Robert Flower, born to a prominent York family during the 1160s. A rock-cut drain separates the domestic area, with a stone bench at the south-west (left) end of the terrace, from the remains of Holy Rood chapel. Spiritually inclined from an early age, Robert entered a Cistercian community at Newminster (Northumberland) but quickly yearned for a more secluded life. He became a hermit at Knaresborough, sharing the cave with a knight in hiding from Richard I. After the king's death in 1199 the hermit-knight returned home to his family; a wealthy widow provided Robert with a cell and chapel at nearby Rudfarlington but these were soon destroyed by bandits. Robert lived for a while under the church wall at Spofforth, south of Knaresborough, and then near Tadcaster with monks too lax for his tastes. Moving back to Rudfarlington, he refurbished the hermitage and kept livestock with the help of four servants. As a charitable holy man, Robert attracted the poor, sick and spiritually needy but the constable of Knaresborough Castle – accusing Robert of helping thieves and outlaws – dispersed the commune and flattened his buildings. According to St Robert's medieval *Life* 'he now returned to the place where he had first lived near Knaresborough, in which he could more quietly occupy himself in contemplating the Lord, and could get away from the ubiquitous harassment of the crowd'. In spite of his desire for solitude Robert continued to attract outcasts and performed miracles of physical and spiritual healing: 'to him both nobles and commoners of both sexes flowed, carrying gifts to him, gladdened by the sight of him and edified by his discourse, and went away roofed in love of Christ'. The constable, William de Stuteville, was again determined to root out the troublesome hermit but, after experiencing threatening visions, he granted Robert cows, land and peace beside the River Nidd. Robert's cave and crude shelter of branches was considered beneath the family dignity by his brother Walter, who brought masons from York to improve the site and build a chapel of 'well-cut and smooth dressed stone'. Robert led a devout life of prayer, taught, healed, and used alms to assist the poor and imprisoned. His reputation for holiness and miracles was such that even King John paid a surprise visit, granting him land despite receiving a pointed homily as a reprimand for disturbing the hermit's prayers. Robert died at his hermitage on 24 September 1218, refusing attempts by the Cistercian monks of Fountains Abbey to gain his body and soul. At his own request Robert was buried in a rock-cut grave visible before the altar-base of his chapel. By 1252 his hermitage was in the care of Trinitarian monks (known as Robertines because of their devotion) who moved Robert's body to their nearby monastery, built in his honour. Oil flowed from his tomb and, although not formally canonized, his cult was given papal approval and became renowned across Europe. Writing around 1250, the historian Matthew Paris considered Robert one of the outstanding saints of that particularly spiritual time.

Fifteenth-century wall paintings at Pickering Church, North Yorkshire, depicting the martyrdoms of St Edmund and Thomas Becket (top)

5.
Martyrs and Militants

This chapter looks at some of those in Britain who fought for their Christian beliefs, were killed because of them, or were declared martyrs out of religious or political expediency. The story of Christian martyrdom goes right back to Jesus, his apostles and the Roman Empire. The emperor Domitian (AD81–96) added himself to the hierarchy of divinities worshipped in Rome. Eastern mystery-religions (such as Christianity and Mithraism), offering spirituality and personal salvation, became attractive alternatives to the increasingly debased and ridiculed state religion. Roman administrators regarded early Christians as suspect members of a secret society: their refusal to take the imperial oath of loyalty to the deified emperor was seen as treason rather than religious principle. Several emperors – including Nero (54–68), responsible for the deaths of SS Peter and Paul; Decius (249–51); Valerian (253–9) who had St Cyprian, Bishop of Carthage, beheaded; Aurelian (269–75); and Diocletian (284–305), under whom New Testament books were removed from libraries and burned – instigated persecutions, feeling their own religious and political plans threatened. The last named martyrs under the Romans in Britain were SS Julius and Aaron, believed to have been killed at Caerleon (Newport) in the mid-fourth century. Missionaries to the pagan Britons ran the risk of being killed, just as hermits were considered fair game for robbers. Germanic incomers killed Christian Britons, who killed one another as well as pagan and Christian Anglo-Saxons.

St Tewdric was a fifth-century Christian prince of south-east Wales recalled from his retirement hermitage to lead his people against an incursion of pagan Saxons. The invaders were defeated in battle near Tintern but the venerable warrior sustained a mortal injury and died at Mathern (Monmouthshire) after his wounds had been washed in the spring which bears his name. St Ethelbert of East Anglia was beheaded in 794 at Sutton Walls fort (Hereford & Worcester) while seeking an alliance through marriage to the daughter of King Offa of Mercia; the hidden body was revealed by a pillar of light, obliging Offa to provide a tomb and church at Hereford where the miracle-making Ethelbert was venerated as a martyr. St Alkmund, exiled prince of Northumbria and patron of Derby, was also declared a wonder-working martyr after being dispatched by a political rival c. 800. The Norse struck terror into the monks and nuns of Britain until they in turn produced Christian martyrs of their own. Credited with converting a few of the Danes plundering the Fife coast, missionary bishop St Adrian was reputedly slaughtered by Vikings on the Isle of May in 875, along with '6,600' companions during 'a most cruel invasion'. The island became a home to monks and a major goal for pilgrims who initially honoured St Ethernan (a seventh-century evangelist of the Picts) until Adrian's legend eclipsed him in the fourteenth century.

Saxon struggles against the Normans threw up politico-religious rebel–martyrs. Christians fought one another across Britain's turf – each with God on his side – and acts of holy bravery added to the ranks of martyrs, which became swollen at the Reformation. As had the Roman emperors, Henry VIII executed religious opponents for treason; Edward VI continued his father's break with Rome and his sister Mary I (1553–8) burned Protestants. Elizabeth I (excommunicated by Pope Pius V) treated Catholics as potential rebels released by Rome from their allegiance to her. St Cuthbert Mayne (canonized 1970) was the first seminary priest to be tried and executed 'as a terror to the papists'; part of his skull is carried in procession each June during the pilgrimage at Launceston (Cornwall) in whose market place he was hung, drawn and quartered. In 1571 a copy of John Foxe's Book of Martyrs *was displayed in every cathedral and collegiate church: it included Christian martyrs from c. 1000, but concentrated vividly on recent Protestant executions, identifying the pope with the Antichrist. Along with those of deep constant beliefs, several professional gadflies were caught by the rapidly changing intolerances. Scottish Covenanters, opposed to a Church run by bishops with the king as its head, were ruthlessly persecuted by the early Stuarts, an estimated 18,000 being killed in the period 1603–88. At Wigtown in 1685, Margaret Wilson (eighteen) and Margaret Lachlan (sixty-three) were staked to the shore to be drowned by the incoming tide.*

St Alban is considered to be Britain's first Christian martyr, the only saint in England to have had a continuous cult from Roman times. Modern scholarship currently places his death on 22 June 209, during the reign of Emperor Septimus Severus rather than the Diocletian persecutions of 303. St Alban is first mentioned in the *Life of St Germanus of Auxerre* written c. 480 by Constantius of Lyons on which Gildas (c. 540) and Bede (c. 700) based their accounts. When Germanus preached against Pelagianism at Roman

Verulamium and the Cathedral, St Albans, Hertfordshire

Verulamium in 429, he visited St Alban's tomb to leave a gift of relics in exchange for bloodstained earth. A pagan Briton with Roman citizenship, Alban was converted by a fugitive priest who sought shelter with him. When soldiers came to search the house, the brothers in Christ exchanged cloaks, the cleric escaping while Alban allowed himself to be arrested. Alban's true identity discovered, he affirmed his Christian faith, refused to sacrifice to the gods and was sentenced to be executed on a hill across the river from the town. After converting one executioner by emptying the river, Alban was beheaded by a second whose eyes fell out. This persecution was halted – possibly by Severus' son Geta Caesar – because it was recognized that Christianity was gaining from 'the slaughter of the saints'. Pilgrims were attracted by miracles and cures occurring at the martyr's tomb. Excavations by Rosalind Niblett on the hill adjacent to the cathedral have uncovered evidence for a Romano-British temple and sanctuary enclosure in use up to the time of St Alban's death. The pagan cult was dedicated to healing (especially eye cures) and the severed head. A human head, a horse's head and urns depicting human faces were buried in pits around the enclosure, and the partly de-fleshed skull of a decapitated teenage boy had been on display in the temple. St Alban may have been executed within the temple precinct, his veneration being a Christian continuation of the earlier healing cult of sacrifice and the human head.

A Saxon monastery established at the tomb of St Alban in 793 by King Offa of Mercia, was supplanted by a Norman one built using Roman materials. The church and pilgrimage grew throughout the Middle Ages and Alban's relics were venerated here until the Reformation, although Ely also claimed to have them. Behind the high altar, the fourteenth-century Purbeck marble pedestal stands in front of a wooden watching chamber used by monks to ensure decorum at the shrine. The pedestal was reconstructed in the 1870s from around 2000 fragments. To celebrate the 1200th anniversary of Offa's foundation an excavation and complete restoration were undertaken in 1992–3 by Martin and Birthe Biddle. Alban's shrine does not mark the position of his original tomb which may have been in a Roman cemetery nearer to the town, or on a site now covered by the nave. The north aisle of the presbytery contains a mutilated remnant of the shrine of St Amphibalus ('cloak'), the medieval name given to Alban's priest whose remains were

OPPOSITE: St Alban's shrine-base and watching chamber (right) *seen from the Cathedral retrochoir*

St Mary's Church, Hennock, Devon.
St Urith (scythe) and St Sidwell (carrying her head) on the
rood screen.

'discovered' in 1177. Alban's martyrdom is commemorated with a special service every June when each member of the congregation lays a rose on the floor around the shrine.

Echoes of pagan Celtic concerns feature in the related stories of SS Juthwara, Sidwell and Urith: virtuous young women beheaded at the instigation of their stepmothers. St Urith (Hieritha) was born in Celtic Devon at a time when Anglo-Saxons from Wessex were moving into the West Country. Devoted to Christianity, she had provoked the envy of her (pagan?) stepmother who incited (Saxon?) harvesters to kill Urith with their scythes. A stream of pure water issued from the grieving earth where she fell in the fields at Chittlehampton; a book of her life and recorded miracles used to be kept at the shrine in her church there. Similar stories are told of St Sidwell, a young girl murdered just outside the city of Exeter (Devon). Although hers is a traditional 'Celtic' tale, Sidwell, whose variant names mean 'virtuous' or 'of good will', is occasionally described as a beautiful Saxon killed by pagan Celts. Through the treachery of her stepmother, the innocent girl was beheaded in her father's fields by the scythes of his hired men. A brilliant shaft of light illuminated the place for three nights, after which shining Sidwell was seen to carry her head close to the east gate. These mixtures of Christian martyrdom and pagan fertility reach back to the rites of early agricultural societies where the sacrifice, transfiguration and rebirth of a nature deity (or human proxy) took place among the crops. The undoing of Sidwell's 'sister' gives the motif a further bizarre twist. St Juthwara was a pious young woman who prayed, fasted and gave alms. After the death of her father she suffered severe chest pains, which her stepmother suggested could be relieved by applying two cream-cheeses to her breasts. At the same time she told her son, Bana, that his stepsister was pregnant. Accusing and examining Juthwara, Bana found that her underclothing was moist with 'milk': he promptly struck off her head which fell to the ground creating a holy spring. Juthwara picked up her head and carried it to an oratory where she lay until her relics were translated to Sherborne Abbey (Dorset). She is depicted with a cream-cheese, a sword or holding her head in her arm.

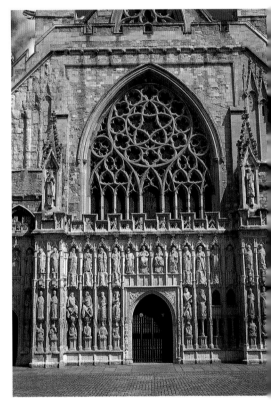

The festivals of Sidwell and Juthwara were celebrated in Exeter Cathedral where Sidwell is illustrated (holding a scythe) in stained glass in the great east window. Her relics were kept in her former church just outside the city's east gate, close to a well which sprang up from her drops of blood. Lights burned at the shrine and 'through her merits' God caused the lame to walk, the blind to see, the sick to find perfect health. The well has gone; a modern church stands in the ancient graveyard on Sidwell Street and the saint is commemorated by a modern mural on the adjacent Tesco supermarket. Although it is unlikely that she ever existed, there are around twenty portraits of her in churches throughout the West Country. At Morebath on the Devon–Somerset border, an altar to Sidwell stood in the north aisle of the formerly richly decorated church. Details from the church account book reveal that she had her own wardens and funds, that on feast days her statue was adorned with a silver shoe and a necklace of silver and jet. In 1533 a thief placed his ladder on the nave roof, climbed through a belfry window and broke open two chests to steal a chalice and Sidwell's silver shoe.

Exeter Cathedral, Devon

At Mylor Churchtown (Cornwall) a granite cross beside the south door, carved from a pagan monolith bearing concentric circles, is reputed to mark the graves of a martyred Breton missionary and a Cornish prince murdered partly for his Christian beliefs. The legend of 'St Mylor' is a confusing *mélange* of personalities, places, and elements from Celtic folklore. Amesbury Abbey (Wiltshire) claimed the relics of a Breton prince named St Melor, possibly obtained in Brittany by King Athelstan. By

Mylor Churchtown, Cornwall

tradition, however, the martyr's body arrived there with wandering monks who placed his coffin overnight on the altar where it became magically, immovably fixed. In Cornwall, Mylor is patron of Linkinhorne where there is a holy well, and of Mylor Churchtown overlooking the inlet of Carrick Roads. Interweaving strands name the saint(s) as a Breton abbot-bishop who founded a monastery at Mylor in the early fifth century, and/or a young prince of Cornwall (or Brittany) whose father was murdered and usurped by his pagan brother. Melor's uncle intended to murder him but was persuaded instead to chop off the young boy's right hand and left foot, as a maimed Celt could not become king. Melor was educated in a monastery where his brass foot and silver hand came to function as efficiently as real ones. Fearful of losing his throne, the uncle bribed Melor's tutor to behead him. Carrying the severed head back to the uncle, the tutor was overcome by heat and thirst, whereupon Melor's head talked to his murderer, advising him to thrust his staff in the ground, which created a cooling spring and grew into a mature shady tree. His wicked uncle died within three days of touching the martyr's head.

Several early Irish annals tell of St Donan, follower and 'soul friend' of St Columba, who set up a monastery on Eigg. Despite the ferocity of their Pictish ruler, Donan believed himself chosen to convert the people of the island, but Columba would not confess the reckless evangelist as he saw 'the red blood of martyrdom' in his eyes. The texts speak of a pagan woman, accustomed to grazing her milking cattle on Eigg, who was resentful of the monks' missionary activities and her loss of pasture. This reputedly awesome Queen of Moydart and her 'Amazonian' attendants gave Eigg its alternative name: 'Island of Big Women'. She sent her own warriors, or paid pirates, to kill Donan's monks, as the herdsmen of Eigg refused to commit such an 'unreligious act'. On Easter night in 617 or 618, armed robbers landed on the island while Mass was being said. Donan negotiated time to complete the service, then led his fifty-two companions to the refectory where they were put to death by fire and sword; it may have been the 'contract killing' of legend or an early opportunistic raid by Vikings. The monastery struggled on into the 750s at least, but did not survive the main Viking onslaught beginning in 794 when the annals record 'devastation of all the islands of Britain by the gentiles'. Scandinavian seafarers often visited Eigg, landing in the bays at Laig and Kildonnan, adding their burial cairns to the Neolithic ones along the coast. Donan's monastery was probably founded in an Iron Age promontory fort beside the sandy bay at Kildonnan, then moved to the higher ground now

OPPOSITE: A holy spring may have attracted early Celtic missionaries to this site where water from St Mylor's well in the churchyard is still used for baptisms

Kildonnan Promontory Fort, Isle of Eigg, Inner Hebrides

occupied by the ruined sixteenth-century church and graveyard. A fifteenth-century schist cross-slab in the graveyard is described as either being brought in pieces to Eigg from Iona, or the remains of two similar but separate crosses. In June 1997 a modern statue of St Donan, once erected inside the fort, lay smashed to pieces on the grass.

The courage and strong religious faith of Oswald of Northumbria, nicknamed 'Shining Sword', ensured his status as an English hero and Christian martyr against the dark forces of Odin.

A wooden cross erected at St Oswald in Lee in 1936 commemorates the battle of Heavenfield fought in 635 between Oswald and Cadwallon, the British ruler of Gwynedd. The sources of their quarrel originated a generation earlier with the rival tribes and territories of the huge kingdom of Northumbria, composed of Deira (approximately modern Yorkshire), and Bernicia (approximately modern Northumberland) which was ruled by Oswald's father, Athelfrith. Edwin, the rightful heir of Deira, was forced into exile by Athelfrith, who took over the whole kingdom which he actively expanded by invading Pictish, Scottish, British and rival Anglo-Saxon kingdoms. However in 616, Edwin, aided by Radwald of East Anglia, raised an army and invaded Northumbria, killing Athelfrith, uniting Deira and Bernicia, and becoming the first Christian king of Northumbria. His influence extended over most of east and central/south England and west to the isles of Anglesey and Man whose ruler, Cadwallon, fled to Ireland after Edwin had besieged him off Anglesey. Meantime Athelfrith's three sons sought asylum among the Picts and Scots, Oswald being converted to Christianity in Iona (see pp. 38). On Edwin's death he returned to Northumbria, now occupied by Cadwallon, and engaged him in battle.

St Oswald in Lee, Wall, Northumberland

Oswald's largely unbaptized forces mustered on raised ground to the north of Hadrian's Wall. Before their advance at dawn Oswald set in the ground a wooden cross, bidding his army kneel to ask God's protection as they fought in a just cause to save their nation. The men of Northumbria defeated the superior British army; skirmishing spread over many miles and Cadwallon, fleeing south, was killed at a stream near Hexham. The site of Oswald's cross became so famous for miracles that people removing the earth created a deep pit. Splinters of wood were mixed with water as medicine, even a piece of moss growing on the cross miraculously mended the fractured arm of a monk who fell on the ice. In memory of Oswald, monks of

Hexham visited Heavenfield on the eve of his death to 'keep vigil for the welfare of his soul'. They also erected a small church on the site of the present eighteenth-century one, which contains paintings of SS Oswald and Aidan, and a Roman stone altar with a slot cut in its top to hold a Christian cross. Oswald ruled for eight years before being killed in battle against Penda at Maserfield (Oswestry) in 642, aged thirty-eight. Surrounded, mortally wounded, he was heard praying for the souls of his bodyguard as the Mercians closed in. On Penda's orders Oswald's head and forearms were cut off and displayed on stakes but his brother Oswy managed to recover them a year later and finally defeated Penda in 655. The spring at Maserfield came in to being when Oswald's arm touched the ground, either dropped by an eagle or during transportation of his remains.

Durham Cathedral: a statue of St Cuthbert holding St Oswald's head

Oswald's head was buried at Lindisfarne, but later taken to Durham inside the coffin of St Cuthbert by monks fleeing the Viking raids. At Durham Cathedral a statue removed from a niche on the central tower depicts Cuthbert holding the head. Oswald's body was moved from Oswestry to Bardney Abbey (Lincolnshire) on the insistence of his niece. Monks washing his bones discovered that earth splashed with the wash-water had acquired the power to heal. Miracles occurred at the tomb, and Athelfled (Ethelfleda, Queen of Mercia) acquired the bones in 909 for her purpose-built church of St Oswald in Gloucester, which became a medieval priory and place of pilgrimage. Oswald's arms went initially to the palace at Bamburgh, his right hand in a silver casket being displayed in Bamburgh church along with the uncorrupt arm later stolen for the monks of Peterborough. (When Oswald spontaneously gave up his own food and silver plate to alms-seekers outside his palace, St Aidan seized the king's right arm saying 'may this hand never perish'.) Oswald's relics multiplied alarmingly; numerous churches in Britain and abroad claimed possession of anything from the whole body down to a pinch of earth from his grave.

The village of Chich was renamed St Osyth in honour of the martyr who established a nunnery here in the seventh century. Osith was a Christian princess from the West Midlands, given in marriage to Sighere, apostate king of the East Saxons. Sighere was

St Osyth Priory, Essex

eventually reconverted and they had a son, but it was not a happy marriage. In her legend a ferociously disruptive white stag appears whenever Sighere tries to make love to his wife; Osith makes a vow of chastity and the frustrated Sighere is persuaded to grant land for her nunnery. Osith was later beheaded by Danish pirates who tried to force her to worship idols; she picked up her severed head and carried it to the church. By around 1000 her cult

was popular beyond Essex, her shrine at Chich a regular stopping-place for pilgrims. In 1121 Augustinian canons were tending the shrine in the monastery which continued until dissolution in 1539. Many of the monastic buildings survive in private ownership, including the thirteenth-century chapel and tower, and the magnificent gatehouse restored in the fifteenth century.

St Wystan's story is told in the *Chronicles of Evesham Abbey* and by the Norman, Florence of Worcester. Heir to the throne of Mercia on the death of his father, Wystan was chosen king when his grandfather, Wiglaf, died in 840. A pious young man with no wish for kingly honours, he was happy for his widowed mother Elfleda to rule as regent. His ambitious kinsman and godfather Britfardus, however, was very eager to gain the throne by marrying Elfleda. Wystan believed that the union would be 'uncanonical' (incestuous), so Britfardus invited him to a conference to discuss the matter. Wystan attended 'innocent as a dove'; as they embraced, treacherous Britfardus dealt him a killing blow on top of the head with his sword hilt. Three of Wystan's attendants were also slain. This happened on 1 June 849 at 'Wistanstowe' (the Holy Place of Wistan). A column of light shot to heaven from the place of his murder, remaining visible for thirty days.

A statue of St Wystan on the south porch of his church at Repton

In the church at Wistanstow (Shropshire) his martyrdom is illustrated in stained glass, but at the more likely location of Wistow (Leicestershire) human hairs grew through the churchyard grass each year on their patron's feast. This miracle was verified in the late twelfth century by a commission sent by the Archbishop of Canterbury, but when I visited shortly after his feast the grass was neatly mown. Wystan's body was taken to the monastery at Repton for burial alongside his father and grandfather. The sequence of events at Repton has been clarified by the architectural studies of Harold Taylor and the excavations of Martin and Birthe Biddle. Wiglaf had created a mausoleum for himself and the Mercian royal family by adding a vaulted roof (in nine bays supported by arches on pilasters and pillars) to a simple, semi-sunken stone crypt where King Ethelbald had been buried in 757. To allow the efficient circulation of pilgrims visiting St Wystan's tomb, two new stairways were knocked through at the north-west (descending) and south-west (ascending) corners. An invading Danish army wintered

OPPOSITE: The crypt of St Wystan's Church, Repton, Derbyshire.

at Repton 873–4 inside a camp made by digging defensive ditches between the church and Old River Trent. They destroyed the timber church and monastery, but Wystan's relics had been safely hidden and were returned to the new church completed in 980. King Cnut (1016–35) transferred the remains of the 'glorious martyr' to Evesham Abbey, where they were later put through ordeals of fire by Normans doubtful of a Saxon saint. Having survived the heat, Wystan's relics were damaged when the falling tower destroyed his shrine in 1207; an arm-bone and part of his skull were returned to Repton.

Goldbrook Bridge, Hoxne, Suffolk

Before St George was adopted as England's patron saint, that honour was shared by Edward the Confessor and Edmund the Martyr. Edmund, who became king of East Anglia at the age of fifteen, was killed in his late twenties by the Danes on 20 November 869. Although based on an account by his armour bearer, the place and exact circumstances of Edmund's death remain controversial. The 'great army' of Scandinavians under their leader Ivar (Ingwar) had been causing trouble in the British Isles since 865. Ivar was considered a pagan sorcerer and did not lose a battle for twenty years. He celebrated victories by offering Christian kings to his god Odin in the 'blood eagle' rite. The victim's ribs were hacked off, the lungs pulled out and spread across his back like an eagle's wings. This may have happened to Edmund although the many versions of his legend tell a different story. The Danish army entered East Anglia in 869 to set up winter headquarters at Thetford (Norfolk) where Edmund engaged them in battle. Soundly beaten, Edmund either surrendered to avoid further bloodshed or escaped to a forest called 'Haeglesdune' where he was caught, tied to a tree, scourged; shot full of arrows and beheaded to prevent Christian burial. Other descriptions refer to a bloody stake being pulled from his midriff which looked as if 'tormented by savage claws'. His head was thrown into a thicket where a wolf protected it and attracted Edmund's followers. The miraculously reunited body and head were buried inside a wooden chapel. As Edmund had died affirming Christ and refusing the Danish peace terms, he was soon regarded as a martyr, saint and English patriot. Hellesdon by Norwich (Norfolk), Bradfield St Clare and Sutton (Suffolk) have all been cited as the place of martyrdom. Since Norman times at least, the villagers of Hoxne have held the strongest belief that the murder took place in their parish which once possessed a woodland chapel dedicated to St Edmund. Local tradition describes him hiding beneath a wooden bridge where a newly married couple, seeing his golden spurs reflected in the water, betrayed him to the Danes. Edmund cursed all those who would in future

St Edmund's Monument, Hoxne, Suffolk.

On a fine still morning in 1848, a huge tree at Hoxne known as Edmund's Oak fell to the ground in pieces. Its growth rings suggested an age of over 1000 years, and the iron point of an arrow was found projecting into the tree's hollow heart about five feet up from the base. Considered to be the tree of sacrifice, its wood was carved to make a church screen illustrating scenes from the martyr's life. A stone cross replaced the oak in an open field close to Abbey Farm, once a Benedictine cell of Norwich Cathedral.

cross the bridge to marry, which causes some modern couples to choose a different route to church.

For over thirty years Edmund's body lay in the forest chapel as legends and patriotic fervour grew around his name. In 903 his incorrupt body was transferred to the Saxon monastery at the place later named after him. Edmund's bones were considered to be miraculous, inducing fertility, avenging wrongs: the sudden death of King Sweyn while trying to force ransom money from the monastery was held to be by 'the Saint's spear'. As a gesture of reconciliation Sweyn's son Cnut, the Danish king of England, had the church rebuilt. He also installed Benedictine monks to tend the shrine which had become an important place of pilgrimage and English national sentiment. Rebuilt by Normans on a huge scale, the abbey became one of the richest Benedictine houses in England. St Edmund's shrine stood just behind the high altar, in the eastern apse of the massive church. It was made of golden plates richly decorated with precious stones and stood on a base of green and purple marble surrounded by candles, crosses and jewels. On St Edmund's Day (20 November) 1214, Archbishop Langton persuaded twenty-five barons to swear on the high altar that they would go to war against King John if he did not abide by the liberties set out in *Magna Carta*. The shrine was dismantled, the abbey dissolved under Henry VIII whose officers carried away the riches. Today, Edmund is honoured in the cathedral church of St James, while his relics are said to lie hidden in the monastery grounds which serve as a public park.

Bury St Edmund's Abbey, Suffolk

Another victim of the Danes was St Alphege, described by St Anselm as a martyr for justice as John the Baptist was a martyr for truth. A monk at Deerhurst (Gloucestershire) Alphege became a hermit in Somerset, then abbot at Bath. As Bishop of Winchester from 984, he was renowned for the contrast between his public generosity and personal austerity. Ethelred the Unready ('evil council') was unwilling to engage the several bands of Danish invaders making war on England, preferring to buy short respites with huge amounts of 'Danegeld' or tribute money. In 994 Ethelred sent Alphege to parley with Danes who had raided London and Wessex; Sweyn was temporarily bought off while Anlaf became a Christian, promising never again to make war on England. Alphege was made Archbishop of Canterbury (1005–12) in seriously troubled times: Ethelred decreed a national three-day fast on bread, water and herbs in 1009 and ordered every man to church and confession, barefoot and unadorned by jewellery. Like the Celts before them, the

St Alfege's Church, Greenwich, London

Anglo-Saxons interpreted the rapacious foreigners as God's punishment. The Danes besieged Canterbury in 1011, capturing it through the treachery of an Anglo-Saxon archdeacon. Along with other worthies, Alphege was taken to the Danish camp at Greenwich and held to ransom for seven months. Silver was unlocked to free his companions, but Alphege forbade Canterbury to pay his separate ransom with 'the money of the poor'. The Danes' rage at the stubbornness of their guest spilled over during a drunken feast when Alphege was pelted with ox-bones before finally being dispatched by an axe-blow. The preserved body of this new national hero was first enshrined in Old St

Paul's, later to be transferred to Canterbury by the recently converted King Cnut who was trying to appease his English subjects. Buried near the high altar, Alphege was venerated by the Canterbury monks at the start and end of each day. Thomas Becket was an admirer

of St Alphege, but his own dramatic death in the Cathedral eclipsed the earlier martyr's cult. Greenwich began as a Roman settlement and the remains of Saxon burial mounds dot the park. The church currently occupying the traditional site of St Alphege's

St Magnus' Cenotaph, Egilsay, Orkney

death dates from 1714–18, built by Nicholas Hawksmoor in the style of a classical pagan temple.

Earl Magnus, born around 1075, was son to one of the Viking rulers of Orkney.

St Magnus' Church, Egilsay, Orkney.

Although he was killed for political reasons, saintly Magnus was declared a martyr and pilgrims visited the scene of his death. A Romanesque church with nave, chancel and a western round tower soon superseded the building where Magnus had prayed. The tower, originally taller and with a conical roof of flagstones, is a navigation mark for ships approaching Kirkwall from the open sea.

Christianity put an end to his early career as a pirate, but he was captured by Magnus 'Barefoot' (king of Norway and overlord of Orkney) who forced him to participate in raiding Britain's western seaboard. According to the Norse *Orkneyinga Saga* Magnus stayed on his ship reading psalms during an attack on Anglesey, saying that he had no quarrel with the men of the island. He escaped to find sanctuary with King Malcolm III of Scotland who allowed him to live as a penitent in the house of a bishop. When 'Barefoot' died, Magnus returned to Orkney to share the earldom with his cousin Hakon, but there was friction between them. At Hakon's request they met on the small island of Egilsay to discuss peace terms. Hakon's murderous intentions soon becoming clear, Magnus decided to sacrifice himself rather than cause the death of his attendants. After spending the night in church, he faced his executioner on 16 April 1116/17. While praying for his murderers he received a great blow to the head from Earl Hakon's cook, Lifolf. Viking sagas record that the area of moss and stones where Magnus was killed, soon afterwards becames green grass. St Magnus's Centotaph, sharing the meadows with corncrakes, was erected in 1938 on the traditional site of the murder.

The body of St Magnus was first taken to Birsay (Orkney Mainland) where the sixteenth-century Earl's Palace and parish church of 1760 can be seen. The *Orkneyinga Saga* says that cures were obtained by those praying at his grave over which a bright, heavenly light was often to be seen. Initially sceptical of Magnus's sanctity, Bishop William was persuaded to move the relics to Kirkwall, and Magnus's nephew Rognvald vowed to build a 'stone minster' in his honour once he had seized power from Hakon. Building began in 1137 and continued into the fifteenth century, changing in style from Romanesque to Gothic. The bones of St Magnus and St Rognvald were kept in reliquaries on display in the choir until hidden at the Reformation. In 1848 a cavity was discovered in one of the northern piers of the choir: inside was a wooden box containing an incomplete male skeleton believed to be Rognvald. In 1919 the bones of St Magnus (the skull showing signs of an obvious death-blow) were found in a similar hiding place in the opposite, southern pier. Each year in June, through the St Magnus Festival of music and culture, Kirkwall celebrates modern excellence and its Scandinavian heritage.

Henry VIII's desperate attempts to produce a secure male heir, his legal and theological manoeuvrings through a succession of marriages and the resulting break from Rome, created an environment rich in opportunities for persecution and sacrifice. Elizabeth Barton, the visionary and prophetic 'Holy Maid of Kent', was persistently critical of the king's divorce from Catherine of Aragon and his rejection of papal authority. She was hanged at Tyburn (Marble Arch) in 1534 after predicting a villain's death for Henry if he married Anne Boleyn. That same year Cardinal John Fisher and Sir Thomas More were imprisoned for refusing to uphold the Act of Succession which sought to confirm the legality of Henry's divorce and

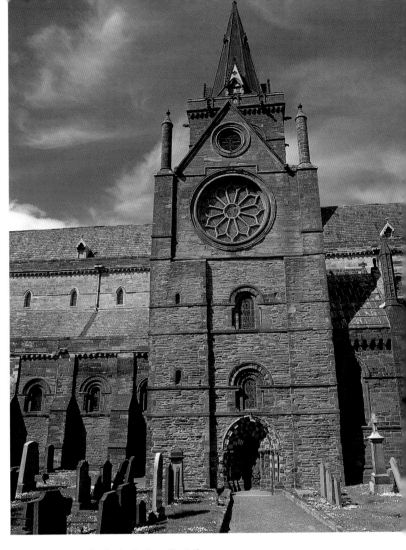

St Magnus' Cathedral, Kirkwall, Orkney

ensure that his hoped-for children with Anne Boleyn would succeed to the throne. Both men were convicted of treason and executed in the following year for denying the king's new title of 'Supreme Head of the Church of England'. More, the former Lord Chancellor and 'Man for all Seasons', was beheaded on Tower Hill. When the Catholic daughter of Catherine of Aragon became Queen Mary I (1553–8) on the death of her half-brother Edward VI (1547–53) it was time to settle old scores with England's senior Protestant clerics and leaders of the Reformation. As Archbishop of Canterbury under Henry's influence, Thomas Cranmer laid the foundations of the Church of England, sent Catholics to the stake and declared Mary a bastard. Imprisoned by Mary, he signed several life-saving recantations of his Protestant beliefs but was burnt at the stake on 21 March 1556 in The Broad outside Balliol College. Retracting previous denials, Cranmer thrust his right hand

Oxford Martyrs' Cross

in to the flames, declaring 'This hand hath offended! Oh this unworthy hand.' On the morning of 16 October the previous year, Nicholas Ridley, Bishop of London, and Hugh Latimer, the former Bishop of Worcester and chaplain to Anne Boleyn, had suffered a similar fate. As the flames went about their deadly business Latimer encouraged his companion: 'Be of good comfort Master Ridley, and play the man. We shall this day light such a candle, by God's grace, in England as I trust shall never be put out'. A memorial to the Oxford martyrs was erected in 1841 in St Giles across the road from the Ashmolean Museum. A cross of cobblestones set into the surface of Broad Street marks the site of the burnings. Mary created nearly 300 Protestant martyrs which did little to prevent the English Reformation that made Christian writings directly available to the people, but much was swept away, including the public veneration of saints.

St Alban's shrine,
St Albans Cathedral, Hertfordshire

6.
Touching Heaven
Relics, Shrines and Miracles

St Ciaran of Clonmacnoise (512–45) ordered that his bones be exposed on a hilltop like those of a stag and only his spirit preserved. This 'pure' approach sat uneasily with the desire for sacred remains as aids to worship, and the innate belief in the miraculous powers of objects. God heard and answered prayers, performed miracles through Christ and, through the special holiness of saints, displayed his supernatural power and mercy. His influence was seen in all aspects of everyday life, anything remarkable being considered a sign of his direct intervention. All nature was regarded as a gift, including the laws of nature which God would alter in a direct and specific way, especially if requested through the agency of a saint. A combination of mental and spiritual forces acting upon the material world could create a miracle, certain places and things might hold spiritual powers and influence the known and unseen worlds: with the aid of saints and their relics it was possible to part the veil and touch heaven.

Bede describes St Germanus curing a young girl's blindness, using relics hung in a casket around his neck. Afterwards he deposited 'relics of all the Apostles and several martyrs' in the tomb of St Alban, taking in return soil stained with that martyr's blood. The monks at Bede's monastery every day 'walked in procession with the relics of the Saints'. The bones of St Botolph could not be moved from Iken (Suffolk) to Thorney (Cambridgeshire) without those of his brother St Adulf, and a reliquary containing St Iwi's bones became immovable when rested on the altar of St Edith at Wilton Abbey. Relics were believed to give or prevent victory in battle, bestow cures and fertility, put out fires and strike offenders dead. When lost or hidden they revealed their whereabouts through dreams, visions and miraculous discoveries: monks were very keen on excavation. A great black stone crucifix was dug up on a hilltop at Montacute (Somerset) in response to the recurring dream of a carpenter. The miraculous Holy Cross chose to be taken to Waltham (Essex) where it cured the future king Harold of paralysis. Harold founded Waltham Abbey to house the Cross and prayed before it for victory against the Normans. Christ's head was seen to bow in sorrow and the Saxon battle-cry of 'Holy Cross' at Hastings (1066) could not prevent their defeat or Harold's true love, Edith Swan-Neck, becoming a widow. For some, the possession of relics became an end in itself, especially the great medieval monasteries, hungry for pilgrim revenues, in competition with neighbouring establishments. In 1445 Salisbury Cathedral (Wiltshire) was the proud owner of no less than 234 relics, including those of their own Bishop Osmund (d. 1099) who was canonized in 1456 after a protracted examination of his life and miracles, first begun in 1228. Relics were traded, manufactured and stolen, and shrine guardians had to prevent pilgrims – including visiting bishops such as St Hugh of Lincoln – from biting away pieces of the remains they were kissing. Disputes were sometimes conveniently settled: when Llandaff, Llandeilo and Penally were competing for the body of St Teilo it was triplicated during the night. An especial sign of sanctity was the spontaneous preservation or 'incorruption' of a body-part or whole corpse. Although the art of total embalming was not practised in medieval Britain, removing the organs, washing with wine or vinegar, packing with salt and spices, wrapping the body in waxed cloth and sealing in an airtight coffin with charcoal or plaster all had some effect, but can hardly explain the lifelike appearance maintained over several hundred years by a few remarkable individuals. In 1198 the body of St Edmund (d. 869) was viewed at Bury St Edmunds by Abbot Samson and twelve companions who pronounced it in perfect condition. As the examination took place at night by candlelight, it is possible that a freshly preserved body had been substituted for the royal martyr – perhaps even a naturally tanned 'bog body' discovered in the fens. Strong belief and the need for magic, theatre and emotionally expressive religion, created a climate conducive to wonders. Statues moved, spoke, shed tears, wept blood – some still do, and not always with the detectable use of speaking tubes or other mechanical aids. The solidified blood and fat relics of martyrs miraculously continue to liquefy on their feast days, especially in southern Italy where St Pantaleon (Ravello) and St Lorenzo (Ameseno) do so each 27 July and 10 August respectively. For the last 500 years some of the dried 'blood' of St Januarius (d. 305) has been kept at Naples. The relic (in a sealed phial inside a glass and silver reliquary) is shown in public three times a year, during which the solid is seen to liquefy: the rate of change varies and occasionally fails. The solidified, rusty mass may be a thixotropic suspension of ferrous chloride and calcium carbonate which changes viscosity when vigorously moved. Temperature variations may account for the physical changes observed in some other sacred liquids containing fats and waxes.

During the Middle Ages the Church had grown generally wealthier, shrines and reliquaries becoming ever more magnificent with the donations of pilgrims and the gifts of the wealthy and powerful, but the mood began to change in the fifteenth century when the popularity of shrines diminished and some preachers took to carrying relics about with them. By the early sixteenth century the Lollards, Martin Luther and other religious reformers were questioning priestly powers, the authority of Rome and the doctrine of transubstantiation at the altar. Avarice, a love of adornment and the sale of indulgences were seen to be corrupting the worship of God. Church practices were obscuring rather than spreading the Word, and the veneration of saints was regarded as little better than pagan idolatry. At the same time, Henry VIII (named by the pope as 'Defender of the Faith' in 1521) was trying to keep the Church in England subject to him and the common law. By 1540 Henry had broken with Rome and dissolved the monasteries, whose treasures were turned into bullion, their roofing lead recast after being melted down in furnaces fuelled with church woodwork. Twenty-six wagon-loads of treasure were carried away from the shrine of Thomas Becket at Canterbury. Most other places of pilgrimage suffered as the king's official Visitors dismantled shrines, smashed images and scattered relics. But not all was swept away: relics survive and are venerated, healing shrines attract the pleas and petitions of Catholic and Protestant alike, and each year over two million visitors file past the body of St Edward the Confessor in his shrine at Westminster Abbey.

St Andrew and his brother Simon (St Peter) were the first disciples to be chosen by Jesus, who, seeing them cast a net into the sea of Galilee, promised to make them 'fishers of men'. Previously a follower of John the Baptist, Andrew went on to spread Christ's message abroad, dying a martyr around AD60. Legends credit him with travels to Ethiopia, Constantinople and north of the Black Sea to Russia but his fourth-century *Acts* link him mainly with Greece where Patras in Achaia (Peloponnese) is claimed as the place of his crucifixion. He preached for two days hanging from a cross, which in medieval times was popularly believed to have been X-shaped. St Andrew's flag is a white saltire on a blue ground, the 'X' being used to represent Scotland on the Union flag. Andrew, considered apostle-patron of Greece and Russia, was extremely

St Helen's Church, Ranworth, Norfolk.
St Andrew holding his saltire cross on the late fifteenth-century rood screen.

St Andrews Cathedral and St Rule's Tower, Fife.

Pinnacled turrets of the long cathedral church compete on the skyline with St Rule's rectangular tower.

popular in Anglo-Saxon England and adopted as Scotland's saint in the belief that his relics had been brought to Fife.

A Syrian monk or native of Patras, St Rule (Regulus) is credited with bringing Andrew's relics to Fife around 345, or in the mid-eighth century during the reign of the Pictish King Angus I. Rule's cult is ancient but his earliest surviving *Life* dates only from the ninth century and the many versions of his legend are contradictory. As guardian of Andrew's relics at Patras, he was instructed by an angel in a dream to carry a portion of the remains to the far north-west; he journeyed in faith until his angel called a halt on the east coast of Fife. It is impossible to know what was brought to St Andrews, when or by whom. Andrew's supposed remains were transferred from Patras to Constantinople whose residents falsely claimed the apostle as their first bishop. After the fall of that city in the early thirteenth century, Andrew's 'body' was taken by crusaders to Amalfi near Salerno (Italy) and his 'head' to Rome. In the late seventh century St Wilfrid brought relics from Rome to his church of St Andrew at Hexham, some of which may have found their way to St Andrews. Certainly by around 800 a Celtic monastery of Culdees ('servants of God') existed at Kilrimont (as St Andrews was then known), and a magnificent stone sarcophagus had been constructed to hold the bones of an important saint or Pictish king. The sophisticated, richly-sculpted altar-tomb (restored from fragments and on display in the cathedral visitor centre) bears biblical scenes of King David with exotic animals, crosses and intertwined serpents. St Andrews became a bishopric and, eventually, the ecclesiastical capital of Scotland. In the late eleventh century St Margaret, English wife of the Scottish King Malcolm III, had St Rule's Church built to house the relics. Only its tall, narrow rectangular tower, reminiscent of Northumbrian work, survives. Such was 'the volume of pilgrims to Fife' that Margaret 'felt obliged to provide a ferry and hostels at the River Forth'. Under David I in the following century, Augustinian canons were brought to tend the relics at St Rule's; the Celtic monks were banished to the cliff top where the remains of St Mary of the Rock can be seen east of the thirty-acre cathedral precinct. The Anglo-Norman cathedral-priory, begun around 1160, was consecrated in 1318 in the presence of King Robert Bruce, who achieved Scottish independence from England.

A major centre of learning and devotion during the Middle Ages, host to thousands of pilgrims arriving by land and sea, St Andrews was later caught up in the Scottish Reformation. The Archbishop of St Andrews executed a string of 'heretics', starting in 1528 with Patrick Hamilton, who was burnt at the stake covered in gunpowder. Following the burning of George Wishart in 1546, Protestant militants including John Knox, assassinated Archbishop Beaton and occupied the castle. After serving time as a galley slave on a French ship, Knox returned to St Andrews in 1559 to preach reforming sermons. Exhorted to 'cleanse their temple' the people responded by sacking it. 'Popish' images were cast down, mass-books burnt, St Andrew's shrine and the thirty-one pilgrim altars reduced to rubble, the buildings left open to stone-robbing and decay.

St Cledarus (Clether) the Aged is reputed to have been a son of King Brychan, or a venerable old man who entrusted his own twenty children to the care of that saintly ruler. Moving from South Wales to north Cornwall, Clether established his hermitage beside a never-failing spring in the tranquil Inny valley. The Normans built their parish church in the village, but in the fifteenth century a new well house and chapel were raised on Clether's Celtic foundations. The chapel was restored in 1895, rededicated in 1909 and renovated (but subjected to vandalism) in the 1990s. Water runs from the northern well house through the chapel in a channel behind the granite altar, to a second well built into the southern wall. Clether's relics were kept in a niche behind the altar, a sunken area to the right being used for baptisms and healing. This ancient arrangement was designed to transfer supernatural power from Clether's bones to the passing water. Those seeking spiritual refreshment or healing collected water from the chapel outflow, placing offerings in the hatchway above to be

St Clether Well Chapel, Launceston, Cornwall

collected by a priest inside. Today's visitors bring such gifts as shells, arrange wild or cut flowers on the altar, and record their appreciation in the book provided. At Ramsey Abbey (Cambridgeshire) spring water flowing close to the relics of the Persian bishop St Ives (Ivo) similarly performed miracles of healing.

Shortly before his death, St Clether may have moved south across Bodmin Moor to St Cleer, where the holy well and now-vanished 'bowssening' pool became famous for

St Cleer Well and Cross, Liskeard, Cornwall

healing and cures of madness. The village is now associated with St Clarus, an Anglo-Saxon monk murdered in Normandy through the spite of a local noblewoman whose persistent advances he had virtuously rejected.

The shrine of St Endelienta stands in the south aisle of her church at St Endellion, near Port Isaac on Cornwall's north-east coast. Bearing eight deep niches, the altar-tomb was carved in the fourteenth century from local catacleuse stone by the 'Master of St Endellion' who was also responsible for the holy water stoup by the south door. The altar-tomb was defaced in Henry VIII's time and later used as a monument over the body of a local landowner. A banner illustrating scenes from Endelienta's life hangs beside the shrine. Nicholas Roscarrock, living in the parish during the reign of Elizabeth I (1558–1603), recorded the stories of Cornish saints while their veneration was being suppressed and he and his fellow Catholics persecuted. He wrote a hymn to St Endelienta in which he asks his 'Patronesse' to 'praye for him whoe humblye prayes to thee' – a task now undertaken by the congregation in response to requests left on the shrine. Although Endelienta was included in the twelfth-century list of the Children of Brychan compiled at her 'brother' Nectan's church at Hartland, almost all we know about this Welsh princess comes from Roscarrock. A virgin, uninterested in marriage, she settled in the same area of north Cornwall as her 'sisters' SS Minver, Mabyn and Teath. In the valley of Trentinney, about half a mile south of the present church, Endelienta lived as a hermit, sustained only by the milk from her one cow. In search of sweeter grass, the cow trespassed on land owned by the lord of Trentinney who killed her. The saint's godfather (a 'great man', possibly even King Arthur) had the lord killed to revenge the insult, but Endelienta miraculously reanimated both casualties. When her own death drew near, Endelienta instructed friends to place her corpse on a sled drawn by certain yearling oxen who would choose the place of burial. The animals freely drew her to an

The altar-tomb at St Endellion, Wadebridge, Cornwall

St Petroc's Church and St Guron's Well, Bodmin, Cornwall.
The church of St Petroc at Bodmin overshadows the well of St Guron, just as Petroc eclipsed the original founder and his cult.

area of waste and quagmire on a slight hill; as the site was close to an ancient burial area and subsequently proved 'fyne, firme & fruitfull', the animals obviously knew their job. By the thirteenth century, a collegiate church for a group of four prebendary priests had been founded on Endelienta's burial place. The present building, dating mainly from the fifteenth century, retains its collegiate status and the surrounding houses of the prebendaries. Moor stone was mainly used but the tower is built of finer, cut stone brought from Lundy Island. The church has a great sense of airy light and space combined with impressive simplicity and a dignity heightened by slate floors and grey walls. Sir John Betjeman (a regular worshipper here,

St Petroc's Reliquary, Bodmin, Cornwall

now buried in the sand of St Enodoc's to the west) described St Endelienta's as giving 'the impression that it goes on praying night and day, whether there are people in it or not.' The church guide makes clear that St Endellion remains a place of 'pilgrimage, prayer, meditation and worship', and invites private prayer to strengthen 'the church's ministry of mission and healing.'

The twelfth-century *Lives* of St Petroc, 'captain of the saints of Cornwall', give colourful accounts of his activities. In addition to an austere regime of prayer and preaching, he found time to receive a miraculous garment from heaven, perform many cures and good deeds, particularly for animals. He saved a stag from the rich huntsman (King?) Constantine who became a convert, rid the Padstow area of a plague of serpents, but also helped a dragon by removing a wooden stake from its eye. The son of a king in south-east Wales, Petroc renounced the throne and withdrew to Ireland with sixty noble retainers for a period of religious instruction. Afterwards, he and his companions sailed to the north-east coast of Cornwall to land in the Camel estuary around 518. Among 'heathenish' people he found a holy hermit and a bishop with a small Christian community. The bishop, St Wethinoc, gave way to Petroc who built a church and monastery on the site now called Padstow (Petroc-stow). Going on pilgrimage to Jerusalem via Rome, Petroc is reputed to have continued eastwards to live for a while as a castaway-hermit on an island in the Indian Ocean. Safely home, he travelled in Cornwall and beyond, founding chapels, a mill, hermitages and monasteries. When he came to a desirable place beside a spring on Bodmin Moor, he found a hermit already in residence. St Guron (Wron) felt impelled to offer the determined newcomer hospitality, before moving away to Gorran Churchtown near Mevagissey. Under St Petroc, the wild moorland spot became Bosvenegh, 'the dwelling of the monks'.

When he died in 564 during a final tour of his communities, he was buried at Padstow which became the centre of his cult, and a stopping-place for Welsh and Irish pilgrims *en route* for continental shrines and the Holy Land. After Vikings sacked Padstow in 981 the community moved with his relics to Petroc's monastery at Bodmin, where the relics were stolen in 1177 by Martin, a Bodmin canon, who took them to the abbey of St Méen in Brittany. An appeal was made to Henry II, who used his considerable influence (and a party of soldiers) in France to have the valuables returned. A consolation rib was left with the Breton monks, the rest of the remains (principally head bones) were brought back to Bodmin in a newly acquired reliquary, an ivory casket of Islamic workmanship from Norman Sicily. A medieval-style festival called Bodmin Riding, held every Sunday nearest to 7 July, celebrates the return of the relics with a procession of horse-riders and countryside garlands. Bodmin also possessed Petroc's staff, and his bell on which people placed their hands during legal ceremonies. Exeter, Glastonbury and Waltham claimed to have relics of the saint, including bones, clothing and hair. According to William

Worcester in 1478, St Petroc lay in a beautiful shrine in front of the Bodmin Priory Lady Chapel, but this was destroyed in the sixteenth century and the reliquary went missing.

The casket was discovered in 1957 hidden over the church porch: it held only a medieval candle.

Renowned as a wonder-working supernatural healer, St Cuthbert was the most popular saint of northern England. Because of his virtues and the incorruption of his body for centuries after death, his shrine at Durham was one of the richest and most visited. Claimed as a Scot from Ireland, a native Briton or a Northumbrian Englishman, St Cuthbert was brought up in an Anglo-Saxon household in the Scottish Borders. An exuberant but pious youth, he spent much of his time tending sheep on the hills around Lammermuir, north of Melrose. One night in 651 he saw angels descending on a track of light to meet, and convey to heaven, a shining soul. On hearing that St Aidan had died that same night, Cuthbert decided to become a monk at Old Melrose. Eventually becoming prior, he undertook arduous missionary journeys to rid the local population of their superstitious attachment to magic, idolatry and amulets. He had a gift for dowsing, and many of his wells and churches are in formerly wild and remote places such as Bellingham (North Tynedale). After the Synod of

St Cuthbert's Cave, Kyloe Hills, Northumberland

Whitby he was appointed prior of Lindisfarne, withdrawing in 676 to the solitude of Inner Farne. He spent the last two years of his life as a busy, conscientious bishop of Lindisfarne before failing health forced his return to Inner Farne, where he died during the night of 20 March 687, a torch being waved as a signal to the monks on Lindisfarne.

Cuthbert had wanted to stay on his own small island but finally agreed to be buried in the priory church. After eleven years, the monks wished to exhume his bones to place them in a new coffin above floor level where he 'might receive the honours due to him'. Bishop Eadbert gave his permission, stipulating that the exhumation should be done during Lent on the anniversary of Cuthbert's burial. Instead of withered remains they found 'the body whole and incorrupt as though still living and the limbs flexible, so that he looked as if he were asleep rather than dead'. His fresh and spotless vestments were removed and taken to the bishop who kissed them in joy, declaring that the miraculous grave would not remain empty for long. Cuthbert's body, clothed in new garments, was placed in the coffin standing on the sanctuary pavement. When Bishop Eadbert died on 6 May he was buried in the original grave beneath Cuthbert's new tomb.

In life, Cuthbert had performed cures of madness, raised the sick from their death-beds, saved with a kiss a child dying of a contagious disease in its widowed mother's arms, and turned the wind to save his foster-mother's house from burning. After death, his garments possessed healing virtues, strands of his hair dissolved a painful eye tumour, his tomb induced a healing sleep removing pain and paralysis.

After nearly a century of Viking raids the community was forced to abandon Lindisfarne in 875. In accordance with Cuthbert's dying wishes they took his body with them. They also carried the remains of St Aidan, St Eadbert, the head of St Oswald and the Lindisfarne Gospels as they wandered for seven years throughout Northumbria. St Cuthbert's Cave in the Kyloe Hills is said to have been one of their temporary resting-places. In 882 the community settled at Chester-le-Street (Co. Durham), sheltering in the ruins of the Roman fort while building a church. King Athelstan visited the shrine in 934 bringing gifts of silver, a maniple (stole) embroidered in silk with figures of saints, and a richly inscribed manuscript of Bede's *Life of St Cuthbert.* Inland raids by Scandinavian pirates in 995 sent 'St Cuthbert's folk' southwards to Ripon.

Venturing north again – led by Bishop Aldhun hoping to return to Lindisfarne – Cuthbert's brethren found themselves beside a rocky piece of land embraced by the River Wear. The coffin suddenly became impossible to move and Cuthbert told them in a vision that he wanted to be buried on Dunholme. Overhearing two passing women discussing a lost cow seen on Dunholme, they followed them up the wooded outcrop with the now-compliant coffin. St Cuthbert's body, sheltered by tree boughs and straw, was set down on the site of the future Benedictine cathedral-priory. By 999 his body had been translated into the 'White Church' built of stone. Around 1022 the sacrist at Durham stole Bede's relics from Jarrow to place them in Cuthbert's coffin. Normans replaced the 'lax' Anglo-Saxon monks and demolished their church, laying the foundations of the present cathedral in 1093. The castle and massive Romanesque church were built together as a fortress, a symbol of Norman domination over raiding Scots and rebellious Anglo-Saxons in northern

St Cuthbert's Tomb, Durham Cathedral

England, and Cuthbert's relics were translated into the Norman cathedral in 1104 after the body had been examined and officially declared incorrupt. His shrine was placed behind the High Altar in the eastern apse, enlarged from 1242 to 1274 to form an eastern transept called the Chapel of the Nine Altars.

The medieval shrine site is marked by a simple slab bearing the name CUTHBERTUS. According to the sixteenth-century *Rites of Durham*, the shrine was 'estimated to be one of the most sumptuous monuments in all England', the miracles of healing endless — 'such help was never denied' — but the Benedictines would not allow women to approach beyond a line of black marble set in the nave floor. The shrine was adorned with valuable jewels, costly woods, marbles, chiming bells, with a gilded cover raised by pulleys. The accumulated treasures included such fabulous items as a griffin's claw and eggs, fragments from Christ's manger, the Apostles' throne and the rod of Moses along with the more humdrum remains of numerous saints.

On 31 December 1540 the priory was surrendered to Henry VIII and contemporary accounts describe the actions of the king's Commissioners sent to demolish the shrine. Rifling through jewels and ornaments, they came to a chest bound with iron which the goldsmith smashed open with his forge hammer. One account says that this broke Cuthbert's leg, another that it wounded his flesh. The vestments, body and face (the beard showing a fortnight's growth) were found to be entire except for part of the nose. Collecting the bones proved impossible as sinews and skin held them together. Placing the body in the vestry, the Commissioners sent to London for the king's instructions. The remains were later buried in a grave dug beneath the site of the shrine. In May 1827 the grave's contents were re-examined: the ancient coffin, vestments and secondary relics were as previously described but accompanied by dry bones with no sign of a body having disintegrated in the coffin. The bones were reburied, the other relics removed. Baring-Gould draws attention to the tradition that Cuthbert's body was spirited away as it lay in the vestry at the Dissolution, the true place of interment remaining a Benedictine secret. The carved coffin of 698, gold *cloisonné* pectoral cross and tenth-century embroidered maniple are on display in the Treasury.

Writing in the early eighth century, Bede described a wooden tomb, shaped like a small house, covering the grave of St Chad at Lichfield. A hand-sized hole in the wall enabled devotees to remove a little dust which was used, mixed with water, to restore health to 'men or beasts'. Bede reported that 'frequent miracles of healing attested to his virtues', and that Chad prayed for God's 'mercy on mankind' during gales and thunder which he regarded as divine reminders of 'the judgment to come'. A Latin manuscript (*c.* 730) of the first three books of the New Testament has long been associated with the shrine but spent some time at Llandeilo (Carmarthenshire) where marginal notes in Welsh were added in the tenth century. Known in England as the Lichfield Gospel (or Gospel of St Chad) and in Wales as the Gospel of St Teilo, arguments over its origins, 'theft' and rightful ownership continue.

Chad was one of four Anglian brothers (Cedd, Cynebil, Caelin, Chad) educated at St Aidan's school on Lindisfarne. He returned from study in Ireland to take over the running of Lastingham monastery after Cedd and Cynebil died there of the plague. He was loved for his great holiness, humility and lack of prejudice. Around 669 he chose Lichfield as his base after being appointed bishop to the kingdom of Mercia – stretching from the Humber to the Thames and spanning England east to west – by Theodore of Tarsus, the Archbishop of Canterbury. Following Aidan's example, Chad chose to walk everywhere to meet the people but Theodore, insisting that he should ride around the huge new diocese, vigorously helped him to mount a horse. At Stowe, a little way north-east of the cathedral,

Lichfield Cathedral, Staffordshire.

Pilgrims used to gather in the south choir aisle, where relics were displayed from the balcony of St Chad's Head Chapel. Chad's skull covered with gold leaf was kept in a painted wooden box. An arm and other bones in portable shrines were available for pilgrims to kiss, and for fund-raising journeys around the diocese. Chad's main reliquary, a thirteenth-century marble shrine adorned with gold and precious stones, stood in the Lady Chapel immediately behind the high altar. Henry VIII initially agreed to spare this shrine but later changed his mind. Four surviving pieces of bone are now kept in reliquaries in Birmingham's Roman Catholic cathedral.

Chad established a small retreat beside a pure spring where he would retire with eight companions for private prayer and study. The area was already sacred (Lichfield = corpse-field), hallowed by the blood of Romano-British Christians slaughtered (according to early Welsh sources) by pagan Britons raiding from the west, after the nearby Roman fort of *Letocetum* (Wall) had been abandoned in the fifth century. Another version attributes the deaths to Roman persecutions a century earlier.

St Chad stood in the well to pray and baptize, and at his cell he tamed a hart and hung his priestly vestments on a sunbeam while chastising King Wulfhere. He died there of the plague after being summoned to heaven by the joyful singing of angels, who returned to collect him a week later (2 March 672) with the spirit of his brother, Cedd.

A great Romanesque vessel moored at anchor on the Fens, Ely Cathedral was a storehouse of royal Anglo-Saxon relics, especially of the female relatives of St Etheldreda (Audrey). One of five saintly daughters of Anna, king of East Anglia, Etheldreda was baptized in a stream near their home at Exning (Newmarket, Suffolk) by St Felix. She remained a virgin during her brief marriage to a young prince, and retired after his death around 655 to her Isle of Ely dowry lands to prepare for a religious life; but she was again required to enter a political marriage, this time with Egfrid (Egfrith) the fifteen-year-old king of Northumbria. Etheldreda received a marriage-gift of land at Hexham which she gave to St Wilfrid to found a monastery. After twelve years of respecting her vow of chastity, Egfrid tried to persuade Etheldreda to consummate the marriage, and offered bribes to her mentor, St Wilfrid, to no avail. Eventually Egfrid allowed her to become a nun at St Abbs, but later determined to abduct her. Etheldreda fled with two handmaidens and was protected on a headland by a miraculous tide which repulsed the king for seven days. Recognizing a 'Divine intervention', Egfrid accepted the situation and married another (Ermenburga). Etheldreda returned to Ely where in 673, with the help of exiled St Wilfrid, she founded a double monastery. At this wealthy family house – funded by her brother King Adulphus – Etheldreda was joined and succeeded by her sisters, nieces and great-nieces. For seven years she led an austere life, keeping vigil in the church from Matins till dawn, wearing itchy wool instead of smooth linen, taking only one meal a day, seldom having a hot wash and always being last to use the water. Despite personal piety and the high reputation of her community, Etheldreda foresaw that she had been chosen to die of the plague and prophesied the number of nuns who would perish with her. Suffering from a large, red burning swelling beneath her jaw, she accepted the necklace of pain as just reward for her youthful vanity in wearing 'the needless burden' of gold and pearls. She died on 23 June 679, a few days after her doctor had cut open the tumour to drain it. At her own request she was buried in a plain wooden coffin in the nuns' cemetery and was succeeded as abbess by her sister Sexburga, former queen of Kent and founder-abbess of Minster-in-Sheppey monastery. After twelve years, Sexburga decided to translate Etheldreda's bones inside the church and place them in a stone sarcophagus brought from a Roman settlement at Grantchester (Cambridge). Quoting the testimony of her doctor and other witnesses, including St Wilfrid, Bede says that Etheldreda's body was found to be intact, her linen wrappings fresh, the gaping wound at her neck healed to a faint scar. The body was

OPPOSITE: Ely Cathedral, Cambridgeshire

washed, freshly robed, laid in the sarcophagus (a perfect fit) and placed in the church on 17 October 695. At the St Audrey's Fairs – held in her honour in later years on that date and 23 June – necklaces of silk and lace (tawdries) were sold, so lacking in taste and worth that the word tawdry (from the Norman French version of her name) became synonymous with showy tat.

Etheldreda became the most popular of Anglo-Saxon women saints and her monastery thrived until 870 when it was plundered and burnt by the Danes; as the first 'satellite of the devil' to strike the sarcophagus 'promptly fell dead', the others left her tomb alone. Ely was refounded in 970 by King Edgar as a strict Benedictine house exclusively for monks. In 1106 Etheldreda's relics were translated into the newly-completed Norman choir along with those of her sisters Sexburga and Withburga, her niece Ermenilda and her great-niece Werburga. The shrine was restored in 1225 after being stripped in 1144 to pay a fine of 300 marks. It was adorned with emeralds, onyxes, pearls and carved stones of precious garnet. On completion of the Early English presbytery built to house the shrine in 1252, another translation of relics took place, this time including remains alleged to be those of St Alban. The position of the shrine, and the possible site of Etheldreda's original church, is marked by a slab in the presbytery floor. In 1541 the abbey was suppressed, the shrines destroyed, but a reliquary containing Etheldreda's hand was secreted away, to be discovered in 1810 at a Surrey farmhouse in a hidden chamber for fugitive priests. The withered hand with parchment-like skin is in the Roman Catholic church in Egremont Street (Ely). At the centre of the cathedral, scenes from Etheldreda's life decorate the pillar-capitals of the octagon, supporting the famous lantern rising above. In the nave is a Saxon cross-base commemorating Etheldreda's faithful steward Ovin (Owini) who joined the monastery at Lastingham, later becoming one of St Chad's close companions at Lichfield where he overheard angels summoning Chad to heaven. The Ely monks had a great appetite for relics, combined with a firm belief in their right to the remains of any with whom they sought to make a connection. In addition to the many relics of King Anna's female descendants, Ely claimed to have parts of St Oswald, and managed to persuade Iken (Suffolk) to give them the head of St Botolph, their founder. Bishop Felix of Dunwich was reputed to have built a church at Cratendune Field, a mile south of Ely, which was destroyed by King Penda. When, for greater protection during Danish raids, his body was being transferred from Soham (south-east of Ely) to Ramsey Abbey to the north-west, the men of Ely set out in force to intercept. In brilliant conditions, the Ely boats were gaining on the single craft bearing St Felix's body until a sudden impenetrable mist enabled the Soham party to escape. But Ely's most audacious piece of relic-snatching involved Etheldreda's sister Withburga.

A sunken well west of the church of St Nicholas in East Dereham (Norfolk) marks the reputed original burial-place of St Withburga, youngest daughter of King Anna. She became a religious solitary after he was killed *c.* 654 in battle against Penda of Mercia. Withburga lived first in an abandoned fort in the salt marshes – perhaps eating the nutritious, fleshy leaves of samphire – at Holkham (Norfolk) where the estate church is dedicated to her. She next established a community of nuns at 'Dereham', usually taken to mean East Dereham although monastic remains have also been located at West Dereham. The nuns and their masons were so poor that they existed on dry bread and the milk of two generous does who appeared each day from the

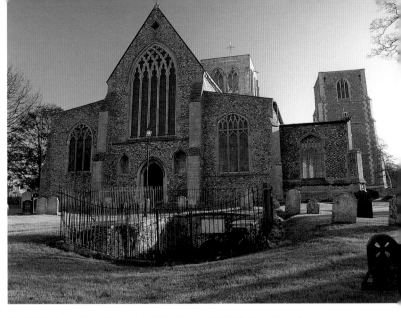

St Nicholas' Church and St Withburga's Well, East Dereham, Norfolk

woods. Withburga died before the completion of her nunnery and was buried in the graveyard, being enshrined in the church when it was rebuilt in the ninth century after a Danish raid. At the translation her body was found to be incorrupt and from the empty grave a clear spring broke forth whose healing power drew pilgrims. In 974 King Edgar agreed with Ely that Withburga should lie with her sisters. Brithnoth, the Ely abbot, went to Dereham with a band of monks to steal the missing sister. By force or deception, the body was removed during the night and taken twenty miles overland to waiting boats on the Little Ouse near Brandon. Armed and angry, the pursuing Dereham monks were left standing as Ely escaped on the water with their precious relic. Legal actions concerning the event were still going on in the late 1980s.

Ely also claimed the relics of another Anglo-Saxon female saint with connections to Anna's royal household at Exning: Wendreda (Mindred, Mildred), who was raised in the river meadows where three springs, sacred from pre-Christian times, formed a well now named after her. Here she cured and comforted the sick and needy and, more recently, the trainers of Newmarket stood their race horses in the water to soothe injured legs. The valley is now very private, guarded land. After King Anna's death and the dispersal of his family, Wendreda moved north-westwards to an island – now a slight hill – known as Merc (boundary) in the Fens beyond Ely. On this remote piece of watery land, six miles long by one mile wide, she used her faith and skills on the agues and malarial fevers of the marsh folk. The good reputation of her advice and healing spread far beyond the growing Christian community on the island. She was buried at 'the village of Merch' but in the late tenth century the Ely abbot desired the holy virgin's bones. King Ethelred 'the Unready' gave permission for translation to Ely, where her relics were 'enclosed in a shrine of gold

St Wendreda's Church, March, Cambridge.
Angels and other figures in the late fifteenth-century double hammer-beam roof, formerly gazed down upon the shrine of St Wendreda.

adorned with precious stones'. Wendreda's remains eventually returned to the specially restored church at March around 1343. Her shrine was dismantled at the Reformation but the church records do not mention the fate of the relics, and the observing angels will not say.

In 1016 Ethelred's son, Edmund Ironside, became king and marched against an army of Danes whose longships had penetrated the Essex waterways. Desirous of miraculous help for a crushing victory, Edmund had Wendreda's relics brought from Ely to his camp on Assa's Hill (Assandun). The Danes were camped to the north-east on Beacon Hill (Canewdon) with their boats on the River Crouch below. For all of St Luke's Day (18 October) the armies joined in battle across fields between the hills and river. Saxon monks carried Wendreda's body against the heathen foe, but Edmund's forces were defeated after Edric Streona of Mercia deserted to Cnut, his former ally; praying clerics were cut down, Wendreda's captured relics carried in triumph to the Danish leader. Then a strange thing happened: Cnut was so moved by her story that he became a Christian, ordering the building of 'a Minster of stone and lime for the souls of the men who were slain'. Cnut had Wendreda's relics enshrined at Canterbury, where they remained for over 300 years. His 'Minster' of St Andrew at Ashingdon became a popular pilgrimage in the thirteenth century, the nave 'Lady Altar' with its statue of the Blessed Virgin Mary was a place of miracles – especially connected with infertility – for those who crawled up the hill in penance on their hands and knees.

Ashingdon Village Sign, Essex

The Saxon font at Ilam may illustrate scenes from the *Life* of St Bertram (borrowed from St Berthelme of France), according to which the grief-stricken Mercian prince became a hermit after the death of his Irish wife. Nearing the end of their journey from her homeland, the princess was devoured by wolves as she gave birth alone in a forest while Bertram sought a midwife. Bertram (Bertelin) is regarded as founder of the nearby town of Stafford: excavations outside the west end of St Mary's uncovered foundation stones of a chapel of *c.* 1000 overlying a much earlier wooden building and cross assigned to St Bertelin.

Medieval pilgrims flocked to St Bertram's shrine where many cures took place, especially of those who managed to crawl through the holes before railings were erected to prevent them. The shrine of *c.* 1386 was originally decorated with a rich canopy bearing figures; it contains the ninth-century tomb cover of St Bertram who was buried a century earlier. His tomb-shrine, bearing petitions, stands in the south chapel of the Norman church which was largely rebuilt in 1618. Bertram converted the pagans of this formerly wild, remote area and founded the first church here in a loop of the River Manifold. His cave and holy well lie half a mile to the north-east.

Peterborough Cathedral occupies the ground of 'Medeshamstede' monastery founded in the seventh century by Peada (first Christian king of Mercia) and Saxulf, a local nobleman who became abbot. Around 1000 a fortified 'burgh' was created by building a defensive wall around the abbey and St Peter's church, which gave the city its present name. There

The Saxon font, Ilam, Staffordshire

was a great interest in relics and the abbey required a good selection to attract donations from pilgrims travelling eastwards over the Fens to the shrine of Our Lady of Walsingham (Norfolk). Abbot Aelfsy (1006–55) was 'like a laborious bee' in collecting and storing sacred remains: in his *Peterborough Chronicle*, Hugh Candidus, a monk at the abbey in the twelfth century, describes the relics of over seventy saints held there. Against fierce competition from other communities, the abbey had acquired relics of local saints, including Cyneburga and Cyneswith (sisters of King Peada) from the ruined church at Castor to the west. Tibba, the virgin anchoress and patron saint of falconers, 'chose' to be translated from Ryhall (Leicestershire) to Peterborough to be with her friends but was later moved to Thorney, then back again to Peterborough. From further afield came such wonders as the swaddling clothes of Jesus, pieces of his manger and cross, fragments from his sepulchre and remains of the miraculous five loaves fed to the five thousand. The sacred jumble of saints, prophets, apostles and other biblical personalities included relics of 'the raiment of Saint Mary', the magic rod used by Aaron in Egypt, a piece of the hair shirt of St Wenceslas, the hand of St Magnus, the arm and head of St George, the hair of St Ethelwold, a tooth of St Sexburga, blood, bones and clothing of St Eutrop(h)ia and a shoulder blade of one of the young boys (holy innocents) slain by King Herod after the birth of Christ.

A twelfth-century watch-tower in the south transept chapel of St Oswald enabled a constant guard to be kept over a relic stolen from Bamburgh c. 1060 by a Peterborough monk named Winegot. Chronicler Candidus wrote: 'There is kept here a thing more precious than gold even, the right arm of Saint Oswald, King and Martyr, abiding entire and uncorrupted alike in its flesh and skin, according to the prayer of Bishop Aidan when he blessed it. This we have seen with our

St Bertram's Shrine, Holy Cross Church, Ilam, Staffordshire

Peterborough Cathedral, Cambridgeshire

eyes and have kissed and handled with our own hands and did wash it at the time it was shewn to Alexander, Bishop of Lincoln and all the convent ...' on 25 March 1129.

The Monks' (or Hedda) Stone, Peterborough Cathedral

The monastery also had a saint and martyrs of its own: in 870, the killers of St Edmund of East Anglia sacked and burned Peterborough. Abbot Hedda, his brethren, and villagers who had sought refuge with them were murdered by the Danish looters who smashed open the church doors. A monk from nearby Crowland recorded his burial of the villagers and eighty-four monks at the scene of devastation. The abbey was refounded in 960 as a Benedictine house but their church burnt down in 1116 and the present building was begun in 1118. A Saxon tomb-shrine surviving from the first abbey (carved *c.* 780 with images of Christ, Mary and ten apostles) was placed in the cemetery over the grave of St Hedda and his companion-martyrs. The tomb was visited as a shrine and the Mass used to be said over it. Holes may once have held relics or fixtures for candles. The stone is in the cathedral apse, close to the burial places of Mary Queen of Scots (moved to Westminster Abbey) and Catherine of Aragon.

St Swithun's remains are said to lie beneath the central bay of the Early English (1200–40) retrochoir of Winchester Cathedral (Hampshire), where a modern memorial (1962) marks the last site of his shrine, a silver-gilt reliquary supported by a tall marble tomb. It was demolished during the night of 21 September 1538 by officers from Henry VIII's Commission for the Destruction of Shrines, who lamented that 'there was no gold, nor ring, nor true stone in it, but all great counterfeits'. From the 1150s to 1472, Swithun's bones had been displayed on a stone 'feretory platform' behind the high altar, a tunnel or 'Holy Hole' allowing pilgrims to crawl underneath the platform to receive healing emanations from the relics above. In 853 Swithun, chaplain to King Egbert of Wessex and tutor to his son Ethelwulf, accompanied the king's five-year-old grandson Alfred on a trip to Rome. On becoming king, Ethelwulf made Swithun Bishop of Winchester, just when 'the ancient capital of England' was under threat from a rampaging Norse army.

Ethelwulf's son, Alfred the Great – himself venerated as an unofficial saint – finally pushed the Danes out of Wessex in 880. Bishop Swithun undertook many practical good works, building and repairing churches, constructing a stone bridge over the River Itchen (on the site of 'City Bridge') and making whole again a basket of smashed eggs dropped by an old woman. He was noted for his charity, and the miracles and cures brought about through his relics. On his own insistence, he was buried in a humble position outside the west door of the seventh-century Old Minster, his tomb exposed to the elements. Bishop Ethelwold, working with King Edgar and St Dunstan, reformed the minster (with its secular canons) as a Benedictine cathedral-priory. On 15 July 971 Ethelwold moved Swithun's remains inside the church; the accompanying torrential downpour was said to represent the saint's displeasure and heaven's tears. Traditional weather-lore states that the conditions on St Swithun's day will prevail for the following forty days. From the moment of his translation miracles began: pilgrims were attracted and a massive

St Swithun's Memorial, Winchester Cathedral, Hampshire

western extension to the church was built over his grave. By 974 there were two shrines to St Swithun in the church, one of which may have contained his head. A contemporary account of the building campaign of 965–95 describes the addition of so many screened chapels, transepts, porticoes and altars (over twenty) that it was impossible for strangers to find their way around the interior without a guide. Walkelin, the first Norman bishop, demolished Old Minster in 1093 when Swithun's relics were carried into an even larger Romanesque replacement. In building the new cathedral the Normans unearthed numerous Anglo-Saxon skeletons which they collected, sorted and reburied in the robbed-out foundation trenches. Many pre-Conquest rulers and bishops were buried at Winchester, including Cnut who married Emma (widow of Ethelred 'the Unready') there in 1043. Around 1525 these accumulated bones were placed in stone mortuary chests on top of the presbytery screens flanking the high altar. Among other saints venerated in the cathedral was Birinus who founded a church here, and used the holy well preserved in the atmospheric Norman crypt below the high altar. Birinus established the first cathedral of the West Saxons at Dorchester-on-Thames but the cathedra and his body were transferred to Winchester in the late seventh century.

Perhaps the greatest miracle at Winchester was performed by deep-sea diver William Walker, who saved the cathedral from subsiding into the mud and peat of former marshland. For five years (1906–11) he spent six hours a day working by touch in deep, murky water, exchanging bags of concrete for the original foundation raft of rotting beech logs. Immediately north of the present cathedral, modern bricks trace the outline of the Old Minster which was excavated in the 1960s by Martin Biddle.

The chapel in St Duthas Old Burial Ground, overlooking the Dornoch Firth north-east of Tain (Ross-shire), held the relics of St Duthac (Duthas) born here around the year 1000. Duthac, who served in the Ross area, was educated in Ireland where he became renowned as a great preacher and wonder-worker. He died in 1065, his relics being brought back to Tain from Armagh in 1253 to be tended by a hermit in the specially built chapel. Duthac's head was encased in a silver reliquary, his breastbone in one of gold. His relics – including a cup, bell, staff and shirt – were believed to have curative powers. The shirt was also said to be sure protection against injury but Huw Earl of Ross was wearing it when he was killed in 1333, fighting the army of Edward III at Halidon Hill (Northumberland).

Tain also possessed an 'immunity' (sanctuary) for fugitives, marked by four 'Girth Crosses' outside the town. Its most famous violation took place in 1306 when the wife and daughter of Robert the Bruce were captured 'within the girth of Tayne' and handed over to the English by the Earl of Ross. After Duthac's chapel caught fire in 1427, the relics were moved into the town to a new church which soon achieved collegiate status. The relics were kept in the eastern part of the church, in aumbries or lockers in the north wall, the highest one probably holding St Duthac's head. A weathered statue in the north-east corner is believed to represent St Duthac; its modern replacement is in an exterior niche on the west end. Miracles and cures drew many pilgrims, and the town became a thriving commercial centre. One of the more colourful miracle stories concerns a hungover party guest who sent gifts to Duthac requesting a cure: the gold ring and piece of pork placed on a grave during prayers, were stolen by a kite but Duthac called back the bird, fed it the pork

OPPOSITE: St Duthac's Chapel, Tain, Ross-shire

St Hugh's Head Shrine (right) *and a memorial to St Gilbert of Sempringham in the Angel Choir of Lincoln Cathedral*

and returned the ring. Between 1493 and 1513, King James IV made at least eighteen penitential journeys to Duthac's shrine. In 1560 the relics were given to Alexander Ross of Balnagown for safe keeping, never to be seen again.

The head shrine of St Hugh of Avalon (Burgundy) survives in the Angel Choir of Lincoln Cathedral, beside pottery memorials to St Gilbert of Sempringham, his monks and nuns. Bishop Hugh's body first lay in a small chapel in the north-east transept, enlarged twenty years after his death when Pope Honorius III sent official confirmation of his sainthood, along with instructions to provide a suitably worthy memorial. To house his shrine and the anticipated crowds of pilgrims, the Angel Choir was then constructed as an eastern extension to the choir built by St Hugh. Translation took place on 6 October 1280 in the presence of Edward I and Eleanor, but during exhumation St Hugh's head and body became separated and were given individual shrines; a restored tomb, which later held the queen's internal organs (viscera), is also in the choir. The head shrine was stripped of its jewels in 1539 on the orders of Henry VIII, the immensely rich body shrine was pulled down from above the altar screen (reredos) and completely destroyed. Shortly after 1641 (during the Civil War) the surviving head and its reliquary went missing. An 'adornment' of bronze-covered stainless steel dates from 1986. St Hugh's funeral features in thirteenth-century stained glass in a rose window called the Dean's Eye, built facing north from the great transept to protect 'against the Devil of cold and darkness'.

A notable Carthusian monk, Hugh was brought to England by Henry II to be prior of the 'Charterhouse' founded at Witham (Somerset) by the king in penance for the death of Thomas Becket. Made Bishop of Lincoln by Henry in 1186, Hugh set about rebuilding the cathedral seriously damaged by an earthquake in the previous year. Among many other duties, he made time to help with the building work, visit far-flung corners of his diocese, consecrate churches, judge church and court matters, tend the sick, bury the dead, keep pets including a tame swan, confirm children and join in their games. In supporting his commoners against the savagely enforced laws of the king's hunting grounds, Hugh excommunicated royal foresters. He stood up to the rages of Henry II and Richard I, deflecting their anger with a joke, a kiss or a shaking. John Ruskin described him as 'the most beautiful sacerdotal figure known to me in history', Hugh described himself as 'peppery', others called him 'fearless as a lion in any danger'. At Lincoln and Northampton he offered sanctuary to the Jews and stood alone against murderous mobs hunting them. In York in 1190, with no similar champion, some 150 Jews were besieged in Clifford's Tower for three days. Offered conversion or death, most of the patriarchs killed their wives and children before committing suicide. The few who agreed to become Christian were abused and foully murdered.

In the south choir aisle at Lincoln, almost unnoticed, is the shrine base of another St Hugh: 'Little St Hugh', a nine-year-old boy buried in the cathedral in 1255, having been found murdered in a well. Against all evidence and reason, it was widely believed that Jews in England murdered a Christian each year, in a ritual based on the Crucifixion. Nineteen of Lincoln's most prominent Jews 'confessed' after torture, and were executed. In 1144 another murdered boy, St William of Norwich, had similarly been claimed as a Jewish sacrifice, another shameful reminder of the evils of ignorance, prejudice, religious intolerance and absolutism which trouble our world.

St Fillan was an Irish monk who came to Scotland in the eighth century as a missionary, following his mother, St Kentigerna, and his uncle, St Comgan. He settled as a solitary at Pittenweem ('the Place of the Cave') studying and writing in darkness, aided by the ghostly glow of his luminous left arm. Fillan was credited with healing powers, and many holy

St Fillan's Cave, Pittenweem, Fife

wells are associated with his name. A spring trickles from a rock cleft to the left of the inner cave, an altar made of fallen masonry in the 1930s stands to the right; both receive small offerings from visitors. A blocked stairway led up to ground level on the hill above, where remains of a twelfth-century Benedictine priory can be seen around the nineteenth-century church. Many people at Pittenweem were tortured and put to death for 'witchcraft' during the seventeenth and eighteenth centuries and the cave and passage were used by smugglers. It was rededicated as a shrine in 1935 and the Holy Eucharist continues to be offered in the cave.

St Fillan was briefly the abbot of a local monastery but retired to Glen Dochart and Strath Fillan near Tyndrum in Perthshire. At Kirkton Farm, beside the West Highland Way long distance path, are the remains of an Augustinian priory founded (1317–18) in his honour by Robert the Bruce, who believed that Fillan had granted him a miraculous victory over Edward II's superior English forces at Bannockburn, fought near Stirling in 1314. At Robert's request, the abbot of Inchaffray had carried into battle St Fillan's left arm enshrined in a casket. The saint's original chapel was beside a pool, up river a little north-west of the priory. Into the early nineteenth century, the mentally afflicted were flung into the dark waters of St Fillan's Pool, then left overnight tied up to the font in his ruined church; if found free in the morning, they were considered cured. In the Middle Ages relics of St Fillan were kept at five farms in Glen Dochart, down river to the east, in the care of hereditary keepers known as 'dewars'. Two are on display in the Museum of Scotland (Chambers Street, Edinburgh): the *Quigrich*, a silver gilt reliquary enclosing a bronze skin which formerly covered the head of Fillan's wooden crozier (staff), and the *Bernane*, a tenth-century cast-bronze bell which used to be placed over a sufferer's head during healing rituals. The crozier reliquary bears a small figure of St Fillan and a rock crystal curing charm. A set of river stones believed to have been given healing powers by the saint himself is still kept in Glen Dochart. The water-shaped stones were considered to resemble and cure different parts of the body, being smoothed around the appropriate area nine times, the direction of movement reversing after the third and sixth circuit.

Oxford's patron, St Frideswide (d. *c.* 735) is a shadowy figure. Her legend, recorded by William of Malmesbury in the twelfth century, claims her as a princess of Wessex, daughter of Didan, a ruler of the upper Thames. Having decided as a child that 'whatsoever is not God is nothing', she fled to the forest of Binsey for three years to avoid marriage to a Saxon prince. When she moved to Oxford he followed, but was struck blind and gave up his quest after Frideswide restored his sight. A variant of the tale describes Frideswide caught at Binsey and

St Margaret's Well, Binsey, Oxford

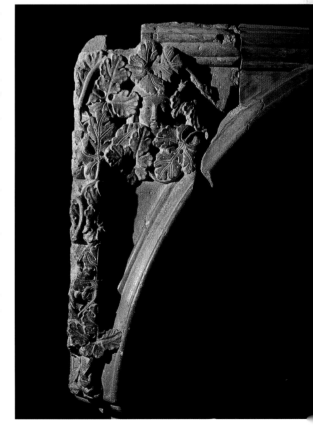

St Frideswides Shrine, Christ Church Cathedral, Oxford

desperately praying for aid to St Margaret of Antioch. Her suitor was blinded, then healed with holy water from a spring which St Margaret caused to flow. The well was much celebrated in medieval times, and the former settlement of Seacourt – west across the Seacourt Stream – had many inns catering for pilgrims.

References to cure and refuge may be seen on a fragment of St Frideswide's shrine in the Lady Chapel of Christ Church Cathedral, Oxford. A wimpled face hides among leaves resembling greater celandine, a plant recommended by Culpeper and other herbalists as a remedy for sore and failing eyes. Frideswide is reputed to have founded a religious house for monks and nuns on the site of Christ Church in the early eighth century, but it was not until the 1980s that excavations located part of a cemetery of that period under the present cloisters. Her monastery was sacked by Danes in 1002 and refounded a century later, when her tomb was given greater prominence; the cathedral is the former priory church dating mainly from the twelfth and thirteenth centuries. Frideswide's relics were examined in 1180 and translated in 1289 to the present shrine which became famous for producing miraculous rays of golden light. By 1434 she had been adopted as patron of the university which twice a year honoured her shrine until Henry VIII ordered its dismantling. It was briefly reinstated in the reign of Mary but finally broken up and dispersed in 1558. At the same time, a Calvinist, James Calfhill, mixed Frideswide's remains with those of Catharine Dammartin, a former nun who had married an Augustinian canon turned Protestant reformer. They lie inextricably mingled beneath the Lady Chapel floor, close to the shrine reconstructed in the nineteenth century with fragments recovered from a well and other parts of the college. The shrine is still overlooked by its watching loft which stood guard over the offerings and relics.

The remains of a shrine in the Lady Chapel of Chester Cathedral once held the relics of St Werburgh, a seventh-century princess, child of Wulfhere (the semi-pagan king of Mercia) and his saintly wife Ermenilda. As a young woman Werburgh prayed, fasted, contemplated heavenly things and determined to become a virginally pure 'bride of Christ'. Her beauty and riches attracted several determined suitors – one of whom brought about the deaths of her two brothers – but she managed to evade them and train as a nun under her great-aunt St Etheldreda at Ely, eventually becoming abbess following her grandmother and widowed mother. Recalled to Mercia by her uncle Ethelred, to regularize discipline in the religious houses of his newly-acquired kingdom, Werburgh reformed or founded monasteries at Threekingham (Lincolnshire), Weedon (Northamptonshire), Repton (Derbyshire), Trentham and Hanbury (Staffordshire). Renowned for humility and purity, she combined extreme fasting and other bodily mortifications with sleepless nights in church, prostrate in prayer. Sensing the approach of her 'heavenly bridegroom' she made a final round of

OPPOSITE: St Werburga's Shrine, Chester Cathedral, Cheshire

visits to her monasteries before dying at Trentham (Threekingham according to some sources) on 3 February 699.

Werburgh's wish was to be buried at her favourite nunnery, but the Hanbury nuns were unable to remove their patroness until those at Trentham fell into a deep sleep. Many came to her tomb, and some experienced miracles after drinking from the 'Pilgrim's Well', formerly near the old Vicarage gateway behind Hanbury church. On being transferred to a rich new shrine in 708, Werburgh's body was found 'entire and whole as when first placed in the ground'. When marauding Danes sailed up the Trent to nearby Repton, the shrine was taken to the safety of Chester, the former legionary city rebuilt in 907 as a fortress (burgh) by 'the lady of the Mercians' (Athelfled, daughter of Alfred the Great) who led her troops against the Danes after the death of her husband, King Athelred. Werburgh escaped the burning of Hanbury, but transfer to Chester caused her preserved body to crumble. Her shrine in the Saxon minster church was tended by secular canons who were replaced in 1092 by St Anselm and his Benedictine monks, brought over from Bec by the Norman earl 'Hugh the Wolf'. Werburgh's relics were translated into the new monastic church, and her *Life* was written by Goscelin of Saint-Bertin, a monk who travelled around monasteries writing up the stories of local saints. Pilgrims made prayers and offerings at St Werburgh's shrine, receiving in return her help and healing.

The monastery also listed among its relics the wonder-working girdle of St Thomas of Canterbury, whose martyrdom is shown on a coloured boss of the Lady Chapel vaulting. The much-restored shrine base was built in 1310 to support and shelter the feretory holding Werburgh's relics. Her remains were scattered at the Reformation, the gilded figures of Mercian saints and royalty spitefully beheaded on the orders of a monarch not impressed by the sanctity of women or Saxons. The stone structure was modified and moved to the choir where it was used as a bishop's throne until the early twentieth century.

One of the carved misericords (turn-up seats with a ledge providing support for standing monks) in the north choir stalls illustrates the legend of the geese, as related by Goscelin who used a similar story for his *Life* of St Amelburga of Flanders. Werburgh was called upon to assist when wild geese began consuming local crops. She sent a servant to summon the birds but, after he had killed and eaten one, its companions became loud and unmanageable. Bringing the bones on a dish, the servant confessed to the saint, who restored life to the bird which flew away, leading the troublesome flock far from the

Misericord, Chester Cathedral

local fields. According to Henry Bradshaw, a monk who died in 1521, St Werburgh also saved Chester from assaults by the Welsh, Danes and Scots, and from a terrible fire which raged throughout the city in 1180 until suddenly extinguished when devoutly praying monks carried her relics in procession against the flames.

Part of the shrine of St Edburga of Bicester rests on a chest tomb at the sanctuary north wall of St Michael's Church, Stanton Harcourt (Oxfordshire). Her relics would have lain on the flat top of the Purbeck marble shrine base, carved by Alexander of Abingdon *c.* 1320 for the Augustinian priory at Bicester, founded in the twelfth century by Gilbert Bassett. It is beautifully decorated with figures, mouldings, leaves, bosses, and shields whose arms link the shrine to the Bassett and Longspee families. Edburga (Eadburgh) is claimed as a daughter of Penda of Mercia and reputed to have lived at Adderbury (Oxfordshire), named after her. She became abbess of Aylesbury (Buckinghamshire) where she was buried around 650, her relics being later transferred to the Bicester priory of Our Lady and St Edburga, thence to Flanders. At the Dissolution, Henry VIII ordered county sheriffs to see all 'Popish' monuments

St Michael's Church, Stanton Harcourt, Oxfordshire

destroyed but Sir Simon Harcourt, High Sheriff of Oxfordshire, had other ideas. In 1537–8 he brought the shrine from Bicester to his own parish church, using part of it to embellish the tomb of his ancestor, Sir Robert (d. 1485), in the Harcourt Chapel. The rest was used in the sanctuary as an Easter Sepulchre ('altar of repose') on which an effigy or the Blessed Sacrament (bread and wine, body and blood) was placed between Good Friday and Easter Morning, to represent Christ's burial and resurrection. The church guide quotes 'an ancient record' referring to Stanton Harcourt: 'Without doubt most, if not all, this Towne were Catholics divers years after the Reformation'. Prayers are still said at the shrine in Edburga's name. The Early English (thirteenth-century) rood screen – believed to be the oldest wooden screen surviving in England – bears a painting of St Etheldreda.

In the later Middle Ages, Llandderfel church (Gwynedd) was rather grand – compared to the generally poor parishes of Merioneth – thanks to the cult and wonder-working image of St Derfel. Styled Derfel Gadarn (Welsh 'cadarn' = mighty or powerful), their patron saint

St Derfel's 'Horse', Llandderfel, Gwynedd

was believed to be a formidable, sixth-century Celtic warrior who fought beside King Arthur at his final battle of Camlann and later became abbot on Bardsey Island. His life-size wooden figure formed part of a shrine on the north side of the church, but only his 'horse' (and a 'staff' or curtain pole) are preserved in the porch. The RCAHMW *Inventory* for Merioneth (1921) confidently describes the mutilated animal as the remains of a fully equipped warhorse painted red, which supported St Derfel dressed as a knight. The animal is described in the 1598–1613 church register as a 'Redd Stagg', its seated posture leading most modern commentators to agree, although the 'horse' may have been performing a special trick or legendary incident from a long-lost story. Whether Derfel ever sat astride the creature, or if it played a separate part in a tableau of some kind, is uncertain. It probably held offerings or relics. On Easter Tuesdays in more recent times, the creature was set up as a rocking horse close to Derfel's well on a hill north-west of his church.

When warrior Derfel's figure was destroyed at the Reformation, an ancient Welsh prophecy that it 'should set a whole forest afire' in a way came true. In 1538 Thomas Cromwell, Henry VIII's chief minister, received a letter from Dr Ellis Price, his appointee for the suppression of image-worship and superstitious practices in the diocese of St Asaph. Price reported up to 600 people attending St Derfel's shrine on his feast (5 April) and pilgrimages made daily by people bringing horses and cattle to be healed or making offerings in order to be personally 'delivered out of hell' by Derfel. Pilgrims also placed offerings before the priestly figure of St Garmon carved on a stone coffin lid at Llanarmon-yn-Iâl (Denbighshire) to the north-east. Cromwell instructed Price to send the image to London, which he did, despite being offered £40 not to. Derfel's 'huge and great image' was added to the blazing pyre in Smithfield which burnt alive the confessor of Queen Catherine of Aragon, a Franciscan friar named John Forrest.

The unfortunate well-shrine of St Triduana in Restalrig (Edinburgh) was one of the first in Scotland to attract the attention of reformers. In 1560 the collegiate church at Restalrig, endowed by several Scottish kings, was declared 'a monument to idolatrie' and 'utterlie ... destroyed'. The upper story of the attached hexagonal well-chapel, built during the reign of James III (1460–88), was also demolished but the lower part survived; it has been excavated and covered by a modern pyramidal roof topped by a replica statue of St Triduana. Steps lead down into a partly sunken vault having a flagged floor and stone benches lining the walls. The water is hidden in pipes but used to cover the whole floor,

St Triduana's Chapel, Restalrig, Edinburgh

forming a bathing pool level with the seat tops. A miniature copy of the well-chapel, known as St Margaret's Well, used to cover a spring nearby. It was moved in 1860 (away from the site of a railway depot) to the base of Arthur's Seat in Holyrood Park, close to the

hermitage-chapel of St Anthony. Relics of Triduana were also claimed by Aberdeen, and a church was dedicated to her at Rescobie (Angus) where she had lived a monastic life with two companions. Triduana, whose name means 'lady of the three days' fast', was especially renowned for eye cures: it was believed she had removed her own eyes and sent them to a local prince who desired her because of their lustrous beauty. She is traditionally linked with the missionary activities of St Rule, and of St Curadán-Boniface to the Picts of eastern Scotland. Usually described as Pictish, Triduana may have been one of two 'virgin abbesses' who travelled from Rome with Pope Boniface IV.

At Munkerhoose on the west coast of Papa Westray (Orkney), the twelfth-century church of St Boniface is associated with monastic and prehistoric remains, including a broch (fort). To the south-east, on a rocky promontory of the Loch of St Tredwell, slight remains of a chapel to Triduana can be traced within the ruins of another broch: it was a popular place of pilgrimage up to the eighteenth century.

Pennant Melangell Church, Llangynog (Powys) commemorates the Irish princess Melangell who, in order to escape her father's idea of a good marriage, sought sanctuary in a Welsh upland valley. She spent many years without human contact but had a spiritual relationship with the wildlife of Cwm Pennant, especially the mystical hares. The Hare of Teutonic myth laid the spring egg, universal symbol of creation and renewal, later adopted to represent Christ's resurrection. Hares were also associated with the goddess Eostre (Easter), 'the rising light' of spring, and used as symbols of lust in medieval art. Melangell proved a worthy protectress: when Brochwel, prince of Powys, came hunting in the valley, a pursued hare sought shelter under Melangell's skirt as she prayed, hidden among dense brambles. Awed by Melangell's spiritual presence, her power over his dogs and huntsmen, Brochwel spared the hare and declared Cwm Pennant a perpetual safe retreat. Canon Allchin (Allchin 1993) describes the valley custom of those out hunting: never to shoot the hares, but to send them off with a shout of God and Melangell be with you. He also quotes a poem of R.S. Thomas, in which Melangell feels God's 'heart beating in the wild hare'.

Church register entries in the eighteenth century describe Cwm Pennant as a 'healing valley' one step away from heaven, and Melangell (with the help of angels) triumphing 'over all the powers of evil'. The legend of St Melangell and the hare is carved on the rood loft in the church. From her remote, seventh-century hermitage a place of medieval pilgrimage and sanctuary grew. By the twelfth century a Norman church had been built with an apse covering Melangell's grave, and a Romanesque shrine installed to hold her relics. The shrine was broken up in the 1540s and the church underwent many changes, including a square-ended 'room of the grave' (Cell-y-bedd) replacing the eastern apse. In the 1950s the shrine was reassembled from fragments visible in the walls of the church and

OPPOSITE: Pennant Melangell Church, Llangynog, Powys

lychgate, and placed in Cell-y-bedd. Archaeological excavations and extensive renovations took place 1988–92 when the fully reconstructed shrine was restored to its original position in the chancel.

The eastern extension was demolished and a new apse built on the original foundations incorporating what is believed to be Melangell's burial marker. The Cancer Help Centre was opened in 1998 on St Melangell's Feast (28 May). Evelyn (now Revd) Davies MBE, her late husband and the Friends of St Melangell have made Cwm Pennant the goal for an increasing number of people seeking healing and a sense of spirit. Thanks to their vision and tireless work, Melangell's refuge is once more a thriving place of pilgrimage.

St James the Great depicted as a pilgrim at Hailes Church, Gloucestershire

7.
Paths To God
Places Of Pilgrimage

Devotional journeys to holy places for penance, thanksgiving or supernatural encounters are a feature of most religions; the desire to 'wander for God' is seemingly an in-built human requirement. Christian pilgrimage to the Holy Land was made popular by Emperor Constantine's mother, St Helen(a), who in 325–6 visited the places connected with the earthly life of Jesus, dedicating churches of his Nativity, Resurrection and Ascension at Bethlehem, the Holy Sepulchre in Jerusalem and the Mount of Olives. On the Jerusalem building site encompassing Christ's tomb and the Rock of Calvary (Golgotha), Helena is reputed to have discovered the True Cross in a rock-cut cistern.

At this time, visiting the tombs of the apostles SS Peter and Paul in Rome came a close second to the tour of Palestine. By the Middle Ages pilgrimages were organized on a grand scale and journeys imposed as penance for the absolution of confessed sins greatly swelled the ranks of pilgrims. The notion that penance could reduce time spent in purgatory was so strong that such symbols as sack-cloth and ashes, hair-shirts and body-constricting bands of iron or leather were worn by some, both in life and in the grave. As Geoffrey Chaucer (1345?–1400) demonstrated in his earthy Canterbury Tales, *featuring a very mixed group of travellers to the shrine of Thomas Becket, medieval pilgrimages were undertaken for a wide variety of reasons: curiosity, wanderlust, forgiveness, healing, spiritual renewal, holiday-adventure or commercial gain. It was even thought possible to obtain the indulgences granted at shrines by hiring a professional pilgrim or by obliging a friend or relative to go on behalf of the rich, lazy, sick or deceased. A hasty vow of pilgrimage made over a short-lived crisis could also be officially discharged by proxy or by a gift of money to the Church. During their meritorious journey towards salvation,* genuinely spiritual pilgrims travelled barefoot, unarmed and unadorned. They fasted, refrained from cutting hair or nails, welcomed difficulty and privation and rested only one night at each stopping place. More casual or wealthy pilgrims travelled on horseback – some with retinues including entertainers and bodyguards – but the privileged could be pious: James IV walked ten miles barefoot over frozen ground to the shrine at Whitekirk near Dunbar (East Lothian), accompanied by the future Pope Pius II. The most popular foreign destinations for noble medieval pilgrims from Britain were the Holy Land, Rome, Santiago de Compostela in Galicia (north-west Spain), Mont Saint-Michel in Normandy and St Patrick's Purgatory on Station Island in Lough Derg (Co. Donegal) where a direct route to heaven could be won by those of true faith, willing to be locked in the cave to face twenty-four hours of '... unknown and unspeakable horrors'. At home, Canterbury and Walsingham were the favoured upper class pilgrimages. The rich placed silver on the altars and left their coats of arms hanging in such places as the church of the Holy Sepulchre, before returning home laden with souvenirs and relics. Poorer pilgrims would carve graffiti or monograms, light candles, obtain such symbolic tokens of pilgrimage as palm-leaves, shells, stone chips from columns adjacent to shrines (I have a leaf from the Mount of Olives and a marble fragment from 'Christ's tomb' collected by my father in wartime Jerusalem), manufactured pilgrim badges, and phials or leaden ampullae of holy water. They also endeavoured to transfer miraculous properties to personal belongings by rubbing them on shrines, relics and statues or dipping them in sanctified liquids.

From early times, oral traditions and the few written lives of saints had given inspiration and direction to pilgrims in Britain. By the eleventh century an anonymous pilgrims' guide, On the Resting-Places of the Saints, was able to list over fifty shrines in Anglo-Saxon England. As the Middle Ages advanced, more lives and legends of the saints were written down and detailed lists of their relics and holy places compiled. Ships were registered specially to carry pilgrims, land routes formalized with networks of official hostels, hospitals, guides, hermits, bridge-keepers and ferrymen established to cater for the increasing numbers setting out on pilgrimage at the customary times of Christmas, Easter, Whitsuntide and after the harvest. Monasteries provided overnight shelter, and parts of the pilgrimage network were protected by various Orders of religious knights, Hospitallers and Templars being the best known. The religious commitment and physical feats of some pilgrims inspired awe but many were seen as tourists to be fleeced or beggars with a constant demand for alms and hospitality. Despite their officially recognized status, pilgrims were often treated with suspicion and resentment by the stay-at-home folks along their routes and were in real danger of being killed, robbed or cheated. At Cremyll, in the south-east corner of Cornwall, there is an ancient crossing-point over the Tamar to Plymouth in Devon. It is associated with St Julian the Hospitaller and his wife, who reputedly built a hostelry here for the poor and sick, and rowed medieval pilgrims and travellers across the estuary. Although most probably mythical, Julian's story was the inspiration for many medieval charitable institutions and he is the patron of hospitals, poor-homes, innkeepers, travellers and boatmen. In legends, he was a nobleman warned by a hunted hart that he would kill his own father and mother. To avoid this Julian moved to a far land, prospered and married but when the inevitable happened the remorseful couple sought absolution in Rome, before returning to Julian's own country for a life of community service. Hidden away in St Mary's at Haverfordwest (Pembrokeshire) is a fifteenth-century effigy of a pilgrim, and a similar figure reposes in the north aisle chapel of St Helen's in Ashby-de-la-Zouch (Leicestershire). His hair is long and cut straight around in the style of the day, his broad-rimmed hat bears a scallop or cockleshell denoting travel overseas, probably to Compostela. Shells also decorate the scrip (satchel) carried on a narrow belt over his right shoulder. He wears a short-sleeved pilgrim cloak revealing the long sleeves of his tunic and reaching to the ankles of short, front-laced pointed leather boots. His string of beads is by the left shoulder, a square-knobbed staff under his left hand. With the addition of a flask, this is the basic outfit of a well-to-do medieval pilgrim seen in manuscripts and repeated on monuments, carvings, rood screens, wall paintings and stained glass throughout the country. There is a fine carving of a pilgrim on the choir stalls of Chester Cathedral and the apostle St James the Great is often depicted as a pilgrim. Excavations inside Worcester Cathedral in 1986 uncovered the grave of a stocky man of sixty-plus, lying on his back beside a long staff with a double-pronged metal tip. His arthritic body, dressed in woollen garments and knee-length leather boots, showed signs of prolonged walking and the right-handed use of his staff. A pierced cockleshell pilgrim badge was in the grave with fragments of willow and bay leaves.

By 1540 Henry VIII had proscribed all pilgrimages, but neither he nor the Reformation could extinguish the love for this form of religious expression with the population of Britain. Covert pilgrimages continued and recent years have seen a steady rise of interest in the pursuit. This latest spiritual awakening, combined with another renewal of popularity in leisure walking, has led to many of the traditional pilgrim ways being regenerated and signposted as sections of long-distance footpaths. The Council of Europe is promoting an extensive network of routes leading to St James's Cathedral in Santiago de Compostela, and many from Britain will be making the pilgrimage through France and Spain. The recently signposted 'Way of St Michael' (Forth Sen Myghal), through Cornwall from St Uny south to St Michael's Mount, is part of the European 'Ways of St James'. The ancient route across Cornwall from Padstow to Fowey, used by Celtic missionaries and later pilgrims, was reopened in 1986 as 'The Saints Way'. 1997 brought the 1,400th anniversaries of St Columba's death on Iona and the arrival of St Augustine in Kent: a modern pilgrimage from Rome to Canterbury was followed by groups walking across England, Wales, Scotland and Ireland, converging at Derry (Co. Donegal) on 9 June to celebrate Columba's feast. The multi-faith 'Sacred Britain' initiative was launched in the same year by the World Wide Fund for Nature, combining a respect for the environment and spiritual landscapes of the United Kingdom. To celebrate the millennium and beyond, sacred sites and ways are being reopened, conserved and made accessible to the general public, while new pilgrimage routes are being established, combining the major faiths of contemporary Britain.

Christ Church Cathedral, Canterbury, Kent.
Thirteenth-century stained glass in Trinity Chapel depicting worshippers at Becket's shrine.

England's first cathedral was established in Canterbury by St Augustine *c.* 602 in a refurbished Roman church granted by King Ethelbert. Danes sacked Canterbury in 1011, took St Alphege hostage and set fire to the late-Saxon church; another fire completed the destruction. Archbishop Lanfranc built the Norman cathedral-priory (1070–77) which became home to one of the most famous shrines of the Christian world.

Thomas Becket, born in London to wealthy Norman parents, became a close friend of Henry II, who made him Chancellor of England in 1155 and Archbishop of Canterbury in 1162. Thomas resigned as chancellor, abandoned 'worldly' ambitions, took to wearing a hair shirt and concentrated his formidable pride and energy on resisting ecclesiastical reform. His relationship with the king breaking down, they engaged in bitter public battles until Thomas fled to France for six years, returning to Canterbury in 1170. Becket excommunicated two bishops and suspended the Archbishop of York, who remarked at a meeting in Normandy that Henry would have neither 'quiet times or a tranquil kingdom' while Thomas lived. The exasperated king exclaimed 'who will rid me of this low-born priest?' and four eager knights immediately left for Canterbury. After confronting Becket, the knights and their followers surrounded the archbishop's palace shouting 'king's men!' Becket's monks persuaded him to withdraw to the cathedral, but he would not allow them to secure the doors. Further angry exchanges followed with Becket taunting the knights, calling Reginald FitzUrse a 'pimp' and pushing him to the floor. Becket received three sword-blows before collapsing, calling on the martyred St Alphege and saying he was willing to die for Jesus and defence of the Church. The force of the final cut removed the top of his skull, the sword-tip shattered on the paving. The Norman floor level has been retained in the north-west transept, at the site of his murder and the former altar of the Sword's Point.

Within hours the cathedral was full of mourners, forgetful of his hubris and mock humility, proclaiming him saint and martyr. Cures and miracles – and punishments for those who did not show enough gratitude – soon began. Thomas's body was placed in the eastern crypt, within a pierced marble tomb allowing access to his wooden coffin smothered with jewels and votives. Inside the coffin his body was further protected by an iron chest. St Thomas was canonized in 1173; by 1180 over 700 miraculous events had been recorded, his ghost was even credited with destroying Henry III's gateway to the Tower of London in 1240. King Henry did public penance in 1174 by walking barefoot through the city to the tomb, allowing himself to be scourged by the monks and prior. The relics were translated in 1220 to the newly built Trinity Chapel, where stained glass windows illustrate scenes from Becket's life and miracles. Those attending the translation were guaranteed a reduction of 540 days from their time in purgatory. A depiction of pilgrims at the shrine gives a double view of the east-facing altar, gold plated tomb chest, draperies and golden lamps. The tomb chest was protected by a painted wooden lid raised on a pulley. The shrine was surrounded by a pavement of inlaid marble (*Opus Alexandrinum*) which – like the stone steps leading up to the Trinity Chapel – became worn and shaped by pilgrims approaching the martyr on their knees. Twelve roundels depict the signs of the zodiac, months of the year, and the virtues and vices. When Henry VIII had the shrine destroyed in 1538, the treasures – including a great ruby sent from France by Louis VII – were carried off in twenty-six wagons. Henry also ordered that images of St Thomas be defaced and his name removed from liturgical books and the official calendar of the Church of England.

The Corona chapel was added on to Trinity Chapel at the east end of the cathedral to enshrine the severed crown of Becket's head. In 1420, 100,000 pilgrims were recorded visiting the internationally famous shrine of St Thomas on the main Dover to London road. Lay pilgrims received board and lodging at the monastic almonry in Green Court, beside the priory gatehouse north of the cathedral. The priory buildings are occupied by the King's School, and the Norman Great Staircase – ascended by pilgrims entering the North Hall – survives. The Eastbridge Hospital of St Thomas, founded in 1180, also provided a place of rest and worship for pilgrims. Travellers from north-east Europe arrived at Sandwich, others from the Continent docked at Portsmouth or Southampton to progress to Canterbury via the shrines of St Richard at Chichester or St Swithun at Winchester. The 'southern route' of the Pilgrims' Way across the Downs from Winchester to Canterbury is something of a Victorian invention, largely popularized by Hilaire Belloc (1870–1953). Despite avoiding most

The Corona Chapel at the east end of Canterbury Cathedral

towns and villages, there are places of interest to pilgrims along the postulated route which makes a fine long distance footpath, arcing north-eastwards from Winchester to Farnham, then eastwards past Guildford on a line now followed partly by the North Downs Way. Once in Kent, pilgrims could visit the Carmelite friary of St Simon Stock at Aylesford and the shrine of William of Perth at Rochester, before heading south-east to Canterbury. William was a saintly fisherman, murdered by his companion outside Rochester *en route* from Scotland to the Holy Land.

The 'northern route' from London also passed through Rochester, following Roman Watling Street (A2) from Westminster to Sittingbourne and Faversham, as did Chaucer's fourteenth-century pilgrims on their way to 'the hooly blisful martir'. On foot or horseback, the 'Pilgrims' Way' was not a precise route: choices of ridge or valley depended on weather or time of year, river crossings varied and there were many diversions for saints and sinners alike as monasteries, holy wells, relic chapels, inns and hospices straddled the ways. Pilgrims on the Farnham route might seek shelter of the Waverley Abbey Cistercians, then enter Guildford or detour slightly south to the Virgin Mary holy well and 'golden ford' across the River Wey. Tracks then led through or above the woods on Colley and Reigate hills, where winter pilgrims slid on greasy silt and those of summer were blinded by bleached chalk. They could drift north a little to Chaldon Church, where one pilgrim found time to carve a Becket 'T' monogram on a pillar near the door. A wall painting depicting St

Whithorn Priory, Wigtown, Dumfries & Galloway.

A Romanesque doorway from the destroyed eastern half of the cathedral-priory has been inserted in the south wall of the much-altered nave.

Michael weighing souls, the terrors of hell and the joys of salvation could also be contemplated.

Whithorn, near Wigtown (Dumfries & Galloway), where the shrine of St Ninian drew countless pilgrims from many different countries, is considered Scotland's 'cradle of Christianity'. In the dying years of Roman rule (Bede says) a British bishop named Nynia (Ninian, 360s–432) established in Galloway a stone church known as *Candida Casa* (White House), after being 'instructed in the mysteries of the Christian Faith in Rome'. Returning through France, Ninian is reputed to have collected relics and masons from St Martin of Tours (d. 397) to whom he dedicated his new church at the place now known as Whithorn, from the Anglian *Hwit-aern.*

A priest and son of a legionary, Ninian was probably sent by the Bishop of Carlisle to minister to an existing community of 'orthodox Roman' (rather than 'irregular Celtic') Christians in south-west Scotland. Bede maintained that Ninian converted the idol-worshipping Picts of south-east Scotland, before being buried in the 'White House' around 432, but he was writing 300 years after Ninian's time and his assertions (and the very existence and identity of 'Ninian') are still being debated.

An inscribed gravestone to Latinus and his daughter, erected around the time of Ninian's death, is the earliest Christian memorial known in Scotland. It was found in 1891 near the medieval cathedral-priory's ruined eastern end, where the Marquess of Bute uncovered slight remains of an earlier building. The dry-stone masonry daubed on the outside with creamy plaster was identified as Ninian's *Candida Casa* – Scotland's earliest recorded Christian church – but its period and usage remain uncertain, especially as the name of Ninian's foundation may have referred to its spiritual intensity. However, excavations by Peter Hill and the Whithorn Trust have confirmed the existence of a Ninian-period monastery centred on the low hill bearing the priory and parish church. Its early Christian buildings and burials were aligned south-west/north-east, echoing pagan interest in the midsummer solstice sunrise and midwinter solstice sunset, an orientation perpetuated by the medieval cathedral-priory.

In Bede's time Galloway was under Northumbrian influence, with an Anglian monastery and bishopric at Whithorn controlled from York. An eighth-century verse *Life of Ninian* indicates that his relics were enshrined and working miracles of interest to pilgrims. Whithorn went through hard times in the ninth century, later becoming a trading settlement for Vikings who buried their dead under cross-inscribed headstones close to Ninian's ancient shrine. A bishop was appointed again in 1128, and work began on a Romanesque cathedral which was soon in the care of Premonstratensian canons. Their church forms the bulk of the visible remains at Whithorn, the roofless nave survives at the west but most of the choir and east end have gone, the space being used as a burial ground. It was in a chapel above the eastern crypts that Ninian's shrine stood, his body wrapped in silken garments provided by the famous eighth-century scholar Alcuin. The vaults (reconstructed in the 1890s) may also have contained relics of the founder and other saints.

A new prose *Life* of Ninian was written by Ailred of Rievaulx (1110–67), in which the saint and his brethren go to the southern Picts who 'worship deaf and dumb idols'. In a rerun of Christ's miracles, the blind see, the lame walk, the deaf hear, the dead are raised, lepers cleansed and those beset by devils are released. Ailred credits Ninian with curing the physical blindness of a stubborn pagan king and persuading a one-night-old child to name his father after the mother had falsely accused a priest. Ninian protected cattle at night against thieves by drawing a line around them with his staff, and could keep the heaviest rain from his open book solely by virtuous concentration.

In the thirteenth century, when the cathedral-priory was built over and around the priory church of *c*. 1150, Ninian's shrine was placed in a special pilgrim chapel (Lady Chapel) east of the high altar in the extended and vaulted (two-level) choir. This is believed to be the site of St Martin's Church (*Candida Casa*) where Ninian was originally buried in a stone sarcophagus and brought about cures of leprosy and other miracles. Between *c*. 1200 and the mid-fifteenth century, over 3000 people were buried on the southern slope below the cathedral-priory, some with nailed coffins and shrouds fastened by pins and lace-ends. Most of the graves contained white quartz pebbles or cattle teeth as symbols or charms. From this period come signs that the medieval Burgh was a thriving commercial centre, catering for a lucrative pilgrim traffic enhanced throughout the Middle Ages by foreign travellers and royal patronage. Prince Edward of England visited the shrine in 1302 at the head of one of Edward I's armies of occupation. King Robert Bruce came to Whithorn in 1329 aged fifty-five, seeking a divine cure for the leprosy which killed him three months later. A visit by his son, David II, had a happier result: the freeing of an English arrow-head trapped in his body since the battle of Neville's Cross in 1346. Even during times of war free access was allowed for foreigners: in 1427 James I issued safe-conduct to Whithorn pilgrims coming from England and the Isle of Man, but their routes and stay (fifteen days in Scotland) were strictly controlled, with different authenticating badges issued for the outward and return journeys. In the period 1460–1542 James III, IV and V all went on pilgrimage to Ninian's shrine. James IV's route led south-west through Biggar, Cold Chapel (near Abington), Crawford Muir, Durisdeer, Penpont and Dalry. His Lord Treasurer's accounts for 1497 record 'to the wife of Durisdeer, where the King lodged 14 shillings'. Whithorn pilgrims used the Roman road (Well Path) through Lanarkshire and Nithsdale still guarded by a Roman fort one mile north of Durisdeer. Mary Queen of Scots made the last royal pilgrimage to Whithorn in 1563, and by 1581 all pilgrimages had been formally banned by parliament. At the Reformation (1560s) Ninian's shrine was stripped of its treasures, including a silver boat donated by the grateful survivors of a storm at sea, but an arm relic may have been smuggled abroad by a Scottish Jesuit. The nave became a

St Ninian's Chapel, Isle of Whithorn, Dumfries & Galloway

Protestant cathedral and then a parish church until the present building was constructed nearby.

The principal harbour for Whithorn was to the south-east on the Isle of Whithorn, once detached from the east coast of the Machars peninsula, now linked to the mainland by a causeway and quay. A partly rebuilt enclosure and chapel of *c*. 1300 stand above a sheltered rocky inlet, the good anchorage used by seaborne pilgrims arriving mainly from Ireland and the Isle of Man. Excavations have uncovered foundations of a twelfth-century chapel but cannot confirm local tradition that this was where St Ninian landed and built his *Candida Casa*. The Whithorn Pilgrimage Trust and Galloway Regional Council have begun signposting cycle and walking routes based on pilgrim paths running in a U-shape through Whithorn and the Machars. The Southern Upland Way coast to coast long distance footpath heading NE from Portpatrick also makes use of ways formerly trodden by pilgrims: a remote pair of prehistoric standing stones, carved with Latin crosses, at Laggangarn (OS 82 NX 222716, Historic Scotland) possibly marked a stopping-place for pilgrims *en route* to Whithorn from western Scotland. Chapel Finian on the western coast of the Machars peninsula was also used by pilgrims from Ireland. Built sometime between 900 and 1100, it is dedicated to the sixth-century Irish abbot-founder of Moville (Co. Down, Ulster) who was educated at Whithorn. The foundations lie beside the coastal road (A747) along the east side of Luce Bay, close to a raised beach and landing-place at Corwall Port. Also overlooking Luce Bay is St Ninian's Cave at Physgill near Glasserton. Contemporary accounts describe St Martin of Tours retiring for periods of contemplation to a cell on the bank of the Loire. Other monasteries copied this practice, the Physgill cave being regarded as Ninian's retreat. Votive crosses on the western rock-face were carved by pilgrims in the eighth and ninth centuries and nineteenth-century excavations uncovered the sculpted slabs and boulders on display in Whithorn museum. The skeleton of a hermit and his eleventh-century grave-marker, bearing Anglian runes, were found separately in the outer part of the cave. Modern votives are left in the form of driftwood crosses, flowers and engraved pebbles. The walk to Port Castle Bay, down through a wooded glen, is particularly beautiful when the bluebells are flowering.

Although both are reputed to have roamed the west-coast lands of Scotland as missionaries to the Picts, Ninian, a conforming Romano-Briton, and Columba, a more individualistic Celt, were as different as their present-day places of pilgrimage.

In 563 Columba and his twelve companions steered their skin-covered currach to the south coast of Iona. The western beach (Port an Fhir-bhréige) of St Columba's Bay is dotted with over fifty small cairns constructed as gradual acts of penitence or devotion by medieval monks and pilgrims. The cairns are still being added to, noticeably changing shape and size over

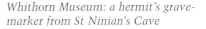

Whithorn Museum: a hermit's grave-marker from St Ninian's Cave

Port an Fhir-bhréige, Iona, Argyll

St Columba's Shrine and St John's Cross, Iona

the last twenty-five years. A grassy mound in the eastern beach (Port na Curraich) is reputed to cover Columba's boat: although a recent construction of pebbles, it may incorporate earlier cairns roughly marking the outline of a sixty-six foot sea-going currach.

After Columba died, aged seventy-five, on Sunday 9 June 597, he lay in his cell for three days and nights while the funeral rituals were carried out. His body, wrapped in pure linen, was laid in a grave-pit whose whereabouts is unknown but traditionally lies under St Columba's Shrine, rebuilt in 1962 on the ninth-century walls of an originally free-standing chapel. A replica of St John's Cross (eighth century) stands in the original stone box-base west of the shrine. Columba's remains were not dug up and enshrined until after St Adomnán's death in 704, but he describes Columba's white garment being taken around the fields and shaken in the air three times to break a spring drought. On the same occasion readings were made on the Hill of Angels from books written in Columba's hand. Vikings looted Iona in 795, 798, 802 and in 806 when sixty-eight monks were killed. In 825 raiders came seeking 'the precious metals wherein lie the holy bones of Columba'. Foreseeing the attack, Abbot Blathmac had the reliquary buried, the sods carefully replaced. Monks who chose to stay were killed next morning by frustrated Vikings, Blathmac being hacked to death at the altar. The undiscovered relics were divided: some went to Dunkeld (Perthshire) others, for temporary safe keeping, to the Columban monastery of Kells (Co. Meath). Although many Norse were Christians by the late tenth century (including a former king of York and Dublin who retired to Iona), Scandinavian 'pirates' murdered fifteen monks and the abbot in 986. Columba's foundation survived the Viking raids, continuing until around 1204 when Reginald, son of Somerled Lord of the Isles, established a Benedictine abbey against the Columbans' wishes. Until the Scottish Reformation of 1560 extinguished the monastic community, pilgrims in great numbers visited the island abbey with its shrine and landscape of miracles. Interest was revived in 1899 by the formation of the Iona Cathedral Trust. Restoration of the ruined complex was completed in 1966 by the Iona Community who have restored a passion for Christian life and worship to the abbey church of St Mary in the monastery of St Columba, though the expensive tasks of maintenance and improvement continue. Historic Scotland has recently taken over responsibility for the abbey complex and nunnery from the Iona Cathedral Trust. Thanks to the work of these bodies, and of the National Trust for Scotland who own much of the

Lindisfarne Priory and Castle, Northumberland

island, Columba's prophecy is on the way to coming true: Iona of my heart,/ Iona of my love,/ Instead of monks' voices/ Shall be the lowing of cattle;/ But ere the world come to an end,/ Iona shall be as it was.

St Aidan founded Lindisfarne in 635 but pilgrims came primarily to the shrine of St Cuthbert, the sixth prior, whose perfectly preserved body provoked wonder and cures. The monastery was fatally weakened by a series of raids starting in 793, when Vikings 'like stinging hornets and ravening wolves' killed monks and livestock, 'trampled the Holy places with polluted feet', dug around the altars and made off with any treasure they could find. Abandoned in 875, the priory was re-founded at the end of the eleventh century by Benedictines from Durham (home of Cuthbert's relics) who rebuilt in warm red sandstone. After Henry VIII dissolved the monastery in 1537, stone was taken to build a fort on the

St Cuthbert's Isle, Lindisfarne (Holy Island), Northumberland.

Each Easter, to honour St Cuthbert and celebrate St Aidan bringing Celtic Christianity from Iona to the Northumbrians, barefooted pilgrims carrying wooden crosses follow marker poles over the tidal sands to Holy Island. To avoid being cut off for several hours, visitors from the mainland and from Lindisfarne to the hermitage site on St Cuthbert's Isle should consult the tide-tables and keep a very careful eye on rising water.

Shave Cross Inn, Marshwood, Dorset.

Pilgrims seeking cures at the shrine of St Wite (Candida) at Whitchurch Canonicorum (Dorset) could meditate on murder and robbery while negotiating a network of tracks and lanes through the Marshwood Vale. After the necessary precaution of being shriven (confessed) and receiving the sacrament at a wayside chapel between Chard and Crewkerne, a wayfarer could set out on the potentially dangerous eight-mile journey clear of conscience and in peak spiritual condition. Beyond lay the safety of Shave Cross Inn which acted as hostel for medieval pilgrims and is a welcome haven yet.

St Candida & Holy Cross Church, Whitchurch Canonicorum, Lyme Regis, Dorset

basalt outcrop protecting the harbour. Lindisfarne 'castle' was restored in 1903 as a holiday house by Sir Edwin Lutyens.

Apart from that of Edward the Confessor in Westminster Abbey, the shrine to St Wite at Whitchurch Canonicorum, Lyme Regis (Dorset) is the only one in an English church to have remained *in situ* containing the original relics, and to have maintained pilgrimage almost continuously since the reign of Alfred the Great (871–99). The mainly regional fame of the saint and pilgrimage probably contributed to their survival. A new shrine for St Wite's tomb was constructed in the early thirteenth century. The reliquary (possibly temporarily removed at the Reformation) was opened in the sixteenth century but the relics were not disturbed. They were examined again in 1900, after settlement in the transept opened a crack in the Purbeck marble tomb chest. An inscribed lead casket was

A modern statue of St Wite (Candida) on the church tower

revealed containing the bones of a small woman aged about forty. Almond-shaped holes below the tomb allowed pilgrims to place ailing heads and limbs close to the healing relics or to transfer their restorative powers on to such items as handkerchiefs belonging to those too sick to travel. While prayers, coin and candles were offered at the shrine, gifts of cake and cheese were also considered acceptable. Those receiving a miracle were 'measured for St Wite': a length of wick, amounting to the dimensions of the part cured, was made into a candle for burning at the shrine. In the case of a whole-body cure, the wick was coiled before being waxed. Modern offerings and supplications and thanks written on printed shrine-cards or pieces of rolled-up paper, are placed in the apertures. A bowl containing water from St Wite's well stands on a shelf between the shrine and the side altar to the right. Her well on Chardown Hill (Morcombelake) is considered to have curative properties for eye complaints, and clear blue periwinkles trailing among the hedgerows of nearby Stonebarrow Hill (part of NT Golden Cap estate) are known as St Candida's Eyes.

Although Wite – known as Candida since the later Middle Ages – is 'surrounded by a curious haze', strong local tradition maintains that she was a Saxon holy woman, with a hermitage near the well, who was martyred in the ninth century during a Danish raid on Charmouth. Pilgrims left gifts of bent pins and other votives in the well, bathed sore eyes – especially as the rising sun first illuminated the water – and filled their leaden ampullae (holy water flasks) for later use.

In the 1930s a farmer built his cattle trough downhill from the well and deliberately allowed the source to disappear under scrub, but this was cleared and fenced in the 1980s by the National Trust. On my last visit, the stone basin contained clear water, coins and an ammonite.

One of the most celebrated appearances of the Virgin Mary took place in Little Walsingham (near Fakenham, Norfolk), a pilgrimage place of the first order, still exercising a fascination over Catholics and Anglicans alike. In 1061 Richeldis de Favarches, the Saxon lady of the manor, was taken in spirit by the Blessed Virgin to her house in Nazareth, *Santa Casa* (the Holy House), home of Jesus and scene of the Annunciation, at which Archangel Gabriel revealed that Mary was blessed among women, chosen to bear God's son. (Luke, 1:28). After the vision occurred three times, Richeldis was encouraged to build a dimensionally accurate replica of Mary's simple dwelling and was drawn towards two sets of mysterious outlines in the grass of a meadow containing twin wells. Her joiners began near the springs, but could not fit wall timbers to the foundations. During a

The eastern window of Walsingham Abbey (Norfolk) and the red-brick Anglican Shrine Church

night of prayer, 'angel hands' moved the house 200 feet away to the second site, west of the wells. Excavations in 1961 confirmed its reputed site abutting the north aisle of the priory church (now marked by a cross-slab set in the grass) and found buried beneath it pagan Anglo-Saxon burials and a possible temple. The marks seen by Richeldis may have been caused by underlying features affecting the appearance and growth rate of the grass.

The split-timber house completed, Richeldis installed a wonder-working wooden statue of Mary holding the infant Jesus, and her son initiated the building of an Augustinian priory. A crystal phial containing 'Mary's Milk' (white dust from the Cave of Our Lady's Milk in Bethlehem) brought back from crusade added to Walsingham's fame as a place where ills were cured, petitions answered. Pilgrims surged along the 'Milky Way' route from London, guided by the stars hanging over 'England's Nazareth'. The priory church was remodelled, with a stone chapel – the *Novum Opus* (New Work) – built around the wooden Holy House. Henry III came here eleven times and provided a golden crown for the brow of Mary's image. His son, Edward I, made over a dozen visits; Edward II came on pilgrimage as did his widow Isabella, and Edward III granted safe conduct to Walsingham for David I of Scotland. Henry VIII made payments to the shrine, he and Catherine of Aragon coming as barefooted pilgrims in 1511 to light candles in the chapel. They sought the health of their infant son but the boy died, as did all of their children except for Mary. A bitter Henry expelled the monks in 1538, stripped the priory, destroyed the Chapel of the Shrine and sent the statue of Our Lady to be burnt in London – but favours continued quietly to be granted at Walsingham.

In 1921 Alfred Hope Patten was appointed vicar of the Anglican parish. He had been influenced by the Oxford Anglo-Catholic movement and the building of replica Holy Houses in Lady chapels at Buxted (Sussex) and the Church of the Annunciation in nearby King's Lynn. Patten commissioned for his parish church a new statue of Our Lady of Walsingham, based on the original illustrated on the priory seal. Prayers were offered before the statue and national interest was stimulated. By 1931, on a site just outside the north wall of the priory precinct and opposite the Knight's Gate, Patten had constructed a brick and stone copy of the Holy House. Regarded by some as the original location of

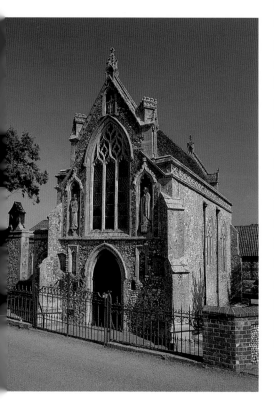

Richeldis's wooden house, the uncovering of a medieval well during building work furthered the misunderstanding. The present red-brick Italianate church was built in 1938 to accommodate the increasing number of pilgrims. It contains Patten's Holy House and statue of Our Lady, a chapel for each of the fifteen mysteries of the Rosary, an Eastern Orthodox chapel, and the well, close to which is a box for intercessions: 'not more than three intercessions from each person, please'. Each evening at 6 p.m. shrine prayers, including intercessions, are offered in the Holy House, other services and masses are held throughout the year. During the pilgrimage season (Easter to end of October) candlelit processions with the statue of Our Lady and processions of the Blessed Sacrament also take place. Comforting draughts and sprinkled blessings of water are administered at the well and everyone is welcome to share in the services. In 1997 the statue of the Virgin was taken on a promotional tour to help relaunch the shrine as an inclusive, vital place of exploration and renewal.

The Slipper Chapel, Houghton St Giles, Norfolk

Built in the reign of Edward III (*c.* 1350) the 'Slipper Chapel' south-west of Little Walsingham was where medieval pilgrims traditionally removed their shoes before walking the final mile barefooted. The chapel was purchased in 1896 on behalf of the Catholic Church, the first public pilgrimage to Walsingham since the Reformation being undertaken in the following year. By 1934 the chapel had been restored as the National Catholic Shrine of Our Lady of Walsingham, and 12,000 pilgrims made reparation for the ancient sin of 'driving St Mary from her English home'. The shrine is restrained in comparison with the unusually ornate and gaudy Anglican one, which features highly coloured images of saints lit by swaying candle-flames. This apparent role-reversal contributes to the ecumenical aims of welcoming 'all people of goodwill' and praying for 'true unity' and 'harmony among Christians'. The Roman Catholic complex includes the attractively barn-like Chapel of Reconciliation, an outdoor altar and fourteen oak crosses which were carried about England in 1948 by groups of men on foot. As part of the WWF Sacred Land project, an old railway track just to the west has been used to create a pilgrim path.

The Red Mount chapel in King's Lynn (Norfolk) was built in 1485, mainly for foreign pilgrims travelling to Walsingham from the port of King's Lynn. With an octagonal shell of early red brick, and three internal storeys topped by a cruciform, fan-vaulted chapel, it is an unusually complete and impressive wayside shrine. The most famous route to Walsingham was the 'Milky Way' from London, following the ancient Icknield Way through Royston, Newmarket, Brandon, Swaffham and Fakenham. At Castle Acre pilgrims could view an arm of St Philip and obtain comfort at the altar in the infirmary. Ely pilgrims also used part of this route and the King's Lynn loop. Others visited Norwich for the cathedral and anchorite cell of mystic and visionary Mother Julian (1342–1416+). Henry III came via the Cluniac priory of Broomholm (near the coast at Bacton, due-east of

Chapel of Our Lady of the Mount, King's Lynn, Norfolk

Walsingham) which possessed a portion of the True Cross or Holy Rood. The quick way to Walsingham was to land at Wells-next-the-Sea and head south directly, or lodge at the Benedictine priory in Binham.

Devotion to the mother of Christ can be seen as a continuation of the timeless respect for a goddess of nature and fertility. Worship of an ancient god of husbandry may also have continued under Christian guise at Bawburgh, where St Walstan's shrine stood in the northern transept of the church. Throughout the Middle Ages, Norfolk farmers and herdsmen – 'mowers and scythe followers' – came to the shrine each 30 May to obtain

SS Mary's and Walstan's Church, Bawburgh, Norfolk.

In a copse to the north of Bawburgh churchyard stands a modernized holy well, once visited by pilgrims to the shrine of St Walstan. Even in the serious drought of 1995 the surrounding grass was damp and lush.

The simple well west of the modern pools below St Kenelm's Church, Romsley, Hereford & Worcester

blessings for themselves and their stock. A surviving Latin *Life* of this local unofficial saint, written on vellum-covered panels, used to hang above his reliquary. Walstan's legend has him deliberately choose to serve God through the hard, humble life of a farm labourer; he excelled at aiding those in need. As Death gathered him out in the fields on 30 May 1061, he uttered prayers for cattle and the sick. Two calves he had raised pulled his body on a cart to Bawburgh church, magically skimming the Wensum at Costessey ford and passing through a solid wall. Offerings to the shrine paid for rebuilding the chancel in 1309 and helped to support a vicar with six priests to chant masses. At the Reformation Walstan's bones were scattered over the fields, the chapel being destroyed so that only foundations are visible outside the north wall. The old fording-place on the north-western outskirts of Norwich is a favourite spot to fish and swim.

Other shrines were also associated with animals: Edward I would send his ailing hawks to Hereford Cathedral to recover beside the shrine of St Thomas Cantelupe which was noted for cures, while pilgrimages to the well and chapel at Llaneilian (Anglesey), by farmers seeking blessings for their animals and crops continued into the mid-nineteenth century.

A spring at St Kenelm's Church, Romsley (Hereford & Worcester) features prominently in the legendary account of his death. The historical Kenelm was a prince of Mercia who died before his father, King Coenwulf (796–821). Killed fighting the Welsh, he was buried at the Saxon minster on the Hwiccian royal family's estate of Winchcombe (Gloucestershire). When St Oswald (Bishop of Worcester) refounded Winchcombe as a Benedictine abbey in the mid-tenth century, Kenelm was regarded as a boy martyr. By the thirteenth century his elaborated legend had him succeeding his father as king at the age of seven. His jealous, ambitious sister Cwoenthryth (Quendreda) was said to have arranged his death.

According to tradition, the murder took place during a hunt in the Clent Hills and Kenelm's body was concealed in a wooded place now occupied by Romsley Church. From his severed head 'a milk-white dove with golden wings soared up to heaven'. A letter describing the brutal deed in Anglo-Saxon was dropped by the dove on St Peter's high altar in Rome where it was translated by English pilgrims, and the body was subsequently uncovered and carried to Winchcombe for burial. Queen Quendreda of the legend came to a sticky end: her eyes fell out while she was reading a psalm backwards to put a hex on Kenelm's funeral; in reality, the historically blameless Quendreda became abbess of a monastery in Kent. A spring created at his death rises underneath the church and fills an ugly complex of concrete pools. The simple well west of the modern pools is dressed with clouties. A modern carving of St Kenelm as a youthful king can be seen above the church gate – he is also traditionally depicted holding a lily or trampling on his evil sister.

Monks conveying Kenelm's body from Romsley to Winchcombe were aided by the miraculous appearance of a series of wells. Chapels were then built along the route which became popular with pilgrims. Sudeley Hill (Gloucestershire) was the last stopping-place before Winchcombe as pilgrims came down one of the ancient salt routes from the west Midlands. The present well chapel is a relatively recent creation of the Sudeley Castle estate. A house beside another spring a little to the south-west, was converted from a chapel in the late nineteenth century. Mr Royle, the owner and a local historian, pointed out to me that the chapel would almost certainly have been sited at the original 'miracle' well.

At the end of a pilgrimage to Winchcombe from the Clent Hills, weary Elizabethans could lodge at the George Inn's pilgrim balcony and soak in a stone bath in the courtyard. The balcony and bath were retained when the hotel was converted to housing in the late 1980s. Pilgrims would revere 'the little saint's body' at Kenelm's shrine in the abbey, beside the site of which is St Peter's parish church, built in 1486 in place of the original Saxon minster. A low mound in the churchyard's northern corner may mark the Hwiccian royal mausoleum where Kenelm and his father were first buried. Two stone coffins (on display in St Peter's nave) dug up from the ruins of the abbey church in 1815

St Kenelm's Well, Sudeley Hill, Gloucestershire

George (Inn) Mews, Winchcombe, Gloucestershire

contained bones claimed as those of father and son.

Pilgrims on the pack-horse and wagon tracks (Salter's Lane, Salter's Hill, Salt Way, White Way) used for carrying salt from Droitwich, could also call in at Hailes Abbey near Winchcombe to see a phial said to contain the blood of Christ: a relic authenticated by the Patriarch of Jerusalem (the future Pope Urban IV) and presented to Hailes in 1270 by a nephew of Henry III. The Cistercian abbey was founded – and the villagers moved to Didbrook – in 1245–6 by Henry's brother, Richard Earl of Cornwall, to fulfil his vow made at sea while in danger of drowning. The phial was housed in the Shrine of the Holy Blood at the abbey church's specially rebuilt east end. Its rectangular stone plinth survives behind the mound of the high altar, surrounded by the lower courses of an arc of five vaulted chapels. Pilgrims processed around the shrine, between the pillars and radiating chapels of this elaborate form of apse called a chevet. After a financially shaky start, Hailes began to thrive on high incomes from wool and pilgrimages, which continued up to the Dissolution. On 28 October 1538 Henry VIII's Commissioners removed the holy blood for examination in London, after which it was publicly declared to be

Hailes Abbey, Winchcombe, Gloucestershire

'honey clarified and coloured with saffron'. The adjacent parish church was founded in the time of King Stephen (1135–54). Shortly after pilgrims began visiting the abbey in the late thirteenth century, the church was decorated with wall paintings of saints, apostles, mythical beasts, heraldic devices and a hunting scene. Nine of the apostles, including St James the Great dressed as a pilgrim, are depicted in fifteenth-century stained glass salvaged from the abbey and placed in the east window.

Those on pilgrimage in Gloucestershire could visit the shrine of a most unlikely royal saint and 'martyr' at St Peter's Abbey (Gloucester Cathedral). The wayward behaviour of Edward I's son dismayed the king and disgusted his barons. At his coronation banquet in 1308, Edward II paid so much attention to his favourite Piers Gaveston – who was dressed in imperial purple trimmed with pearls – that the relatives of his twelve-year-old queen, Isabella of France, walked out. Edward's inadequate behaviour continued, his defeat by the Scots at Bannockburn in 1314 being followed by civil war. With the support of bishops and barons, his estranged queen raised an army of mercenaries against the king in 1326, and had his new best friend executed for alleged 'unnatural practices': Hugh Despenser's genitals were cut off, his stomach slit open and his entrails set on fire while he still lived. Edward was held prisoner at Kenilworth Castle and in January 1327 Isabella and her lover, Roger Mortimer, forced him to abdicate in favour of

An alabaster effigy of Edmund II in the choir of Gloucester Cathedral

Prince Edward. Later that year the deposed king was imprisoned and tortured at Berkeley Castle (Gloucestershire) where his chamber may still be seen. His ordeal came to a terrible end when a heated soldering iron was forced into his bowels. In fear of Isabella, the abbots of Bristol, Kingswood and Malmesbury refused to bury their former king. A month later, the shrewdly brave Abbot of Gloucester collected the body in his own carriage, interring it in St Peter's Church after a magnificent and crowded funeral. Edward III imprisoned his mother, sent Mortimer to the scaffold and persuaded the Benedictines to convert their choir into a lavish mausoleum for his murdered father. Beneath an intricately pinnacled canopy, Edward's exquisite alabaster effigy lies in the Perpendicular choir, bathed in colour and light from the great east window.

The acquisition of a popularly acclaimed royal 'saint' did wonders for the abbey's crumbling buildings and ailing finances. The New Inn was built in the fifteenth century

The New Inn, Northgate Street, Gloucester

to accommodate the influx of pilgrims which was threatening to overwhelm the town's facilities. As well as King Edward II, St Peter's also possessed healing relics of St Arild of Thornbury (a virgin beheaded by a tyrannical suitor), and an arm of St Oswald was kept at his priory nearby. The New Inn courtyard was used for Tudor theatrical performances, viewed from its first-floor gallery where the ill-fated Lady Jane Grey was proclaimed Queen in 1552.

Similar cults of royal martyrs grew up around Thomas of Lancaster at Pontefract, Henry VI at Windsor, and nationally for the publicly executed Charles I.

Sir John Schorne was another uncanonized but extremely popular saint, patron of those with toothache, the blind and the unhappy. In the Middle Ages he was esteemed for great holiness and for his miraculous cures of fevers and gout. Sixteenth-century reformers considered him a superstitious semi-saint and disapproved of his curing the symptoms of overindulgence. A defaced image on the fifteenth-century rood screen at Cawston (Norfolk) illustrates the jingle 'John Schorne, Gentleman born/Conjured the Devil into a boot'. Schorne is said to have entertained congregations with a mechanical toy 'devil in a boot', a precursor of the 'Jack in a Box'.

He was vicar of North Marston (1290–1314) where he dramatically created a holy well for his parishioners during a drought, performed cures and prayed so often that his knees grew hard and leathery. Healing continued at the well after his death, and at a shrine in the south aisle of St Mary's where a small ground-level niche is believed to have held his bones. Sir John's relics were forcibly removed in 1478 to Windsor Castle (Berkshire) to bring fame and funds to its expensively remodelled Chapel of St George. Edward IV eased his conscience and pacified the villagers of North Marston by building them a new chancel.

The spiritual home of many contradictory beliefs, Glastonbury (Somerset) was a powerfully sacred place long before Christian times. The Tor is regarded as a spiral maze-mound, symbol of the Mother Goddess and the hub of a zodiac mapped out in the surrounding watery landscape: an island of the dead, home to the king of the Celtic underworld, key point for ley lines and other earth forces, and a centre of electromagnetic, supernatural and alien activity. Every inch of Avalon's topography is associated with the Arthurian quest for the Holy Grail, in which Christian ideas of redemption combine with the magically restorative cauldrons of pagan Celtic legend. The abbey site is of great symbolic significance; it is claimed as the burial place of St Patrick, Arthur and Guinevere, and the location of the first Marian shrine in Britain, a wood and wattle church built by Jesus himself. England's true national anthem, the poem 'Jerusalem' by William Blake, is based on the legend that Jesus and Mary visited Britain with Joseph of Arimathea, a tin trader who provided his own tomb for Christ's use. A variant of the tradition credits Joseph with building the church, after he and twelve companions had brought the Faith from Palestine to Britain within thirty years of Christ's death. They came to Glastonbury by boat, alighting on Wearyall Hill where Joseph's staff, thrust into the ground, became a winter-flowering thorn tree. Joseph carried the Holy Grail (the Chalice of the Last Supper) which he had used to collect drops of blood falling from Christ on the Cross. This was reputedly handed over to an ancient priesthood, then buried, possibly beneath Chalice Hill. Pre-Roman links between south-west England and the trading empire of Phoenicia (Syria) are certain, and modern analysis of trees grown from cuttings of the ancient thorn finds them to be of Syrian origin. Christian

St Mary's Church, North Marston, Buckinghamshire

yearnings fuse with more ancient instincts to form a belief that Britain as a whole, but England specifically, was, is, will be again, the New Jerusalem: a sacred country, a vast hidden symbolic landscape of enhanced natural features and designed structures incorporating magical numbers, relationships and shapes.

The Celtic foundation at Glastonbury passed remarkably peacefully into Anglo-Saxon control. King Ine of Wessex (689–728) refounded the monastery and built a new abbey

church in 705 but retained, untouched, the ancient wattle one. St Dunstan – regarded as such a determined character that he was depicted holding the Devil by the nose with a pair of tongs – brought Glastonbury under Benedictine rule when appointed abbot in 940. Written around 1000, his *Life* states that the ancient chapel was 'not built by art of man, but prepared by God Himself', and that pilgrims from Ireland flocked to Glastonbury because St Patrick, their Romano-British patron, was buried there. (St Patrick's true burial place is unknown, the relics probably belonged to a different but contemporary St Patrick.) St David of Wales was also considered an early patron of Glastonbury. William of Malmesbury, writing in the 1120s, claimed that St David had heard Christ at Glastonbury saying he had dedicated the 'Old Church' to his mother, Mary. William also described the floor design of the (by then) lead-covered wooden chapel as containing a 'sacred mystery', most likely a configuration of alchemical symbols. The present Lady Chapel replaced that ancient and deeply mysterious St Mary's, which was burned down in 1184 along with the abbey church and much of the monastic range. Rebuilding was aided by grants from Henry II and donations from visitors to the tomb of King Arthur. In 1190 a vision prompted the discovery of a stone slab, seven feet below the ground, in the area south of the destroyed Marian chapel. With the slab was a lead cross – drawn by Camden *c.* 1607 but since disappeared – bearing the Latin inscription 'Here lies buried the renowned King Arthur in the Isle of Avalon'. Bones of a tall man with a fractured skull and the remains of a smaller individual with yellow tresses lay deeper still in a tree-trunk coffin, reputedly bearing the name Guinevere. The heads and knee joints were kept out for public display, the other remains placed inside a black marble tomb before the high altar of the extravagantly long new church. The leaden cross lay on top of the tomb which bore the inscription 'King that was, and King that shall be'.

The monument to a heroic Christian royal couple must have had particular resonance for King Edward I and Queen Eleanor, who were present in 1278 when the excavated remains were placed in a casket and transferred to a black marble tomb before the high altar in the main abbey church. Froissart, the French court chronicler, describes how the royal Christian couple went on a romantic pilgrimage to Glastonbury before embarking on a heroic quest in the Arthurian mould to save their nation, i.e. to repel and conquer the Scots and Welsh. Edward managed the Welsh but died on the way to one last go at the Scots. Their attendance at Glastonbury lent credence to the discovery.

Throughout the Middle Ages Glastonbury was the richest monastery in England: hordes of pilgrims were attracted by its high-profile burials, famous patrons, international relics and biblical memorabilia, offers of over sixty years' exemption from purgatory, and the

OPPOSITE: Glastonbury Abbey, Somerset.
Looking eastwards through the Galilee Chapel arch, down the nave of the abbey church to the site of King Arthur's tomb in the choir.

reputation of being the oldest Christian sanctuary in the British Isles. Free lodgings were available inside the abbey; important visitors and wealthy paying guests could stay at the abbey's inn, now the George and Pilgrims Hotel in High Street, rebuilt in the 1470s by Abbot John Selwood; it is said that from here Henry VIII watched the abbey being dismantled in 1539. The sixtieth abbot, Blessed Richard Whiting, was executed on the Tor with two of his monks for resisting suppression and hiding Church treasures from the king. His head was displayed on the abbey gate, his quartered body shared out between Bath, Bridgwater, Ilchester and Wells.

The original grave was located, about fifty feet from the south door of the Lady Chapel, by Dr Ralegh Radford in 1962–3. Disturbed slabs at a deep level suggested that a significant burial, of the right date and general description given by the monks, had been exhumed. Glastonbury's romantic ruins continue to exert a beguiling charm over uncomplicated tourists and deep seekers alike. Verifiable history, legends, half-truths, bogus claims and a genuine spirit of place create an uncomfortable *mélange* of the mercenary and authentically sacred. Beneath soaring shoulders of masonry, 'sensitives' have trouble with their leg muscles on the site of Arthur's tomb, and designer gypsies or style-conscious witches lead open-palmed acolytes in swaying pavanes around the points of power.

Known as 'Water-man', St David of Wales demanded total obedience, poverty, temperance and hard labour from his monks, on a diet of bread, salt and vegetables. He brought them from the 'White House' monastery, established by St Patrick near

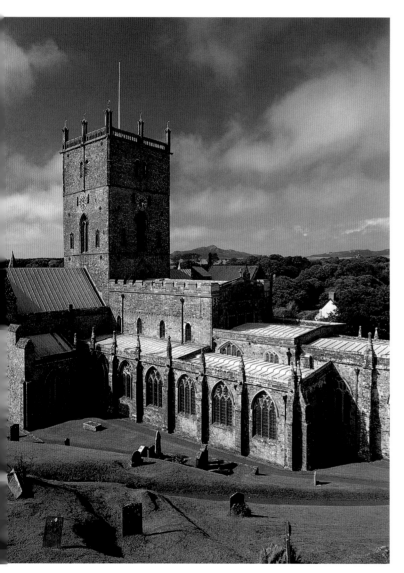

St David's Cathedral, Pembrokeshire

Whitesands Bay, to the more remote inland valley of the River Alun where they were not welcome. Boia, a local tyrant, saw their fires from his stronghold; on discovering where they came from, he and his wife determined to be rid of them. Armed slaves, verbal abuse, naked maidservants, human sacrifice all failed to dislodge the monks; Boia's wife went mad and he was burned in his fort, Clegyr Boia, by rival freebooters. The monks' spartan regime included work on the monastery farm, wielding mattocks and pulling ploughs. This was followed by reading or writing, then chanting psalms, praying and vigils into the night, starting with prayers again at dawn. Aspiring monks were made to wait ten days at the monastery gate, then further tested with hard work before being granted admission to the community. Several killings and attempted murders took place in the heady atmosphere. After David's death (traditionally 589) his relics were kept in the monastery church which burned down in 645. The community suffered various disasters, including numerous Viking raids, up to the late eleventh century when the site lay derelict, the shrine vandalized and overgrown. Menevia (the medieval name for the monastery and diocese) was reorganized under a Norman bishop who, in 1123, obtained from the Pope a form of canonization for the patron of Wales. This, along with a decree that two pilgrimages to his shrine should equal one to Rome, ensured that St David's (Pembrokeshire) became a major centre for medieval pilgrims. Henry II visited the cathedral on his way to and from Ireland in 1171–2, using Porth Clais, the ancient harbour where David had been baptized by an Irish bishop. Pilgrims landing there could see the summit of Carn Llidi, on which angels attended St David. Massive rebuilding was begun in the 1180s, from when the present cathedral mainly dates.

A new shrine was built in 1275 to celebrate the 'rediscovery' of David's body, missing since around 1090; Edward I prayed there in 1284. The shrine was destroyed at the Reformation but the stone base remains: murals filled the arches, while a silver arm reliquary and the portable head reliquaries of David and

St David

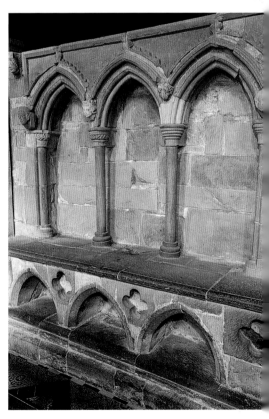

St David's Shrine Base

his friend and confessor Justinian stood on top, covered by a wooden canopy. Bones believed to be those of David and Justinian were found in a walled-up recess behind the high altar during Victorian restorations and were placed in a modern oak casket. Recent analysis has assigned them to a twelfth-century fish-eater, making the local St Caradoc, buried in the cathedral in 1124, a more likely candidate. Caradoc was harper at the court of Rhys ap Tewdwr, becoming a monk and maritime hermit after losing the king's greyhounds. William of Malmesbury tried to steal a finger from Caradoc's incorrupt body as it lay in his shrine, part of which survives between the choir and north transept. Even without his relics, the palpably ancient sanctity of 'David's House' (Tyddewi) has a profound effect on visitors.

St David's was the premier goal for pilgrims in medieval Wales, often combined with visits to Bardsey Island (Gwynedd) and Holywell (Flintshire). Designated pilgrim routes led to and between the major shrines, with travellers praying at holy wells, chapels and crosses along the way, seeking shelter at inns, hospices and monasteries. Those taking the west coast route would call at Nevern church to meditate on St Brynach – David's Irish colleague who conversed with angels on Carn Ingli and survived a murder attempt arranged by his wife – and pray for a safe journey at this cross cut in the rock face.

Nevern Pilgrims' Cross, Newport, Pembrokeshire

Six tombs in the lonely churchyard of ruined St Michael's, west of the Afon Cywyn where it meets the Taf estuary, are associated with pilgrims. Details on the decorated grave slabs between head and foot stones suggest the Norman family who founded the church and a motte-and-bailey castle at Trefenty Farm. There are two ridged or 'hog-backed' tombs bearing long crosses, as well as four flat slabs with two female figures and, possibly, a knight and a child. Despite the indications of a local family group, legend stubbornly claims them as a band of destitute pilgrims who came to the church dying of hunger. Known as the Pilgrims' Church, St Michael's is just north of an ancient crossing point of the Taf estuary. South-east of the smaller river, at Llandeilo Abercywyn, there is another ruined church and a farm called Pilgrims' Rest. These features are reputed to be on a pilgrim path leading north-westwards via Whitland Abbey to St David's.

St Winefride's Well near the northern coast of Wales, is linked to St David's by Celtic miracle stories, healing, sea routes and pilgrim paths. It is the only shrine in Britain that can reasonably claim an unbroken history of pilgrimage from the seventh century. The holy spring traditionally appeared in the year 660, when the religious and virginal daughter of a local chieftain was beheaded by her spurned suitor. Hearing the commotion outside his church, St Beuno, Winefride's (Gwenfrewi) 'uncle' or spiritual tutor, came to her aid by cursing the murderer who disappeared into the ground. Gwenfrewi's head and body were reunited, her spirit rekindled with Beuno's breath and prayers, a white scar around the neck being the only outward sign of her 'martyrdom'. She became a nun and then abbess at Gwytherin (Conwy) where she was buried. A shrine

'Pilgrim Graves', Llanfihangel, Abercywyn Carmarthenshire

St Winefride's Well, Holywell, Flintshire

chapel dedicated to her stood in the southern part of the churchyard until the early eighteenth century. Edward Lhuyd mentioned it around 1698 and published a drawing of Gwenfrewi's triangular-shaped reliquary: a 'tent-shrine' of *c.* 800 (with detachable lid) made of oak covered in ornamental metal plates and roundels. Gwenfrewi's relics were removed to Shrewsbury Abbey in 1138; the shrine remained at Gwytherin into the nineteenth century when fragments of it were being sold as religious souvenirs. In 1416 Henry V made a pilgrimage on foot from Shrewsbury to Holywell to honour the saint for her part in his remarkable victory at Agincourt. Some, like the king, came for ritual cleansing, others to renew their baptism by the Celtic rite of triple immersion or to pass through the water three times in search of a boon or cure.

A sick pilgrim and his supporter, depicted above St Winefride's Well, Holywell, Flintshire

Those too ill to walk are carried through the healing waters on the backs of stronger companions, as depicted by a carving overlooking the well. The lower part of the two-storey chapel, built around 1500 by the mother of Henry VII, has a vaulted roof illustrating incidents from the life of Gwenfrewi. Water fills the inner chamber – star-shaped in remembrance of the healing well at Bethesda used by Jesus – before flowing outside to a long rectangular pool. From 1240 the well was in the care of Basingwerk Abbey which offered wines from Aragon, Spain and Brittany to guests, who were so numerous in the fifteenth century that two sittings were held at every meal. After Henry VIII dissolved the Cistercian abbey in 1537, varying degrees of official repression were used to discourage pilgrimages and rid Holywell of Catholic priests. Despite the dangers of capture and execution, St Winefride continued to draw the faithful: Edward Oldcorne was cured of cancer of the tongue on a pilgrimage in 1601, but Winefride could not save him from execution in 1606. Later, the images were defaced and pilgrim's names recorded, but action was not always taken against them and innkeepers would refuse to give Justices of the Peace details of their 'Romish recusant' customers. When James II and Queen Mary of Modena came to Holywell in 1686 to pray for the gift of a son, they presented the chapel with money and part of the dress worn by Mary Queen of Scots at her beheading. In 1712 the Bishop of St Asaph complained of pilgrims coming to Holywell from all over Britain and Ireland and declared 'the enemy we have to deal with grows more numerous, is active, vigilant and daring ... and under no discouragement but that of laws ...'. Dr Johnson's visit of 1774 yielded the following comment: 'the bath is completely and indecently open: a woman bathed while we all looked on'. In 1795 Pennant recorded that most of the pilgrims came from Lancashire (they were ferried across the Mersey, then walked over the Wirral and Dee sands at low tide) and could be '... seen in water in deep devotion up to their chins for hours, sending up their prayers ...'. He also said that Protestants going to the well on the first Sunday after St James' Day were there for '... most unsaintly ends' and involved in '... every species of frolick and excess'. In 1840 crutches and hand-barrows were still being abandoned by those cured at the well. By 1875 wooden screens and cubicles had been erected around the outer bathing pool and by 1900 the town was, in the summer months, openly 'crowded with zealous pilgrims from all parts of Britain'. Although the water flowing through St Winefride's is not from the original underground source cut off by mining in 1917, pilgrimages and cures continue.

Mwnt Bay and Holy Cross Chapel, Ceredigion

St Beuno's Church, Pistyll, Llŷn, Gwynedd

Pilgrimage to Bardsey, an island with an ancient reputation for sanctity, off the tip of north-west Wales' Llŷn peninsula, was firmly established by the twelfth century. The unwarranted belief that 20,000 saints were buried on the island encouraged the faithful to risk their lives on arduous journeys by land and sea, or desire to be buried there 'among the saints'. Pilgrims (dead or alive) collected from the mortuary chapel and beach at Mwnt in Cardigan Bay were carried northwards, like silt, by prevailing currents and winds, to the mysterious isle where Merlin lay in a cave sleeping. Those from Ireland, the Continent and other parts of Britain also travelled directly by sea but other hardier souls would visit Bardsey on a pilgrimage around Welsh coastal shrines – from Holywell in the north to St David's in the south-west – or tramp through the central valleys and the mountains of Snowdonia.

Shorter pilgrimages along the northern coast, with Bardsey as final destination, began at, or visited, such places as Chester, Holywell, St Asaph, Bangor or Caernarfon (from where holy places on the island of Anglesey could be visited) and, especially, Clynnog Fawr. From the shrine and well of St Beuno at Clynnog, the pilgrim route led south-westwards along the north coast of Llŷn marked by holy wells, stone crosses, inns, hospices, chapels and churches: Llanaelhaearn, Pistyll, Nefyn, Tudweiliog and Llangwnnadl were among the stopping-places before reaching Aberdaron. At Pistyll there was an inn and monastery with a hospice growing medicinal plants, some of which are still used to decorate the church. A small wayside cross survives in walling on the south side of the B4417, just under a mile south-west of St Beuno's. Once at Aberdaron, pilgrims could claim food and shelter at Y Gegin Fawr (the Big Kitchen) rest-house and visit St Hywyn's Church before crossing through the treacherous winds and currents of Bardsey Sound. In difficult conditions the two-mile trip can become a tooth-crunching sea journey of six miles. Several embarkation points were used by pilgrims, including the modern choice of Porth Meudwy around the bay to the west.

Before the Reformation, Bardsey was regarded as a waiting room for heaven; three crossings to 'fair Mary's isle' were considered equivalent to a pilgrimage to Rome. Today its heady atmosphere and special, 'holy' feel attract many on pursuits of the mind, body and spirit. Except for the Bardsey Bird and Field Observatory based in Cristin farmhouse, the island has been owned and managed since 1979 by the Bardsey Island Trust which wishes to maintain its unique character and strike a balance between natural, physical and spiritual history. Holidays and 'breaks' involving archaeology, conservation, ornithology, seal watching, yoga, meditation, retreats, healing and recuperation are all available, and it is not unusual to see a group performing lotus postures outside Elgar's (Merlin's) Cave on the hillside north-east of Cristin or doing head stands in one of the lovely gardens. In the words of Father Derwas Chitty, who contributed to Bardsey's spiritual revival in the 1950s, '[it is] the island of hermits, the island of the solitude where we are least alone'. Bardsey is a good place to ponder meaning and the mysteries of existence; the nature and variety of this earth, the planets and stars; infinite time and space or the eternal now; faith or its absence; self-belief or acceptance of something eternal and universal; the paradise of Christ or the Celtic land of the blessed beyond the setting sun.

St Mary's Abbey, Bardsey Island, Gwynedd

Orkney Islands

*St Tredwell's
St Magnus (Egilsay)
St Magnus (Kirkwall)

Tain
Applecross
Urquhart Castle & Loch Ness
Kildonnan
Lismore
*St Fillan's
Iona
*Luss & Loch Lomond
*Glasgow
Edinburgh
*Dunfermline
St Andrews
St Fillan's Cave
*Isle of May
Lindisfarne
Inner Farne
St Cuthbert's Cave
Bamburgh
Scott's View & Old Melrose
Coquet Island
Holy Island & Shiskine
*Lady's Well
St Oswald in Lee
Jarrow
Hexham
Monkwearmouth
Whithorn
Finchale
Durham
Whitby
St Herbert's Isle
*Rievaulx
Lastingham
Pickering
*Ripon
St Robert's Cave
York
Beverley
Hatfield Chase
*Llaneilian
Llanbabo
Penmon
Holyhead
Llangelynin
Llangwyfan
St Trillo's Chapel
Ilam
*Hanbury
King's Lynn
Walsingham
East Dereham
Holywell
Repton
*Cawston
Ranworth
Chester
Llanddwyn
*Gwytherin
Anchor Church
*Norwich
Clynnog Fawr
Ffynnon Degla
*Ryhall
Crowland
Burgh Castle
Pistyll
*Oswald's Well
Lichfield
*Ashby-de-la-Zouch
Peterborough
March
Hoxne
Bawburgh
Bardsey Island
Llanddderfel
*Shrewsbury
Ely
Bury St Edmunds
Dunwich
*Aberdaron
*St Cybi's Well
Pennant Melangell
*Brixworth
*Llanbadarn Fawr
Romsley
Winchcombe
St Osyth
Mwnt
Worcester
St Kenelm's Well
King's Sutton
Bradwell-on-Sea
Nevern
Llanfihangel Abercywyn
Newport
North Marston
St Albans
Ashingdon
St David's
*Hereford
Gloucester
Binsey
Oxford
*Waltham Abbey
Greenwich
St Non's
*Caerwent
Hailes
Dorchester
*Minster in Thanet
St Govan's
*Capel Gwladys
*St Tewdric's Well
Stanton Harcourt
*Westminster
*St Augustine's Cross
Caldey Island
*Llandaff
Llancarfan
Canterbury
Llangennith
*Llantwit Major
Hawkesbury
*Wells
St Edith's Well
*St Barruc's Chapel
St Aldhelm's Well
Pilgrims' Way
*Chittlehampton
Oare
Glastonbury
*Salisbury
Winchester
Steyning
Hartland
St Decumans
St Clether
Crediton
Shave Cross
St Neot
St Endellion
St Cleer
Exeter
Roche
Bodmin
Hennock
Whitchurch Canonicorum
St Piran's
*St Keyne
*Shaftesbury
*Madron
St Levan
Golant
St Cuby's Well
St Michael's Mount
Mylor
St Nonna's Well
Sithney

• site illustrated eg • St Michael's Mount
* site not illustrated eg * Waltham Abbey

188   THE WAY AND THE LIGHT

8.
A Pilgrim's Way
Gazetteer

This book was written during a time of considerable activity in Britain: county names and boundaries seemed to change almost monthly and many of the sacred places mentioned have been receiving attention to make them more recognizable, attractive and accessible to the public. There are also increasing numbers of specialist organizations and interest groups being set up to study and conserve such neglected features as holy wells or yew trees. A list of all the Christian sites in Britain worthy of a modern pilgrim's attention would be a book in itself, so I have limited the gazetteer to those illustrated in this volume, plus a few of the more significant and rewarding ones mentioned in the text. Used in conjunction with the distribution map, the following information will be of help in planning visits, or serve as a quick reminder to the 'what, where and why' of a particular place.

Name and location are given along with the Ordnance Survey 1:50,000 Landranger map sheet and National Grid Reference (in brackets): some of the sites (even churches) can be difficult to find using only a motoring atlas or general tourist map. The name of the owner or organization responsible for the site is followed by a brief summary of what is to be seen, with comments on access etc. For security and other reasons many churches are now kept locked and, understandably, not all incumbents relish the churches in their care being treated as museums or amusement galleries; some give details in the porch of the key holders (who are not always available), others offer no such assistance to casual visitors.

Cadw: Welsh Historic Monuments, English Heritage, Historic Scotland and the National Trust all have membership schemes, publications, events and displays to help visitors appreciate and enjoy the properties and landscapes in their care.

The Council for British Archaeology, based in York (tel: 01904 671384), also has a national and local membership scheme (and the Young Archaeologists Club) designed to inform and involve those interested in all aspects of archaeology. Increasingly, local councils and trusts are responsible for the maintenance and presentation of a wide range of 'heritage sites', and the World Wide Fund for Nature is running the multi-faith Sacred Land project of environmental and religious conservation work across the United Kingdom until 2002.

Other sites of interest are described in the works listed in the bibliography and in my own *Holy Places of Celtic Britain*. Local tourist information offices can supply up to date details of opening times, exhibitions and special events etc.

Sites marked * are mentioned but not illustrated in this book.

*Aberdaron: St Hywyn's Church and Y Gegin Fawr
Llŷn, Gwynedd, Wales
OS 123 (SH 173264)

Shore-side, former monastic church used by Bardsey Island pilgrims; twelfth-century west door and inscribed gravestones of two sixth-century priests from Capel Anelog. The Big Kitchen (café and shop) was a pilgrims' rest-house.

Anchor Church
Ingleby, Melbourne, Derbyshire, England
OS 128 (SK 339272)

A cave beside the River Trent romantically associated with hermits. Access via footpaths from Ingleby or Foremark NW of Melbourne, minor roads off the A514.

Applecross: St Maelrubha's Churchyard and 'Grave'
Wester Ross, Highland, Scotland
OS 24 (NG 713459)

Heavenly bay facing Raasay and Skye; approach by mountainous 'Pass of the Cattle' or new coastal road around Loch Torridon to N. Ninth-century cross-slab.

*Ashby-de-la-Zouch: Pilgrim Monument
St Helen's Church, Leicestershire, England
OS 128 (SK 361168)

Fifteenth-century effigy in N aisle of parish church in NE part of town, just S of A50. See also finger pillory in nave beside font and nearby castle (English Heritage).

Ashingdon: St Andrew's Church
Southend-on-Sea, Essex, England
OS 168 (TQ 866936)

N of Southend off B1013. Founded by Cnut after battle of Assandun fought with St Wendreda's relics in fields to N and E. Once held a miraculous statue of the BVM.

Bamburgh Castle and *St Aidan's Church
Northumberland, England
OS 75 (NU 178350)

Modern shrine in chancel on reputed site of Aidan's death; former relic-crypt below occasionally open. Restored Norman castle on site of St Oswald's stronghold.

Bardsey Island (Ynys Enlli)
off Aberdaron, Llŷn, Gwynedd, Wales
OS 123 (SH 120222)
Bardsey Island Trust

Visits to the island must be arranged in advance through the Trust, or Bardsey Bird and Field Observatory. Good views from National Trust land SW of Aberdaron.

Bawburgh: St Mary's and St Walstan's Church, and *Well

Norwich, Norfolk, England

OS 144 (TG 153087)

W of Norwich off B1108: destroyed N transept of eleventh- to twelfth-century church held the shrine of St Walstan. Agricultural pilgrims would also visit his well, N of the churchyard.

Beverley Minster

East Yorkshire, England

OS 107 (TA 037392)

Beautiful and impressive collegiate church on site of St John's eighth-century monastery. Very attractive market town; former sanctuary, and pilgrimage destination.

Binsey: St Margaret's Church and Well

Oxfordshire, England

OS 164 (SP 485080)

NW suburb of Oxford; lane off A420 ends at church. Holy well brought into being by the prayers of St Frideswide to St Margaret of Antioch. Cures and pilgrimage site.

Bodmin: St Petroc's Church and St Guron's Well

Cornwall, England

OS 200 (SX 073671)

Off the A30: twelfth-century ivory reliquary in S aisle, well house outside W end with water spouts by steps. Carving of St Petroc beside the altar of his church at *Padstow.

Bradwell-on-Sea: St Peter's Chapel

Maldon, Essex, England

OS 168 (TM 031082)

Access by car, then on foot, along the Roman road NE of Bradwell. Chapel and Roman fort are situated by the marshy shore with the Othona Community to the N.

*Brixworth: All Saints' Church

Northamptonshire, England

OS 141 (SP 748712)

Off A508 N of Northampton. Saxon basilica-style church possibly built in honour of St Boniface. Displays a reliquary containing a human (Boniface's?) throat bone.

Burgh Castle Roman Fort

Great Yarmouth, Norfolk, England

OS 134 (TG 475046)

English Heritage and Norfolk Archaeological Trust

'Saxon Shore' fort and site of St Fursey's seventh-century monastery. Access via minor roads off A143 SW of Yarmouth. Views across Breydon Water to Berney Mill.

Bury St Edmunds Abbey

Suffolk, England

OS 155 (TL 859642)

English Heritage/St Edmundsbury Borough Council

Benedictine abbey remains, site of King Edmund's shrine: landscaped precinct, impressive gateway, Norman tower, visitor centre, cathedral. Angel Inn opposite NW gate built 1452 as a pilgrim hospice.

*Caerwent Roman Town

Chepstow, Monmouthshire, Wales

OS 171 (ST 469905)

Cadw

Village S of A48 Chepstow–Caerleon road. Impressive remains of a walled Roman town: site of the monastic school founded by Irish St Tathan in the fifth and sixth centuries.

Caldey Island Monastery and *Old Priory

off Tenby, Pembrokeshire, Wales

OS 158 (SS 141963 priory)

Reformed Cistercian Order

Boat trips from Tenby harbour, weekdays early May to late September. Guided tours of monastery for men only, other facilities and monuments open to all.

Canterbury World Heritage Site

Kent, England

–Cathedral Priory

OS 179 (TR 151579)

Sites of death and shrine of St Thomas.

–St Augustine's Abbey

(TR 154577)

English Heritage

Visitor centre, museum.

–St Martin's Church

(TR 158578) off A257 E of cathedral and abbey.

*Capel Gwladys

Gelligaer Common, Caerphilly, Wales

OS 171 (ST 125993)

Modern cross marks site founded by mother of St Cadoc. Church and Roman forts beside B4254 in Gelligaer with *Maen Cattwg to NW on footpath at ST 127974.

*Cawston: St Agnes Church

Aylsham (NW of Norwich), Norfolk, England

OS 133 (TG 134239)

Late fourteenth-century 'wool' church with hammer-beam roof and rood screen with Flemish paintings of saints, some (including John Schorne) defaced by sixteenth-century reformers.

Chester Cathedral

Off Eastgate, Cheshire, England

OS 117 (SJ 406665)

Within Roman city walls: Norman abbey complex, cathedral since 1541. Restored shrine in Lady Chapel; choir stall carvings include a pilgrim, geese and St Werburgh.

*Chittlehampton: St Hieritha's Church

South Molton, Devon, England

OS 180 (SS 636256)

Imposing late-Perpendicular church – largely paid for by offerings to St Urith's shrine – in village E of the river Taw and A377 Crediton–Barnstaple road.

Clynnog Fawr: St Beuno's Church, Chapel and Well

Caernarfon, Gwynedd, Wales

OS 115/123 (SH 414497 and SH 413494)

Parking at hotel. Impressive pilgrims' church and shrine chapel. Exhibition in N transept. Sundial in churchyard. Well SW of village beside A499; dangerous, no parking.

Coquet Island

Amble, Northumberland, England

OS 81 (NU 293045)

RSPB/Trinity House

Henry the Dane's island, about one and a half miles offshore: lighthouse, bird reserve. No landing, but boat trips around island arranged through Amble Tourist Office/RSPB.

Crediton: St Boniface Statue

Devon, England

OS 191 (SS 834003)

1960s statue of Winfrith in Newcombes Meadow at the E end of his home town.

Croyland Abbey

Crowland, Lincolnshire, England

OS 142 (TF 242103)

S of Spalding off A1073: parish church in Benedictine ruins, site of St Guthlac's hermitage. Sculptures of Guthlac's life, saints, abbots and royalty on nave façade.

Dorchester Abbey

Dorchester-on-Thames, Oxfordshire, England

OS 164/174 (SU 579942) Churn Knob OS 174 (SU 522847)

SE of Oxford off A4074. Beautiful and interesting light-filled church with modern 'shrine' to St Birinus. Annual pilgrimage from Churn Knob to abbey at start of July.

*Dunfermline Abbey

Fife, Scotland

OS 58/65 (NS 089873)

Historic Scotland

Palace and abbey off Canmore Street in town centre. Romanesque nave with impressive pillars: burial place of Scottish royals including its founder St Margaret (body moved to Madrid), her son St David, and Robert Bruce (heart at Melrose Abbey).

Dunwich (Lost Town)
Southwold, Suffolk, England
OS 156 (TM 479704)

Roman fort, St Felix's see, medieval town, nine churches claimed by the waves. Graves on cliff close to E wall of friary, leper hospital and Victorian church to W.

Durham Cathedral World Heritage Site
County Durham, England
OS 88 (NZ 273421)

Norman priory church containing tombs of St Cuthbert and the Venerable Bede. Cuthbert's coffin, pectoral cross and other relics on display in the Treasury.

East Dereham: St Nicholas' Church and St Withburga's Well
Norfolk, England
OS 132 (TF 987133)

Off the A47, W of Norwich. Sunken well below W end of the church: reputed site of Withburga's tomb and monastery. Detached sixteenth-century bell-tower.

Edinburgh: St Triduana's Chapel
Restalrig, Scotland
OS 66 (NT 283744)
Historic Scotland

In E of city, off Restalrig Road South. Lower storey of a well-house and shrine-chapel: *St Margaret's Well* on Queen's Drive (NT 271738) is a miniature copy.

Ely Cathedral
Cambridgeshire, England
OS 143 (TF 541802)

Former island in the Fens N of Cambridge on A10. Site of Etheldreda's shrine, cathedral-priory, magnificently preserved medieval buildings of the King's School.

Exeter Cathedral
Devon, England
OS 192 (SX 921925)

Decorated Gothic with 'image screen' of *c.* 1400 on W front. St Sidwell's churchyard and Tesco mural are on the eastern continuation of High Street.

Ffynnon Degla (St Tecla's Well)
Llandegla, Ruthin, Denbighshire, Wales
OS 116 (SJ 194522)

St Tecla's Church is on a minor road between the B5431 and A5104 SE of Ruthin. Healing well to SW, in alder trees E of River Alun: footpath and private land.

Finchale Priory

County Durham, England

OS 88 (NZ 297471)

English Heritage

Thirteenth-century priory ruins on site of Godric's hermitage and burial. Beautiful setting three miles NE of Durham beside the Wear: access/parking S of river via minor road off A167.

*Glasgow Cathedral

Strathclyde, Scotland

OS 64 (NS 602655)

Historic Scotland

Between Castle Street and necropolis, E city centre: thirteenth to fifteenth century, on site traditionally founded in sixth century by St Kentigern (Mungo) whose shrine is in the Lower Church.

Glastonbury Abbey

Somerset, England

OS 182/3 (ST 501388)

Church of England

Car park/entrance on Magdalene Street; open every day except Christmas. See also: the George and Pilgrim's Hotel and the Tribunal in High Street; to the SE, Chalice Well Gardens in Chilkwell Street (A361); to the E, the Tor and St Michael's Tower (NT) N of the A361; WSW, Wearyall Hill with 'Holy Thorn' planted in 1951, between A39 and housing estate; and more!

Gloucester Cathedral and Abbey of St Peter

Gloucestershire, England

OS 162 (SO 831188)

Tomb of 'saint' Edward II; impressive abbey cloisters and precinct. ***St Oswald's Priory** (SO 830190) to N held relics of the seventh-century Northumbrian king. The New Inn on Northgate Street was built as a pilgrim hostel.

Golant: St Sampson's Church and Well

Fowey, Cornwall, England

OS 200 (SX 121552)

Traditional (uncertain) site of Samson's monastery: beautiful location above River Fowey and a vineyard. The Tristan Stone (SX 113521) and Castle Dore fort (SX 104548) connected with King Mark are to the S and W.

Greenwich: St Alfege's Church

London SE10, England

OS 177 (TQ 383776)

Corner of A206/Greenwich Church Street, just W of Greenwich Museum. Hawksmoor church on site of Alphege's martyrdom by Danes. Saxon barrows in park.

*Gwytherin: St Winifred's Church

Llanrwst, Conwy, Wales

OS 116 (SH 876615)

On B5384 in the Cledwen valley: shrine chapel to Gwenfrewi stood in S of the large churchyard. A row of four stones, one with fifth- to sixth-century Latin inscription, by church.

Hailes Abbey and Parish Church

Winchcombe, Gloucestershire, England

OS 150 (SP 050300)

National Trust/English Heritage

NE of Winchcombe on Salter's Lane off the B4632. Cistercian abbey with shrine base of the Holy Blood. Parish church to N was used by pilgrims; wall paintings.

*Hanbury: St Werburgh's Church

Burton upon Trent, Staffordshire, England

OS 128 (SK 171279)

E of A515; former site of St Werburgh's shrine and her monastery destroyed by Danes. Statue of saint on tower and stained glass in S aisle. Good monuments.

Hartland (Stoke): St Nectan's Church and Well

Bideford, Devon, England

OS 190 (SS 235248 church, SS 236247 well)

Magnificent fourteenth-century church held Nectan's shrine. Well to SE, down a path running N from Stoke–Hartland road. Hartland Abbey half mile NE, now a country house.

Hatfield Chase

Thorne, South Yorkshire, England

OS 112 (SE 7162100)

General area of battle where St Edwin was killed in 633. Farmland and peat extraction NE of Doncaster between thundering lorries on the A18 and M180.

Hawkesbury: St Mary the Virgin

Chipping Sodbury, South Gloucestershire, England

OS 172 (ST 768869)

Quiet hamlet off A46 with fine Perpendicular church, manor-house and farmhouse once owned by Pershore Abbey. Former Saxon minster where Wulstan officiated.

Hennock: St Mary's Church

Newton Abbot, Devon, England

OS 191 (SX 830809)

Minor roads off B3193 SW of Exeter: rood screen paintings (c. 1450) of around forty saints including Sidwell and Urith, who can also be seen at Higher Ashton to NE.

*Hereford Cathedral

Hereford & Worcester, England

OS 149 (SO 510398)

N of the Wye, E of A49. Originally founded to house the miracle-working tomb of St Ethelbert, 'martyred' by King Offa in 794. The N transept contains the shrine of St Thomas Cantelupe, its marble base decorated with figures of Knights Templar.

Hexham Abbey
Northumberland, England
OS 87 (NY 935641)

Beside River Tyne, S of Hadrian's Wall. Twelfth-century Augustinian priory overlying Saxon monastery destroyed by Danes: St Wilfrid's crypt and chair survive.

Holyhead: St Cybi's Church and Roman Fort (Caer Gybi)
Holy Island, Anglesey, Wales
OS 114 (SH 247827)
Cadw (Roman walls)

Site of Cybi's sixth-century monastery and grave (Eglwys y Bedd) within Roman naval base.

Holy Island
Lamlash Bay, Arran, Scotland
OS 69 (NS 059296)
Rokpa Trust (Samyê-Ling) (tel: 013873 73232) for work/retreats

Cave hermitage of St Molaise on rugged and beautiful island used as retreat by Tibetan Buddhists. Boat trips from Lamlash. Possible grave-slab of Molaise at **Shiskine Church**, Blackwaterfoot, Arran. OS 69 (NR 910294).

Holywell (Treffynnon): St Winefride's Chapel and Well
Flintshire, Wales
OS 116 (SY 183763)
Cadw

Two-storey well-chapel and bathing pool: lies between the A55 and A548 in the Dee estuary NW of Flint. Basingwerk Abbey (its former owner) is to the S.

Hoxne: Goldbrook Bridge and St Edmund's Monument
Eye, Suffolk, England
OS 156 (TM 179769 and TM 183767)

Screen and bench carved with Edmund's legend in church on B1118 SE of Diss. Modern bridge at minor junction to S, stream where Edmund was betrayed: scene illustrated on adjacent wall. Stone cross in field to E of the road to Cross Street.

Ilam: St Bertram's Shrine in Holy Cross Church
Staffordshire, England
OS 119 (SK 132507) (*Well SK 137514)
National Trust

Just over the border from Derbyshire, NW of Ashbourne off the A52 or A515. Medieval shrine containing Saxon tomb; Saxon font; hermit's cave and holy well.

Inner Farne Island

Off Bamburgh, Northumberland, England

OS 75 (NU 218360)

National Trust/National Nature Reserve

Remains of medieval monastery, and tower of 1500 on site of St Cuthbert's cell. Boat trips from Seahouses April-September, weather and nesting times permitting.

Iona Island

Off the Ross of Mull, Argyll, Scotland

OS 48 (NM 287245)

Historic Scotland and National Trust for Scotland

Passenger ferry from Fionnphort (Mull) where there is an Iona visitor centre. Working visits and retreats may be arranged through the Iona Community.

*Isle of May: St Adrian's Priory

Firth of Forth, Fife, Scotland

OS 59 (NO 658991)

Scottish Natural Heritage

Six-mile boat journey from Anstruther (summer ferry). Bird reserve and medieval pilgrimage site: excavated remains of ninth-century relic-chapel of St Ethernan and twelfth-century Benedictine priory on reputed site of St Adrian's martyrdom by the Danes.

Jarrow: St Paul's Church and Monastery

South Shields, Tyne & Wear, England

OS 88 (NZ 338652)

English Heritage/Jarrow 700AD Ltd

In Jarrow S of the Tyne on minor road N of the A185. Parish church with Saxon chancel, remains of monastery, and Bede's World Museum and reconstructions.

Kildonnan Graveyard and Fort

Isle of Eigg, Inner Hebrides, Scotland

OS 39 (NM 488853 and NM 491847)

Isle of Eigg Heritage Trust

Ruined church, cross-slab, promontory fort: possible sites of St Donan's monastery and martyrdom. Boat trips from Arisaig, or ferry from Mallaig, both on the A830.

King's Lynn: Chapel of Our Lady of the Mount

Norfolk, England

OS 132 (TF 625199)

Beautiful medieval market town and port in NW Norfolk. Chapel for Walsingham pilgrims near S gate of town: in The Walks Park, SE of railway station.

King's Sutton: St Rumbold's Font and *Well

Northamptonshire, England

OS 151 (SP 497361 font, SP 506362 replica well)

SE of Banbury. Font in SS Peter's and Paul's Church. Original spa well in private grounds of Astrop House: replica on N side of road to Charlton, E of King's Sutton.

*Lady's Well

Holystone, Rothbury, Northumberland, England

OS 81 (NT 953029)

National Trust

Footpath from forestry car park beside road leading W from village. Used for baptisms by St Ninian and later, with nearby Pallinsburn stream, by St Paulinus.

Lastingham: St Mary's Church

Kirkbymoorside, North Yorkshire, England

OS 94 (SE 728904)

Former monastic site in secluded valley in N York Moors National Park NW of Pickering. Norman crypt built as shrine to St Cedd, his well on village bridge to E.

Lichfield Cathedral

Staffordshire, England

OS 128 (SK 115098)

On W side of city, N of Birmingham. Head Chapel to S of choir, site of fourteenth-century shrine in Lady Chapel, scenes from Chad's life in presbytery floor, nineteenth-century statue outside N door. At *Stowe to NE, **St Chad's Church and Well** (SK 122102).

Lincoln Cathedral

Lincolnshire, England

OS 121 (SK 978718)

Majestic Gothic cathedral on a hill; former Celtic site and Roman town. Head shrine of St Hugh, memorial to St Gilbert of Sempringham, shrine base of Little St Hugh.

Lindisfarne (Holy Island)

Berwick-upon-Tweed, Northumberland, England

OS 75 (NU 126418)

English Heritage (priory, museum), National Trust (castle), National Nature Reserve

Vehicle causeway and tide-table at Beal Sands E of A1. Inaccessible two hours before/three hours after high tide; pilgrim route across flats is flooded sooner and longer. St Cuthbert's Isle SW of the priory also becomes cut off.

Lismore Island: St Moluag's Church

Loch Linnhe, Argyll, Scotland

OS 49 (NM 860434) Port Moluag (NM 872433) Tirefour Broch (NM 867429)

Car ferry from Oban, passenger/bicycle ferry from Port Appin. Church is at Clachan on B8045 in the N of the island. Stone fort and Moluag's landing-place are SE of church, via track to Balure off road NE of the church.

Llanbabo: St Pabo's Church

Amlwch, Anglesey, Wales

OS 114 (SH 378868)

Ancient circular graveyard SW of Amlwch, just W of Llyn Alaw reservoir. St Pabo's memorial slab is inside the twelfth-century church, his 'head' above the S doorway.

*Llanbadarn Fawr: St Padarn's Church

Aberystwyth, Ceredigion, Wales
OS 135 (SN 599810)

Established sixth century by St Padarn (Paternus) on land reluctantly granted by Maelgwn Gwynedd. Important monastic and 'clas' (pre-Norman clergy) site which once had its own bishop. Early thirteenth-century church contains a Celtic cross-shaft showing Padarn(?) holding a spirally-folded cloak.

Llancarfan: St Cadog's Church

Vale of Glamorgan, Wales

OS 170 (ST 051702)

NW of Barry. Large graveyard, and fourteenth-century double-aisled church, in a wooded hollow beside a stream; probably the site of Cadoc's Celtic monastery.

*Llandaff Cathedral (St Teilo's Church and Well)

Cardiff, Wales

OS 171 (ST 155781)

Just S of the River Taff, NE of Cardiff centre. Norman cathedral: one of the four dioceses of medieval Wales. St Dyfrig and St Teilo, whose tombs are in the church, are unconvincingly claimed as founder-patrons. Teilo's silver shrine was destroyed in the time of Henry VIII but his well survives in the precinct wall.

Llandderfel: St Derfel Gadarn's Church

Bala, Gwynedd, Wales

OS 125 (SH 981371) Holy Well (SH 977374)

E of Bala at meeting of B4401/B4402. Wooden 'horse' in church porch from fourteenth-century shrine of St Derfel: peek through window, or key at Tirionfa Home uphill on right.

Llanddwyn Island

Newborough Warren, Anglesey, Wales

OS 114 (SH 387627)

National Nature Reserve, Countryside Council for Wales

Ruins of St Dwynwen's Church, sites of well and hermitage. Exhibition in Pilots' Cottages. Island occasionally cut off by high tides. Access/parking via Forestry toll-road SW of Newborough. A mile's walk along beach. Views of mountains of Llŷn.

*Llaneilian: St Eilian's Church and Chapel

Amlwch, Anglesey, Wales

OS 114 (SH 469928)

Church is W of Amlwch near Point Lynas. A footpath leads N to Porth yr Ychen then NW along coast to ruined well-chapel by a stream at SH 46569329.

Llanfihangel Abercywyn 'Pilgrims' Graves'

St Clears, Carmarthenshire, Wales

OS 159 (SN 302133)

Six decorated tombs in churchyard of St Michael's Old Church; N of the Taf, W of the Cywyn. Take Llanstephan road off the A40 E of St Clears. Continue S and straight past Foxhole to Trefenty. Footpath through farmyard, then SE to church.

Llangelynin: St Celynin's (Old) Church and Well

Garnedd Wen, Conwy, Wales

OS 115 (SH 751737)

Rebuilt medieval well house over ancient spring, hut circle. Steep, narrow lanes to Garnedd Wen then footpath: three miles SW of Conwy via Hendre; map essential.

Llangennith: St Cenydd's Church

Gower, Swansea, Wales

OS 159 (SS 429914) ·Burry Holms (SS 401926)

Former priory church on site of monastery founded by St Kyned in sixth century. Monastic remains also on a tidal island to NW of Llangennith, through The Burrows (dunes).

Llangwyfan: St Cwyfan's Church

Aberffraw, Anglesey, Wales

OS 114 (SH 336683)

Twelfth-century church situated on a rocky islet between Porth China and Porth Cwyfan, SW of Aberffraw which has a coastal heritage centre at Llys Llywelyn.

*Llantwit Major: St Illtud's Church and Celtic Crosses

Cowbridge, Vale of Glamorgan, Wales

OS 170 (SS 966687)

Llanilltud Fawr, near the coast SW of Cardiff, founded by St Illtud *c.* 500: his monastery, missionary centre and school were internationally renowned.

*Luss and Loch Lomond

Argyll and Bute, Scotland

OS 56 (NS 361928)

St Mackessog's Church: stone head, effigy, cross-slabs, Viking hogback tomb, visitor centre. St Kessog was martyred at Bandry opposite his monastery on Inchtavannach (NS 365910). St Kentigerna's Church is on Inchcailloch (NS 411906).

*Madron Chapel and Well

Penzance, Cornwall, England

OS 203 (SW 445328)

NW of Penzance on B3312: signed track and footpath NW of village to 'wishing well' and chapel linked with healing pilgrimages (my car was broken into here in May 1997).

March: St Wendreda's Church
Wisbech, Cambridgeshire, England
OS 142 (TL 415953)

S of the present village, off the A141. Former site of Wendreda's nunnery; shrine-church with magnificent double hammer-beam roof adorned with soaring angels.

*Minster in Thanet Church and Abbey
Kent, England
OS 179 (TR 311642)

NE of Canterbury off A28/A253. St Mary's and Abbey built on sites of nunneries founded by saintly Saxon princesses Ermenburga and Edburga in seventh and eighth centuries. Part of St Mildred's tomb found by excavation. Monastery tours, at limited times.

Monkwearmouth: St Peter's Church
Sunderland, Tyne & Wear, England
OS 88 (NZ 402577)

Parish church and visitors' centre incorporating remains of Wearmouth Saxon monastery. In a labyrinth of streets E of the A1018 and N of the River Wear.

Mwnt Beach and Holy Cross Chapel
Cardigan, Ceredigion, Wales
OS 145 (SN 195520)
National Trust

Embarkation point and thirteenth-century mortuary chapel on the pilgrimage route to Bardsey Island. Minor roads off the A487 NE of Cardigan; NT car park, information, snacks.

Mylor Churchtown: St Mylor's Church
Penryn, Cornwall, England
OS 204 (SW 820353)

Holy well and monolithic cross, associated with a Breton missionary and martyred Cornish prince, where Mylor Creek meets Carrick Roads off the A39.

Nevern: Pilgrims' Cross and *St Brynach's Church
Newport, Pembrokeshire, Wales
OS 145 (SN 081400 and SN 083400)

Fifteenth-century church in wooded valley on St David's pilgrim route. Fifth-century memorial stones, tenth-century Celtic cross, bleeding yew. Pilgrims' cross to W cut in cliff off Frongoch road.

Newport: St Woolos Cathedral
Stow Hill, Newport, Wales
OS 171 (ST 309876)

On site of Gwynllyw's settlement W of the Usk. Former clas (mother) church of the area became cathedral of the new diocese of Monmouthshire in 1949.

North Marston: St Mary's Church and *The Schorne Well

Winslow, Buckinghamshire, England

S of Winslow off A413 Aylesbury–Buckingham road. Remains of Sir John Schorne's shrine in S aisle. His well is downhill to the SW, along Schorne Lane.

*Norwich: St Julian's Shrine

St Julian's Alley, Norfolk, England

OS 134 (TG 235081)

One of the great medieval cities of England with an exquisite cathedral and precincts. A few pilgrims used to visit the cathedral shrine of the dubious boy 'martyr' St William of Norwich but Mother Julian (1342–1416+), who became a 'recluse atte Norwyche', is a more authentic saint best known for fifteen mystical 'shewings' (visions) recorded in her *Revelations of Divine Love*. Julian's cell-shrine and church are off Rouen Road SE of the Castle Museum.

Oare: St Mary the Virgin's Church

Porlock, Somerset, England

OS 181 (SS 802473)

Off A39; wild, remote spot on the edge of Exmoor, near the Devon border. Piscina representing St Decuman's head in chancel: scene of shooting in *Lorna Doone*.

*Oswald's Well

Maserfield, Oswestry, Shropshire, England

OS 126 (SJ 278297)

Oswestry Town Council

Holy well created by St Oswald's uncorrupt arm. In sunken garden below road bordering modern estate at Maserfield about a mile E of Oswestry centre.

Oxford: Christ Church Cathedral

England

OS 164 (SP 527035)

In Christ Church College off St Aldates. Former priory church on site founded by St Frideswide whose grave and shrine are in the Lady Chapel. See **Binsey** entry.

Oxford Martyrs' Cross and Memorial

Oxford, England

OS 164 (SP 513064 and SP 512065)

A cross set in the surface of Broad Street outside Balliol College marks the site where Protestant clerics were burnt at the stake. Memorial nearby in St Giles.

Penmon: St Seiriol's Priory, Church and Well

Beaumaris, Anglesey, Wales

OS 114/115 (SH 630806)

Cadw (not church)

Holy well, parish church with Viking-age crosses and other carvings, Augustinian priory buildings, fish-pond, and post-Dissolution dovecote. **Puffin Island** may be viewed from Penmon Point (toll road): it is a SSSI with no public access.

Pennant Melangell Church, Shrine and Cancer Help Centre

Llangynog, Powys, Wales

OS 125 (SJ 023265)

Tel/fax 01691 860408

Cwm Pennant is W of Llangynog on A4391 Bala–Oswestry road. Valley cul-de-sac, single-track road: advance booking required for group pilgrimages and Help Centre.

Peterborough Cathedral

Cambridgeshire, England

OS 142 (TL 194987)

In city centre: formerly housed many shrines and relics; monk's watching stair in St Oswald's chapel; Hedda Stone in apse. Monastic complex, cathedral close, Bishop's buildings, precinct wall, outer gates, herb garden, visitor centre.

Pickering: SS Peter's and Paul's Church

North Yorkshire, England

OS 100 (SE 799840)

Norman church with wall paintings of 1450–60 including SS George, Christopher, Thomas Becket and Edmund the Martyr. On small hill in town centre, W of A169.

Pilgrims' Way

Colley Hill, Reigate Woods, Surrey, England

OS 187 (TQ 246519)

National Trust

One of the many tracks used by pilgrims travelling between the shrines at Winchester and Canterbury. Access off A217, N of Reigate.

Pistyll: St Beuno's Church

Nefyn, Llŷn, Gwynedd, Wales

OS 123 (SH 328423). *Wayside Cross at (SH 319418)

Pool and ancient Celtic church on the pilgrim route to Bardsey Island; formerly had an inn, monastery and hospice. Turn N off B4417 between Llithfaen and Nefyn.

Ranworth: St Helen's Church

South Walsham, Norfolk, England

OS 134 (TG 356148)

Edge of Norfolk Broads National Park, off B1140 NE of Norwich. Magnificent late fifteenth-century paintings of saints on rood screen and parcloses etc. Visit Ranworth Broad.

Repton: St Wystan's Church

South Derbyshire, England

OS 128 (SK 303272)

On the B5008, off the A38 Burton–Derby road. Historic village beside the Trent: famous school in former priory, Anglo-Saxon mausoleum/relic-crypt of St Wystan.

*Rievaulx Abbey

Helmsley, North Yorkshire, England

OS 100 (SE 577849)

English Heritage

Off the B1257. E part of church housed the tomb of St Ailred, twelfth-century Cistercian abbot, friend and biographer of saints, who became the subject of a local cult.

*Ripon Cathedral

North Yorkshire, England

OS 99 (SE 314711)

Off A61 N of Harrogate. Norman minster church built over cave-like Saxon crypt of 672, styled by St Wilfrid on Christ's tomb and the relic-crypts of Rome.

Roche Rock: St Michael's Chapel

Roche, St Austell, Cornwall, England

OS 200 (SW 991596)

Rock outcrop, hermits' cell and chapel beside a minor road running SE from St Gonan's Church, which is on the B3274 NW of St Austell.

Romsley: St Kenelm's Church and Well

Clent Hills, Hereford & Worcester, England

OS 139 (SO 944807) N of Clent Hills Country Park: NT/H&WCC

Traditional site of Kenelm's murder: church built over spring; clouty well, pools. Statue over gateway. On Clent–Romsley minor road E of Hagley off A456 or A491.

*Ryhall: St John the Evangelist's Church

Leicestershire, England

OS 130 (TF 036108)

Two miles N of Stamford (Lincolnshire) off A6121. Remains of hermitage against W wall of N aisle; associated with cult of anchoress Tibba, patron saint of falconers.

St Albans Cathedral

Hertfordshire, England

OS 166 (TL 145070)

Former abbey church containing shrine of St Alban. Roman walls of **Verulamium** (English Heritage) lie to SW across River Ver. Also, museum and Roman theatre.

St Aldhelm's Well

Doulting, Somerset, England

OS 183 (ST 645432)

Off A361 E of Shepton Mallet. Look around church, then take footpath and lane down hill to W. Well is behind (over) the wall by the stone trough as the lane ends.

St Andrews Cathedral and St Rule's Tower

North East Fife, Scotland

OS 59 (NO 513166 and NO 514167)

Historic Scotland

On coast at end of A91: colleges, castle, harbour; cathedral-priory complex includes remains of one of the longest churches in Britain and 108-foot tall tower.

*St Augustine's Cross

Cliffs End, Isle of Thanet, Kent, England

OS 179 (TR 340641)

English Heritage

Site of Augustine's meeting with King Ethelbert; E of Minster off B2048. Ebbsfleet and Pegwell Bay landing area for Romans, Saxons, missionaries and Norse.

*St Barruc's Chapel

Barry Island, Vale of Glamorgan, Wales

OS 171 (ST 119667)

Excavated remains of a medieval pilgrimage- and shrine-chapel. At E end of the island on Friars Road off A4055: masked by the wire and spikes of a vandal fence.

St Cleer Well and Cross

Liskeard, Cornwall, England

OS 201 (SX 249683)

Restored fifteenth-century well-house/baptistery with bathing pool, niches for clothes, statue of saint, Latin stone cross with crucifixion: NE outskirts of village, N of Liskeard.

St Clether Well Chapel

Launceston, Cornwall, England

OS 201 (SX 203846)

St Clether village is S of A395, W of Launceston. A footpath marked by white posts runs from S of the church, NW to chapel and wells above N bank of River Inny.

St Cuby's Well

Duloe, Liskeard, Cornwall, England

OS 201 (SX 240579)

Well-house beside B3254, SE of Duloe Church, between East Looe and Liskeard.

St Cuthbert's Cave

Kyloe Hills, Northumberland, England

OS 75 (NU 059352)

National Trust

Cuthbert's body may have rested for a while beneath this outcrop. NE of Wooler via B6349 and minor roads to car park at Holburn Grange Cottages, then on foot.

*St Cybi's Well (Ffynnon Gybi)

Llangybi, Llŷn, Gwynedd, Wales

OS 123 (SH 429413)

Cadw

Sheltered location NE of Pwllheli: holy well and eighteenth-century spa buildings with a latrine, and cottage where patients slept after treatment. Access signposted off A499, or through churchyard. Cross-inscribed stones by lychgate.

St David's Cathedral

St David's, Pembrokeshire, Wales

OS 157 (SM 751254)

Cadw (Bishop's Palace)

Small, peninsular city: church and palace stand within a cathedral close defended by wall and gatehouses. *Porth Clais (SM 742238, National Trust) at outflow of River Alun to SW: ancient harbour for Irish pilgrims, kings and raiders.

St Decuman's Well and Church

Watchet, Somerset, England

OS 181 (ST 062427)

At St Decumans off B3190 SW of Watchet. The modernized, but ancient holy well is W of the church which has a figure of St Decuman on the S face of the tower.

St Edith's Well

Kemsing, Kent, England

OS 188 (TQ 555586)

Off A225, NE of Sevenoaks and N of M26. Holy well in a small sunken park S of church, on site of nunnery where St Edith (see village sign) spent her early days.

St Endelienta's Church and Shrine

St Endellion, Cornwall, England

OS 200 (SW 997787)

A beautiful collegiate church, prebendaries' houses, fourteenth-century altar-tomb and holy water stoup. Near Port Isaac on the NE coast, beside B3314 N of Wadebridge.

St Fillan's Cave

Pittenweem, Fife, Scotland

OS 59 (NO 549025)

Off A917, SE coast of Fife. Door to cave is in Cove Wynd below nineteenth-century Episcopal Church of St John. Key and leaflet available at the Gingerbread Horse, High Street.

*St Fillan's Priory and Pool

Strath Fillan, Stirling, Scotland

OS 50 (NN 351288 and NN 359285)

On West Highland Way NE of A82 between Crianlarich and Tyndrum. Priory ruins and information at Kirkton Farm; the pool is opposite St Fillan's Church.

St Govan's Chapel and Well

Bosherston, Pembrokeshire, Wales

OS 158 (SR 967930)

Car park via lane S of Bosherston Church, or coastal walk from parking at Elegug (to W) or NT parks at Broad Haven/Stackpole (to E). View from cliff, or risk the steps.

St Herbert's Isle
Derwentwater, Cumbria, England
OS 90 (NY 259212)
National Trust

Island home of seventh-century hermit: visible along the lake-side walk from Keswick jetties.

St Kenelm's Well
Sudeley Hill, Winchcombe, Gloucestershire, England
OS 163 (SP 044278)
Sudeley Castle Estate

'Folly' well house on footpath running N from minor road SE of Winchcombe and W of the Salt Way. Original well chapel (SP 043277) is now a private house.

*St Keyne's Well
Liskeard, Cornwall, England
OS 201 (SX 248602)

On minor road off B3254 SE of St Keyne village. Medieval well-house over the spring where a Celtic princess planted four sacred trees and laid a spell on the water.

St Levan's Chapel, Well and Church
St Levan, Land's End, Cornwall, England
OS 203 (SW 380223; church) (SW 381219; well)
National Trust

Well-baptistery and chapel-oratory on slope above Porth Chapel cove. Footpath SW, then SE from church, or coastal path W from Porthcurno and Minack open-air theatre.

St Magnus' Cathedral
Kirkwall, Orkney Mainland, Scotland
OS 6 (HY 449109)

Twelfth-to fifteenth-century church of red and yellow sandstone; contains relics of its founder St Rognvald and his uncle St Magnus. Earl's and Bishop's palaces (Historic Scotland).

St Magnus' Cenotaph and Church
Egilsay, Orkney, Scotland
OS 5 (HY 470300) (HY 466303)
Historic Scotland (church)

Memorial on site of Earl Magnus's martyrdom and twelfth-century church built in his honour. Egilsay is a small island reached by ferry from Tingwall on Orkney Mainland.

St Michael's Mount
Marazion, Cornwall, England
OS 203 (SW 515299)
National Trust (tel: 01736 710265 for tide/ferry details only)

Tidal island with priory and castle converted to a private house in seventeenth century. Access on foot at low tide along causeway from Marazion E of Penzance, or summer ferry.

St Neot: St Anietus' Church

Liskeard, Cornwall, England

OS 201 (SX 187679)

NW of Liskeard off A38: fifteenth-century church; crosses; magnificent stained glass depicting Old Testament scenes and saints' lives. Oak branch on tower renewed every Oak Apple Day (29 May) as a symbol of Royalist support for Charles I during the Civil War. **St Neot's Well** (SX 183681) in meadow NW of church.

St Nonna's Well

Pelynt, Looe, Cornwall, England

OS 201 (SX 224564)

Well-house beside lane W of the West Looe River SE of Muchlarnick, NE of Pelynt. Ferns, mosses and a decorated basin glow green in the dark interior.

St Non's Well and Chapel

St David's, Pembrokeshire, Wales

OS 157 (SM 751243)

St Non's Retreat; Cadw (chapel)

Overlooking St Non's Bay, S of Cathedral. Modern 'Celtic' chapel beside retreat-house; well, shrine, ruined chapel and standing stones downhill from car park.

St Oswald in Lee: St Oswald's Church and Heavenfield Battle Site

Wall, Hexham, Northumberland, England

OS 87 (NY 937695)

Beside B6318 (which follows the line of Hadrian's Wall) E of junction with A6079.

St Osyth Priory

Clacton-on-Sea, Essex, England

OS 169 (TM 120157)

Remains of medieval Augustinian monastery on site of St Osith's nunnery and shrine. Privately-owned but open to the public at limited times.

St Piran's Cross

Perranporth, Cornwall, England

OS 200 (SW 772564)

Celtic cross beside Norman church ruins in dunes of Penhale Sands. Piran's oratory (SW 768564) to W (N of modern Latin cross) buried beneath a mound with commemorative stone. Access via Gear Sands holiday complex or long distance path off Perranporth–Mount road. **⁺St Piran's Church** (SW 770520) is at modern Perranzabuloe. **St Piran's Round** (SW 780545) a circular enclosure used as a 'Playing Place' for sixteenth- to seventeenth-century religious performances, is SE of Rose.

St Robert's Cave

Knaresborough, North Yorkshire, England

OS 104 (SE 361561)

Harrogate Museums and Art Gallery Service

Hermit's cave, site of chapel and grave on NW bank of R. Nidd at E end of Abbey Road off B6164 Wetherby Road SE of town. Information panels, limited parking. Park at Briggate (W) end of Abbey Road (no through road) for pleasant walk passing cave-shrine of **Our Lady of the Crag** (SE 351565) guarded by a carved knight.

*St Tewdric's Well

Mathern, Monmouthshire, Wales

OS 162 (ST 523911)

SW of Chepstow off A48. The spring where Tewdric's wounds were washed is nearly under the M4, N of the church traditionally built over his grave.

*St Tredwell's Chapel and Loch

Papa Westray, Orkney, Scotland

OS 5 (HY 496508)

Former pilgrimage site and chapel to St Triduana in ruined fort on E shore of loch. See also *St Boniface Church** at Munkerhoose (HY 488526).

St Trillo's Chapel

Rhos-on-Sea, Colwyn Bay, Conwy, Wales

OS 116 (SH 842811)

Stone-roofed well chapel below road between Colwyn and Penrhyn bays.

*Salisbury Cathedral

Wiltshire, England

OS 184 (SU 143295)

E of the Avon, W of A30/A338 ring road. Part of St Osmund's shrine-tomb with 'healing holes' survives in the nave's S aisle: he was first buried at the original cathedral site of *Old Sarum** (SU 138327) English Heritage, to the NW off A345.

Scott's View

Melrose, Borders, Scotland

OS 73 (NT 593342)

Viewpoint on Bemersyde Hill, E of Melrose on B6356, over the Tweed encircling site of Old Melrose, precursor to *Melrose Abbey** (Historic Scotland).

Sempringham: St Andrew's Church

Pointon, Bourne, Lincolnshire, England

OS 130 (TF 106329)

Down track W of B1177: Norman church with memorial to St Gilbert on S wall, and well to SE. Gwenllian memorial and priory site at stream, as track branches N.

*Shaftesbury Abbey

Dorset, England

OS 183 (ST 864227)

Abbey Ruins Museum

Excavated Benedictine nunnery founded 888 by Alfred the Great. Rich, famous medieval pilgrimage site through royal patronage and relics of St Edward the Martyr: museum and modern shrine among the ruins on Park Walk; limited opening.

Shave Cross Inn

Marshwood Vale, Bridport, Dorset, England

OS 193 (SY 415980)

Free House

A hostelry for medieval pilgrims to the shrine of St Wite at Whitchurch Canonicorum; hidden away in lanes S of Pilsdon, S of the B3164, NW of Bridport.

*Shrewsbury Abbey (Holy Cross Church)

Abbey Foregate, Shropshire, England

OS 126 (SJ 498124)

Off A458, E of town and English Bridge over the Severn. Nave of Abbey Church of St Peter: remains of St Winefride's fourteenth-century shrine; Brother Cadfael trail and herb garden.

Sithney: St Sithney's Church

Helston, Cornwall, England

OS 203 (SW 637290)

Off A394 W of Helston. Wooden figure of St Sithney, site of shrine in N transept.

Stanton Harcourt: St Michael's Church

Oxfordshire, England

OS 164 (SP 417056)

Off the B4449 W of Oxford. Parts of the shrine of St Edburga in sanctuary and Harcourt Chapel. Thirteenth-century rood screen. Attractive manor-house complex with ponds.

Steyning: St Andrew's Church

Shoreham-by-Sea, West Sussex, England

OS 198 (TQ 184106)

Romanesque church on site of former pagan sanctuary taken over by St Cuthman. Village sign, and Bramber Castle (EH/NT) to SE beside roundabout on A283.

Tain: St Duthac's Chapel and *Collegiate Church

Ross-shire, Highland, Scotland

OS 21 (NH 794824)

Beside the Dornoch Firth off A9 N of Inverness. Chapel on the Links NE of town marks Duthac's birthplace. Collegiate complex in town with a museum and The Pilgrimage visitor centre telling the story of 'Tain Through Time'.

Urquhart Castle and Loch Ness

Drumnadrochit, Inverness, Scotland

OS 35 (NH 531286)

Historic Scotland

Possible site of Pictish King Bredei's stronghold visited by St Columba. **Craig Phadrig Vitrified Fort**, Inverness [OS 26 (NH 640452)] is another contender.

(Little) Walsingham Abbey and Shrines of Our Lady of Walsingham

Fakenham, Norfolk, England

OS 132 (TF 935368)

Information at Shire Hall in the Common Place

Remains of Augustinian priory (entrance in High Street, opening times variable), holy wells, bathing pool, and former site of the Holy House of Nazareth. The Anglican Shrine Church is just to the N. The village has pilgrim shops and hostels. The National Catholic Shrine complex is 1m S at **Houghton St Giles** (TF 921353).

*Waltham Abbey: Holy Cross Church

Essex, England

OS 166 (TL 381007)

N of London, M25 junctions 25/26. Minster founded 1060 by King Harold who is buried there. The miraculous Holy Cross drew pilgrims until dissolution in 1540.

*Wells Cathedral, St Andrew's Church and Well

Somerset, England

OS 182/3 (ST 551458)

Founded 705 by King Ine, present building 1148–1363, *c.* 400 statues on W front. Cult of St Decuman. Four sacred springs in garden of moated Bishop's Palace (tel: 01749 672552 for opening times, Easter–end October).

*Westminster Abbey

Parliament Square, London SW1

OS 176 (TQ 301795)

Shrine containing the body of the abbey's founder: Anglo-Saxon king, St Edward the Confessor. Since 1066, every ruler of the kingdom has been crowned here.

Whitby Abbey

North Yorkshire, England

OS 94 (NZ 904115)

English Heritage

Destroyed by Danes 867, refounded by Benedictines; thirteenth-century pilgrimage church which held St Hilda's shrine. Cliff top parking or ascend steps from town.

Whitchurch Canonicorum: St Candida (Wite) and Holy Cross Church

Bridport, Dorset, England

OS 193 (SY 397954)

Early thirteenth-century shrine containing the relics of St Wite, inside a church begun by Norman monks: N of Morcombelake, off A35 Bridport–Lyme Regis road. *St Wite's Well (SY 399937) National Trust (Golden Cap Estate) is S of the A35 on Chardown Hill, off minor road from Morcombelake to Stonebarrow Hill.

Whithorn Cathedral-Priory and Museum
Wigtown, Dumfries & Galloway, Scotland
OS 83 (NX 444403)
Historic Scotland/Whithorn Trust

Royal burgh, priory gatehouse, remains of church which held St Ninian's shrine, reputed site of fifth-century Candida Casa. Inscribed stones, finds from the area, details of recent excavations. Signed pilgrim route runs to/from Newton Stewart via Whithorn to/from Glenluce/New Luce. Related pilgrimage sites: **St Ninian's Chapel**, Isle of Whithorn, OS 83 (NX 479362) Historic Scotland; *St Ninian's Cave, Physgill, OS 83 (NX 422359) Historic Scotland; *Chapel Finian, Mochrun, OS 82 (NX 278489) Historic Scotland.

Winchcombe Abbey, St Peter's Church, George (Inn) Mews
Cheltenham, Gloucestershire, England
OS 163 (SP 026284 area)

Sixteenth-century pilgrim balcony and stone bath in alley on S of High Street; abbey ruins on Gloucester Street beside St Peter's which contains stone coffin of 'St Kenelm'.

Winchester Cathedral
Hampshire, England
OS 185 (SU 482293)

St Swithun memorial; mortuary chests; black marble font with scenes of St Nicholas; fourteenth-century Pilgrim's Hall. King Alfred statue (Broadway); 'Arthur's round table' in the castle; St Cross Hospital; fort and maze on St Catherine's Hill.

Worcester Cathedral
Hereford & Worcester, England
OS 150 (SO 850546)

On E bank of the Severn in city centre off Deansway. Former Benedictine priory and pilgrimage centre: effigy of King John, pilgrim exhibition in Norman crypt.

York Minster
North Yorkshire, England
OS 105 (SE 603523)

Cathedral Church of St Peter on site of legionary headquarters; re-erected Roman column opposite S door. Head of St Edwin, body of St William, pre-Christian well.

Bibliography

I found many interesting details in the history leaflets produced by most of the churches included in this book; the information panels and booklets at monuments in care, the series of abbey and cathedral guides published by Pitkin, and articles in the following:

Archaeology in Wales: published annually by CBA: Wales

British Archaeology: six issues a year published by the Council for British Archaeology, editor Simon Denison.

Current Archaeology: published six times a year by Andrew and Wendy Selkirk.

I also consulted the *Royal Commissions Inventories* and the *Victoria County Histories* for several counties/regions.

My other main sources are listed below.

Adair, J. & Chèze-Brown, P. *The Pilgrim's Way*, Thames & Hudson, London, 1978
Adkins, L. & Adkins, R. *A Thesaurus of British Archaeology*, David & Charles, Newton Abbot, 1982
Allchin, A. *Bardsey: A place of pilgrimage*, Bardsey Island Trust, 1991
—*Celtic Christianity, Fact or Fantasy?*, Gwasg Santes Melangell, 1993
—*Pennant Melangell Place of Pilgrimage*, Gwasg Santes Melangell, 1994
Anderson, W. & Hicks, C. *Holy Places of the British Isles*, Ebury Press, London, 1983
Austerberry, J. *Chad Bishop and Saint*, English Life Publications, Derby, 1984
Barber, C. *Mysterious Wales*, Paladin, London, 1987
—*More Mysterious Wales*, Paladin, London, 1987
Baring-Gould, S. & Fisher, J. *The Lives of the British Saints*, 4 vols., London, 1907–1913
Bede, the Venerable, *A History of the English Church and People*, (trans. Sherley-Price, L.) Penguin, Harmondsworth, 1968
Bevis, T. *Fenland, Saints, Shrines and Churches*, T. Bevis, March, (Cambs.) 1986
Bible, The Holy; Authorized King James Version, Collins, Glasgow, 1934

Blair, J. & Pyrah, C. (eds.) *Church Archaeology: Research Directions for the Future*, Council for British Archaeology, York, 1996

Bond, A. *The Walsingham Story*, The Guild Shop, Walsingham, 1988

Bowen, E. *The Settlements of the Celtic Saints in Wales*, University of Wales Press, Cardiff, 1956

—*Saints, Seaways and Settlements in the Celtic Lands*, UWP, 1977

Butler, A. (rev. Thurston, H. & Attwater, D.) *Lives of the Saints*, Burns & Oates, London, 1956

Butler, L. & Given-Wilson, C. *Medieval Monasteries of Great Britain*, Michael Joseph, London, 1979

Carew, R. *The Survey of Cornwall*, London, 1602

Chitty, M. *The Monks on Ynys Enlli*, W. Alun Jones, Aberdaron, 1992

D'Arcy, M. *The Saints of Ireland*, The Mercier Press, Cork, 1985

Dafydd ap Gwilym *Selected Poems*, (ed. Bromwich, R.) Penguin, Harmondsworth, 1985

David, Revd C. *St Winefride's Well: a history and guide*, Holywell, 1990

Davies, W. *Wales in the Early Middle Ages*, Leicester University Press, 1982

Dixon, J. *Gairloch and Guide to Loch Maree*, Nevisprint, Fort William, 1984 (reprint of the 1886 edition by Co-operative Printing Company, Edinburgh)

Doble, G. *'Cornish Saints'* pamphlet series published *c.* 1925–46

—*The Saints of Cornwall*, (ed. Attwater, D.) Truro, 5 vols., 1960–70

Dowse, I. *The Pilgrim Shrines of England*, The Faith Press, London, 1963

Dunbar, J. & Fisher, I. *Iona*, HMSO, Edinburgh, 1993

Edwards, N. 'The Dark Ages' in *The Archaeology of Clwyd*, Clwyd C.C., 1991

English Heritage Visitors' Handbook 1998–99, London, 1998

Evans, J. (ed.) *The Book of Llan Dav*, Oxford, 1893

Farmer, D. *The Oxford Dictionary of Saints*, Oxford University Press, Oxford, 1979

Ferguson, J. *An Illustrated Encyclopaedia of Mysticism and the Mystery Religions*, Thames & Hudson, London, 1976

Geoffrey of Monmouth, *The History of the Kings of Britain*, (trans. Thorpe, L.) Penguin, Harmondsworth, 1978

Gerald of Wales, *The Journey Through Wales/The Description of Wales*, (trans. Thorpe, L) Penguin, Harmondsworth, 1978

Gildas, *The Ruin of Britain*, (ed. & trans. Winterbottom, M.) Phillimore, Chichester, 1978

Godwin, M. *The Holy Grail*, Labyrinth/Bloomsbury, London, 1994

Hall, J. *Dictionary of Subjects and Symbols in Art*, John Murray, London, 1989

Heald, H. (ed.) *Chronicle of Britain*, Chronicle Communications, Farnborough, 1992

Heighway, C. *Anglo-Saxon Gloucestershire*, Alan Sutton, Gloucester, 1987

Henig, M. *Religion in Roman Britain*, Batsford, London, 1984

Hole, C. *English Folklore*, Batsford, London, 1944–5

Hughes, H. & North, H. *The Old Churches of Snowdonia*, Snowdonia National Park Society, 1984 reissue of 1924 edition

John, C. *The Saints of Cornwall*, Dyllansow Truran, Redruth, 1981

Johnson, S. *Later Roman Britain*, Routledge & Kegan Paul, London, 1980

Jones, F. *The Holy Wells of Wales*, University of Wales Press, Cardiff, 1992

Jones, G. & Jones, T. (trans.) *The Mabinogion*, Dent (Everyman), London, 1975

Kightly, C. & Cyprien, M. *A Traveller's Guide to Places of Worship*, Routledge & Kegan Paul, London, 1986

Labarge, M. *Medieval Travellers*, Hamish Hamilton, London, 1982

Lamont, Rev. D. *Strath: in Isle of Skye*, Skye Graphics, Portree, 1984 (reprint of Celtic Press, Glasgow, 1913 edition)

Levi, P. *The Frontiers of Paradise*, Collins Harvill, London, 1987

Livingstone, E. (ed.) *The Concise Oxford Dictionary of the Christian Church*, Oxford University Press, Oxford,1977

Lynch, F. *A Guide to Ancient and Historic Wales: Gwynedd*, HMSO, London, 1995

MacDonald, A. *Curadán, Boniface and the early church of Rosemarkie*, Groam House Museum Trust, Rosemarkie, 1992

Macdonald, A. M. (ed.) *Chambers Twentieth Century Dictionary*, Edinburgh, 1977

Metzger, B. & Coogan, M. (eds.) *The Oxford Companion to the Bible*, Oxford University Press, New York, 1993

Mildren, J. *Saints of the South West*, Bossiney Books, Bodmin, 1989

Millard, Dom B. (ed.) *The Book of Saints*, A & C Black, London, 1989

Morris, R. *Churches in the Landscape*, Dent, London, 1989

National Trust, *Properties of the National Trust*, London, 1997

National Trust Countryside Handbook, (compiled, Spouncer, C.) London, 1993

National Trust Handbook 1998, London, 1998

Olson, B. *Early Monasteries in Cornwall*, Boydell, Woodbridge, 1989

Palmer, M. & Palmer, N. *Sacred Britain*, Piatkus, London, 1997

Patterson, A. *A Way to Whithorn*, Saint Andrew Press, Edinburgh, 1993

Pennant, T. *A Tour of Scotland and a Voyage to the Hebrides*, London, 1776

Pepin, D, *Discovering Shrines and Holy Place*s, Shire, Princes Risborough, 1980

Phillips, Fr. A. *The Hallowing of England*, Anglo-Saxon Books, Pinner, 1994

Pochin Mould, D. *Scotland of the Saints*, Batsford, London, 1952

RCAHMS, *Exploring Scotland's Heritage*, 8 vols., HMSO, Edinburgh, 1985–7

Redknap, M. *The Christian Celts*, National Museum of Wales, Cardiff, 1991

Ritchie, A. *Iona*, Batsford/Historic Scotland, London, 1997

Rodwell, W. (ed.) *Temples, Churches and Religion in Roman Britain*, BAR no. 77, Oxford, 1980

—and Bentley, J. *Our Christian Heritage*, George Philip, London, 1984

Romer, J. *Testament: the Bible and History*, Henry Holt, New York, 1993

Roscarrock, N. *Lives of the Saints: Devon and Cornwall* (ed. Orme, N.), Devon & Cornwall Record Society, Exeter, 1992

Russell, V. *West Penwith Survey*, Cornwall Archaeological Society, Truro, 1971

Salway, P. *The Oxford Illustrated History of Roman Britain*, OUP, Oxford, 1993

Sharkey, J. *Celtic Mysteries*, Thames & Hudson, London, 1975

—*Pilgrim Ways*, Ancient Landscapes, Cardigan, 1994

Sugden, K. *Walking the Pilgrim Ways*, David and Charles, Newton Abbot, 1989

—*In the Footsteps of the Pilgrims*, Pitkin Guides, Andover, 1997

Thomas, C. *Celtic Britain*, Thames & Hudson, London, 1986

—*And Shall These Mute Stones Speak?*, University of Wales Press, Cardiff 1994

Urquhart, J. & Ellington, E. *Eigg*, Canongate, Edinburgh, 1987

Vince, J. *Discovering Saints in Britain*, Shire, Princes Risborough, 1979

Wade Martins, S. *Eigg – An Island Landscape*, Countryside Publishing, Scotland, 1987

Waters, C. *Who was St Wite?*, Whitchurch Canonicorum Church, Bridport, 1980

Weatherhill, C. *Belerion, Ancient Sites of Land's End*, Alison Hodge, Penzance, 1989

Woodward, A. *Shrines and Sacrifice*, Batsford/English Heritage, London, 1992

Yeoman, P. *Pilgrimage in Medieval Scotland*, Batsford/Historic Scotland, London, 1999